CAMBRIDGE LIBRARY COLLECTION

Books of enduring scholarly value

British and Irish History, General

The books in this series are key examples of eighteenth- and nineteenth-century historiography which show how centuries of political, social and economic change were interpreted during the height of Britain's power. They shed light on the understanding of dynasty, religion and culture that shaped the domestic, foreign and colonial policy of the British empire.

A Topographical and Historical Account of the Parish of St Mary-le-Bone

Little is known about Thomas Smith, the author of this 1833 local history of the parish of St Marylebone in London, where, as he states in his preface, he was born and had lived for thirty-six years. His motive for writing the book, aside from 'an inherent affection for the place of his nativity', was an awareness that with the passing of the great Reform Act of 1832, by which Marylebone was designated a borough with its own Member of Parliament, the district was likely to grow rapidly, with both the loss of memories of earlier times, and a swiftly changing built environment. The illustrated book surveys the boundaries of the original parish, the etymology of its name, its churches, schools and hospitals, the new shopping district of Oxford Street and the ancient gallows at Tyburn, and some of the famous people who had lived in the parish.

Cambridge University Press has long been a pioneer in the reissuing of out-of-print titles from its own backlist, producing digital reprints of books that are still sought after by scholars and students but could not be reprinted economically using traditional technology. The Cambridge Library Collection extends this activity to a wider range of books which are still of importance to researchers and professionals, either for the source material they contain, or as landmarks in the history of their academic discipline.

Drawing from the world-renowned collections in the Cambridge University Library and other partner libraries, and guided by the advice of experts in each subject area, Cambridge University Press is using state-of-the-art scanning machines in its own Printing House to capture the content of each book selected for inclusion. The files are processed to give a consistently clear, crisp image, and the books finished to the high quality standard for which the Press is recognised around the world. The latest print-on-demand technology ensures that the books will remain available indefinitely, and that orders for single or multiple copies can quickly be supplied.

The Cambridge Library Collection brings back to life books of enduring scholarly value (including out-of-copyright works originally issued by other publishers) across a wide range of disciplines in the humanities and social sciences and in science and technology.

A Topographical and Historical Account of the Parish of St Mary-le-Bone

Comprising a Copious Description of Its Public Buildings, Antiquities, Schools, Charitable Endowments, Sources of Public Amusement, &c. with Biographical Notices of Eminent Persons

Thomas Smith

CAMBRIDGE
UNIVERSITY PRESS

CAMBRIDGE
UNIVERSITY PRESS

University Printing House, Cambridge, CB2 8BS, United Kingdom

Cambridge University Press is part of the University of Cambridge.

It furthers the University's mission by disseminating knowledge in the pursuit of education, learning and research at the highest international levels of excellence.

www.cambridge.org
Information on this title: www.cambridge.org/9781108079037

This edition first published 1833
This digitally printed version 2017

ISBN 978-1-108-07903-7 Paperback

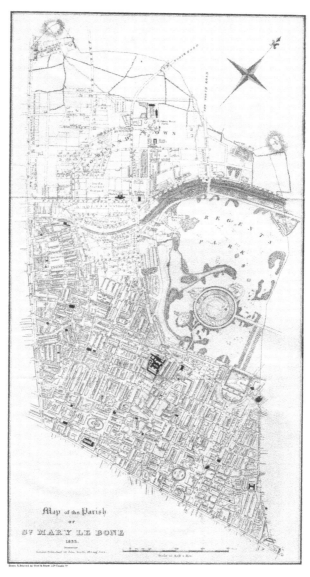

Map of the Parish
OF
ST MARY LE BONE
1833.

The material originally positioned here is too large for reproduction in this reissue. A PDF can be downloaded from the web address given on page iv of this book, by clicking on 'Resources Available'.

A TOPOGRAPHICAL

AND HISTORICAL ACCOUNT

OF THE

PARISH OF ST. MARY-LE-BONE,

COMPRISING

A COPIOUS DESCRIPTION

OF ITS

PUBLIC BUILDINGS, ANTIQUITIES, SCHOOLS, CHARITABLE
ENDOWMENTS, SOURCES OF PUBLIC AMUSEMENT, &c.

WITH

BIOGRAPHICAL NOTICES OF EMINENT PERSONS.

Illustrated with

SIX VIEWS AND A MAP.

THE WHOLE COMPILED AND ARRANGED BY

THOMAS SMITH.

LONDON:

PRINTED AND PUBLISHED BY JOHN SMITH,
49, LONG ACRE:

AND SOLD BY GARDINER AND SON, PRINCES STREET, CAVENDISH
SQUARE; BOWDERY AND KERBY, OXFORD STREET; J. BOOTH,
DUKE STREET, PORTLAND PLACE; V. ELKINS, BAKER STREET;
T. & J. HOITT, UPPER BERKELEY STREET; W. J. CLEAVER, KING
STREET; J. LANGDON (CLERK OF ST. MARY'S), UPPER YORK
STREET; AND ALL OTHER BOOKSELLERS.

1833.

LONDON:
PRINTED BY JOHN SMITH, 49, LONG ACRE.

TO

EDWARD BERKELEY PORTMAN, Esq.

MEMBER OF PARLIAMENT

FOR THE

BOROUGH OF MARY-LE-BONE,

THIS WORK

IS RESPECTFULLY DEDICATED;

AS A HUMBLE

BUT HEARTY TRIBUTE TO HIS PRIVATE WORTH,

AND PUBLIC INTEGRITY.

BY

HIS FAITHFUL AND OBLIGED SERVANT,

THOMAS SMITH.

PREFACE.

It has been well observed by an eminent writer, " that the Public have a right to require of him who addresses them through the Press, and thereby calls upon them to sacrifice no small share of their time and attention, to render some account of his pretensions." The Compiler of the present Volume, therefore, feels himself bound to comply with what has been so sensibly advanced.

A continued residence of thirty-six years in the Parish of St. Mary-le-bone, and a constant observation of its progressive improvement, even in that short period, combined with an inherent affection for the place of his nativity, has induced the Compiler to devote a considerable portion of his time in collecting information, and preparing a full and authentic account of its rise and progress from the earliest period, to the present time; presuming that the importance of this populous district gives it a peculiar claim to an accurate and ample description.

The close of the year 1832, has become memorable to all who feel an interest in the welfare of this division of the metropolis, from the extension of the elective franchise by an Act of the Legislature, and the creation of the *Borough of Mary-le-bone :*—by which means " a population equal to that of most Capitals, and in intelligence and wealth not inferior to any on the globe," became for the first time represented in the Great Council of the Nation.

The utility of a Work of this description will not be denied; and if, after making a recent personal survey, and using the most unwearied industry in collecting materials, and procuring valuable information and communications, the writer shall have succeeded in producing a miscellany, at once interesting to the general reader and the lover of antiquarian research, he will have attained the highest point of his ambition.

The following pages are, therefore, respectfully submitted to a generous and enlightened Public; with the entire confidence that the intention of the author will be duly appreciated, and in the hope that it will be found worthy of general approbation.

The sincere and grateful acknowledgments of the Compiler are due to Sampson Hodgkinson, Esq. for many useful communications and free access to his library; to John White, Esq. for the inspection of many valuable plans and documents relating to the Portland Estate; to James Hugo Greenwell, Esq. for his uniform kindness, and readiness to oblige; to the Rev. Dr. Dibdin, for occasional advice and assistance; to the Rev. Bryant Burgess, and to William George Paux, Esq. for the facility afforded to the Writer in the gratuitous inspection of the Parochial Registers.

CONTENTS.

CONTENTS.

CONTENTS.

LIST OF EMBELLISHMENTS.

AN

HISTORICAL ACCOUNT

OF THE

PARISH OF ST. MARY-LE-BONE.

THE Parish of St. Mary-le-bone is situated in the
County of Middlesex, and Hundred of Ossulston.
This County derives its name from its position
relatively to the three surrounding kingdoms of
the Heptarchy; namely, the East, West, and
South Saxons; of the first of which, or East Sex,
it formed a part during the long period of about
three centuries. Though of an irregular figure it
resembles a parallelogram, 20 miles long, and 14
broad, with an area of 288 square miles, or 179,200
acres. It is also divided into six Hundreds,
exclusive of the Cities and Liberties of London and
Westminster, and the Tower Hamlets. It contains 230 parishes, precincts, and extra parochial
places: of which 98 are exclusive of London and
Westminster; 122 are within the City of London;
and 10 in the City and Liberty of Westminster.

The Hundred of Ossulston * comprehends the

* *Ossulstan.*—The word *Ossulstan* is probably of Saxon origin;
and a writer on the Antiquities of Middlesex conjectures that it
was named after the original proprietor of this part of the Country,
who was called *Ossul*, or that the word is a corruption of *Ossul's
Tuna*, or oldest Town; alluding to London as being the most
ancient town in the County at the period when Middlesex was
divided into tythings and hundreds. But this supposition does

whole of the Middlesex environs ol the metropolis. On the west it abuts on the Hundreds of
Isleworth and Elthorne; on the north it meets the
Hundred of Gore and Edmonton; and the latter
district runs in contiguity with its limits on the
east, until the river Lea forms a natural boundary
on the Essex side. The great increase of buildings and population in a division of the county
so intimately blended with the metropolis, have
caused, for the convenience of internal political
arrangements, several subdivisions to be made at
various periods; one of which took place in the
year 1822, when, by an Act of Parliament, 3 Geo.
IV. cap. 84. sec. 45., a new and distinct division
of the Hundred of Ossulston was created, to be
described by the name or style of " *The Division of
the Parish of St. Mary-le-bone, within the Hundred
of Ossulston, in the County of Middlesex.*"*

This Hundred also affords the title of Baron, to
Charles Bennet, Earl of Tankerville. The Bennet
family was anciently seated in Berkshire. Sir John
Bennet (made Knight of the Bath at the Coronation of Charles II.), was a faithful adherent to the
royal cause during the darkest periods of internal
convulsion in the seventeenth century; and in
consequence of such services he was, in the year
1682, advanced, by the restored Monarch, to the
dignity of a Baron of this realm, by the title of
Lord of Ossulston, Baron of Ossulston. His
Lordship was twice married. His first lady was
Elizabeth, Countess of Mulgrave, daughter of
Lionel Cranfield, Earl of Middlesex. Charles,

not appear to be supported by sufficient authority. It has been
suggested, as a more probable conjecture, that it derives its name
from the old German word *Waasel*, which signifies *water;* the
Hundred being surrounded and intersected, with rivers and water-
courses —*Faulkner's Hist. of Kensington.*
 * By 3d Geo. IV. cap. 84, sec. 46 —The Magistrates for the
County of Middlesex are empowered to hold General Meetings, for
the purpose of granting Licences, &c. in the Court-House of the
said Parish.

second Lord Ossulston, was created Earl of Tankerville in 1714, which honour has descended
uninterruptedly, from father to son, upon Charles
Augustus, present and fifth Earl, through the
intervening Earls, all named Charles. The first
Earl died in 1722; the second in 1753; the third
in 1767; and the fourth Earl, who was succeeded
by his eldest son, the present Earl, in 1822.

The Parish of St. Mary-le-bone derives its name
from the ancient village of Ty-borne, or Ty-bourne,
which was situated on the eastern bank of a brook
or rivulet (Bourn being the Saxon word for a
brook), which passed, under different denominations, from Hampstead into the Thames. When
the site of the church, which was originally
dedicated to St. John the Evangelist, and subsequently to the Blessed Virgin Mary, was removed
to another spot near the same brook, it was called
St. Mary at the Bourne, afterwards corrupted to
Marybourne, Marybone, Mary-la-bonne, and now
styled in the preambles of its various local legis-
lative enactments, ST. MARY-LE-BONE.* †

Tyborne Brook, which appears to have been
formerly of some consequence, from the circumstance of a bridge over it in Oxford Street, having
been widened in 1737, has long since been converted into a sewer, running from the high grounds
on the south side of Hampstead, entering Mary-
le-bone by its northern boundary near the west
end, and passing through the Park in a direction
from north to south, crossing the New Road at
Alsop's Buildings; Oxford Street, at the corner
of Stratford Place; Piccadilly, at the lowest part;
and passing down the Green Park below the
Basin; continues through Buckingham Gate, to
Charlotte Street, Pimlico; from whence it is an

---

* In the Valor of Pope Nicholas, written in the reign of Edw. I.
it is called *Ecclesia de Tyborne :* in a Record of the reign of
Hen. VIII. (Pat. 17, Hen. VIII.) it is called Tyborne, alias Ma-
ryborne, alias Marybourne.—*Lysons's Environs,* vol. iii. p. 224.

open sewer, through the low lands on the west side of Tothill Fields, crossing the Vauxhall Road, and discharging itself into the Thames, at a place called King's Scholars' Pond, a little above Vauxhall Bridge. It is described by the Commissioners of Sewers as *King's Scholars' Pond Sewer*.

The Parish of St. Mary-le-bone is bounded by the parishes of St. Giles and Pancras, on the east; by Hampstead on the north; Paddington on the west; and on the south by St. George's, Hanover Square, St. James's, and St. Anne's, Soho. It is two miles and a half W. N.W. from St. Paul's Cathedral,* eight and a quarter miles in circumference, and contains about 1,700 acres of land; of which, till within the last 70 years, two-thirds were chiefly occupied as pasture-fields. This parish is charged the sum of 564*l*. 5*s*. 1*d*. to the land-tax, which, as early as the year 1794 (such had been the improvement of property by the increase of buildings), was raised by a rate of only one farthing in the pound.†

The order of the strata observed on digging wells, as exhibited in the southern parts of the Parish, is, immediately under the surface, from five to ten feet of flinty gravel; leaden coloured clay from 1 to 300 feet in thickness; loose sand, gravel, and water ; while sand and gravel, intermixed with loam, constitute the prevailing ingredients of the soil in the northern or uppermost parts.

Comparative Account of the Population of this Parish, in the years 1801, 1811, 1821, and 1831, from the Returns printed by Order of the House of Commons, Oct. 19, 1831.

Population, in 1801,	.	.	63,982
1811,	.	.	75,624
1821,	.	.	96,040
1831,	.	.	122,206

* Carlisle's Topog. Dict. 1808.
† Lysons's Environs, vol. iii. p. 243.

Annual Value of the Real Property, as assessed
April, 1815,   .   .   .   £509,244
  Ditto, as assessed March, 1828 .   692,085
  Ditto, as assessed in 1832, - -   732,134

The ancient Roman military way (the *Watling Street*), formed the western boundary of this parish, coming from Edgware, and continuing over part of Hyde Park, and through St. James's Park to the street by Old Palace Yard, anciently called the Wool Staple, to the Thames. This road was continued, on the opposite side of the river, from Stangate Ferry to Canterbury, and so to the three famous sea-ports, Rutupiæ, Dubris, and Lemanis.

The Roman road, which Dr. Stukeley calls "Via Trinovantica," and which began at the sea-coast in Hampshire, and ended at the sea-coast in Suffolk, near Aldborough, running from south-west to south-east through London, also passed through the southern extremity of this parish. Dr. Stukeley says, " This is the common road at present from Staines towards London, till you come to Turnham Green, there the present road through Hammersmith and Kensington leaves it, for it passes more northward upon the Common; then it goes over a little brook called from it Stanford Bridge, and comes into the Acton Road, at a common and a bridge, a little west of Camden House, so along Hyde Park wall, and crosses the *Watling Street* at Tyburn, then along *Oxford Street*, and continued to *Old Street (Eald Street)* going north of London. This road was originally carried north of London, in order to pass into Essex, because London was then not considerable, but in a little time became well nigh lost, and Holborn (Oldbourne was struck out from it, as conducting travellers thither, directly entering the City at Newgate, originally called Chamberlain's Gate, and so to London

Stone, the *lapis miliaris*, from which distances are reckoned."*

The following accurate account of the Manor of Tybourn, with its descent to the present proprietors is taken from Lysons's Environs, vol. iii. p. 243-4.

MANOR OF TYBOURN.

The Manor of Tybourn, containing five hides, is described, in Domesday-Book, as parcel of the ancient demesnes of the Abbess and Convent of Barking,† who held it under the Crown. " The land," says the Survey, " is three carucates.‡ Two hides are in demesne, on which is one plough ; the *villans* employ two ploughs ; there are two *villans* holding half a hide, one *villan* who holds half a virgate ;§ two *bordars* who have 10 acres, and three *cottars*.|| There is pasture for the cattle

* Stukeley's Itinerarium Curiosum, Iter vii. p. 205, &c.

† *Abbey of Barking in Essex.*—" Erkenwald son of Anna, King of the East Angles, and afterwards Bishop of London, founded here a monastery of Religious Virgins, A. D. 675 ; which continued till the general dissolution, *temp.* Hen. VIII., when it appeared to be 862*l.* 12*s.* 5*d. ob. per ann.* as Dugdale, and 1084*l.* 6*s.* 2*d. ob. q.* as Speed. It was of the Order of St. Benedict, and dedicated to the Blessed Virgin Mary, and St. Ethelburgha, or Alburgh, the first Abbess, sister to the Founder. The site of this House was granted, 5th Edw. VI. to Edward Lord Clinton."—*Tanner's Notitia Monastica.*

" The Abbess was Lady paramount in all the Manor within this half hundred, *i. e.* Becontree, as is still the Lord of Barking Manor, and she held of the king by an entire Barony, there being but three more of the kind in England, viz. the Prioresses of Wilton, Shaftsbury, and Winchester."—*Morant's Essex*, p. 2 and 4, vol. i.

‡ " Dr. Thoroton, says, *carucates* and *hides* were the very same, and contained 100 acres, six score to the Hundred, more or less, according to the stiffness of the soil."

§ *Virgate.*—The fourth part of one carucate or hide.

|| *Villanus* and *villain*, which can in its original use only be construed a *villager*, is by a modern writer distorted into a *slave, villain*, &c. Lee, in his History of Lewes and Brighthelmstone, published 1795, candidly observes : " We frequently meet in almost every part of Domesday, with *servus, cotarifus* or *coterellus, bordarius*, and *villanus*, which I take to be only accidental distinctions, and not any discriminate classification, as to the origin and degrees of bondage."

of the village, *pannage** for 50 hogs, and 40 pence arising from the herbage. In the whole valued at 52 Shillings; in K. Edward's time at 100 Shillings."

Robert de Vere, who held this manor under the Abbey of Barking, gave it in marriage with his daughter Joan, to William de Insula, Earl Warren and Surrey,† whose son John dying without issue, it descended to Richard, Earl of Arundel, son of his sister Alice.‡ After the death of Richard the succeeding Earl, who was beheaded in 1394,§ his estates became the joint property of

* *Pannage.*—" This was an usual method of stating the quantity of wood upon an estate ; which seems to imply that the woods were considered as of no other value than to afford pannage for hogs. Indeed, a wood that yielded neither acorns nor beech mast, is in the Domesday Survey called *Silva infructuosa.* The ancient inhabitants of England subsisting principally upon salt meat during the winter, the rearing of swine was an important article of rural economy. Dr. Whitaker remarks, "that though the hog would of course be put up to fatten, at that time as at present, he was in his general habits more of a wild animal than now, feeding, as his snout imports, upon roots, mast, &c. and very far from the filthy impounded glutton to which we have degraded him."—*Park's Hist. Hampstead,* p. 91.

† *Dugdale's Baronage,* vol. i. p. 192. There was a grant from the Crown to William de Insula, in 1285, perhaps by way of confirmation. Pat. 13, Edw. I. m. 15. William de Insula and Joan his wife, confirmed a life interest in this manor, to Alice de Vere, Countess of Oxford, who died seised of it in 1813. The manor was then valued at 5*l.* 13*s.* 5*d. viz.* A capital messuage, 12*d.* ; 120 acres of arable, at 4*d.* per acre ; 5 acres of meadow, at 1*s.* ; 2 of pasture, at 4*d.* each ; services of the tenants 10*s.* 5*d.* ; quit-rents from the freeholders, 48*s* ; rents from the copyholders, 8*s.* 4*d.*—(Esch. 6 Edw. II. No. 39). After this, Ralph de Cobham was lessee under John de Insula, and died seized of the manor so held, anno 19 Edw. (Esch. No. 93.)

‡ Inquisition taken after the death of John de Insula. The manor then contained, a capital messuage ; 130 acres of arable, valued at 4*l.* 6*s.* 8*d.* ; 136 of pasture, 55*s.* ; 4 of meadow, 4*s* ; and quit-rents, 58*s.* 2*d.* (Esch. 21 Edw. III. No. 58.) In the year 1345, there was a grant from the Crown to Richard Earl of Arundel of the reversion of this manor, which he had before given to the King after the death of John de Insula.—Pat. 12. Edw. III. pt. 1. m. 1.

§ Richard, Earl of Arundel, had granted it for life to his cham-

his daughters and coheirs.* William, Marquis of
Berkley, who had an interest in this inheritance,
as descended from John Fitzalan, through the
Mowbrays, is said to have given the manor of
Marybone to Sir Reginald Bray, prime minister
to Henry VII.;† but I imagine it was only his

berlain, Stephen Hyndercle, *alias* Clerk, in consideration of his
good services; the reversion to vest in the Earl and his heirs.—
Bund. Forisfact. 21 Ric. II. (In the Tower.)

This unfortunate nobleman fell a sacrifice to the cruel and in-
flexible temper of Richard II. He was accused of High Treason,
for being one of the Commissioners appointed by the Parliament
of 1386, to whom was committed the inspection of the administration of the Public affairs, and for which the King had granted a
pardon nine years before; he was tried, and sentenced to die by
the Parliament, on the 21st September. *Froissart* says, " the
King would be present at Arundel's execution." Another Historian adds, " that the spectacle remained so deeply impressed on
his memory, that his sleep was often interrupted by dreams, representing to him the Earl covered with blood, and upbraiding
him with injustice." To this contributed perhaps the rumour
that several miracles were wrought at the tomb of the deceased,
which was in the church of the Augustin Fryers in London, and
that his head was miraculously rejoined to his body. Though to
prevent the ill consequences of this false notion, the King had
ordered the corpse to be taken up and exposed to public view, ten
days together in a church, it was not possible to cure the people of
their prepossession.—*Rapin's Hist. of England.*

* It appears by an Inquisition taken 1 Edw. IV. (No. 46), that
the inheritance came between the Nevills, Mowbrays, and Lent-
halls. Edward Nevill, Lord Abergavenny, died (anno 1477)
seised of a third part of the manor, in right of Elizabeth his wife,
daughter and heir of Richard Earl of Worcester.—Esch. 16 Edw.
IV. No. 38.

† Dugdale's Baronage, vol. i. p. 3.

August 5, 1503.—Died Sir Reginald Bray, a man distinguished
for his bravery in the field, and for his skill in architecture, of
which science he was a complete master : the existing testimonies
of his great ability are Henry VIIth's Chapel in Westminster Abbey, and St. George's Chapel Windsor; the former structure he
has the credit of being the draughtsman of, and the latter he was
concerned in finishing and perfecting. From these great performances in art, we turn to his feats in arms; passing over the
fight in Bosworth Field, where he behaved valorously for Richard,
we come to the battle of Blackheath, where he was instrumental
in taking prisoner the Lord Audley, who had joined the Cornish
rebels, and in suppressing the rebellion; for which services he
was rewarded by Henry VII. with the land of the traitorous noble-

share in it; for it appears that Thomas Hobson, about the year 1503, purchased three parts of this manor of Lord Abergavenny, the Earl of Derby, and the Earl of Surrey.* It is probable that he purchased the remaining part of Sir Reginald Bray. In the year 1544, Thomas Hobson, son (it is supposed) of the last-mentioned Thomas, exchanged this manor with the king for some church lands.† Queen Elizabeth, in 1583, granted a lease of this manor to Edward Forset, for 21 years, at the yearly rent of 16l. 11s. 8d.; and in 1595, to Robert Conquest and others (trustees it is probable), on the same terms.‡ In the year 1611, King James granted the manor with all its appurtenances, *excepting the park*, for the sum of 829l. 3s. 4d., to Edward Forset, Esq.§ in whose family it continued several years, and then passed into that of Austen, by the intermarriage of Arabella Forset, with Thomas Austen, Esq.|| In the year 1710, it was purchased of John Austen, Esq. (afterwards Sir John Austen, Bart.) by John Holles, Duke of Newcastle¶, whose only daughter

man. Sir Reginald received many other marks of the King's bounty and favour, which he died enjoying. By historians he is called " the father of his country, a sage and grave person, and a fervent lover of justice, and one who would often admonish the King when he did any thing contrary to justice or equity."— *Universal Chronology.*

* From MSS. in the possession of John White, Esq. of Devonshire Place.

† Particulars for Leases in the Augmentation Office.

‡ Ibid.   § Pat. 9. Jac. pt. 7. No. 10. || Newcourt, v. i.

¶ From the information of John White, Esq. The purchase money was 17,500l.; the rental then 900l. per annum.

John Holles, first Earl of Clare, (so created 1624), died 1637, leaving John, second Earl, who dying 1665, left Gilbert, third Earl, who dying, 1689, left John, fourth Earl, who marrying Margaret, daughter and coheir of Henry Cavendish, Duke of Newcastle, was himself created Duke of Newcastle, in 1694; His Grace died July 15, 1711, when his titles became extinct. He was buried in Westminster Abbey on the 9th of August, and a magnificent monument was erected to his memory. His daughter Henrietta married Edward Harley, 2d Earl of Oxford; and his sister marrying Thomas Lord Pelham, was mother of Thomas Lord Pelham, created Duke of Newcastle.

and heir, married Edward Harley, Earl of Oxford and Mortimer. This manor is now the property of His Grace the Duke of Portland; William the second Duke of Portland, having married Lady Margaret Cavendish Harley, Heiress of the two noble families of Newcastle and Oxford.

Having thus given Mr. Lysons's Account of the Descent of the Manor, with additional notes, it may not be improper to introduce here some account of the families of the Proprietors.

HISTORICAL ACCOUNT OF THE HARLEY FAMILY.

The Harleys can be traced with great lustre to a very early period. In 3 Edw. I. Richard de Harley held the manor of Harley, in Shropshire; and 28 Edw. I. represented that County in Parliament; he died about 13 Edw. II. His son Robert, by marriage with the heiress of Brampton, obtained Brampton Castle, in Herefordshire, the future residence of the family. His descendant, Thomas Harley, Esq. of Brampton, born about 1548, had a grant 1 James I. of the honour and Castle of Wigmore; he died aged, in 1631. Sir Robert, his son was born 1579, at Wigmore Castle, was made Knight of the Bath, 1603, and Master of the Mint, 1626; he afterwards embraced the side of the Parliament, and was Captain of a troop of Horse in their service. His wife heroically defended his Castle at Brampton, which was besieged in 1643, and after a noble defence, was surrendered and burnt, as well as that of Wigmore. In that destruction perished a rich library of books and MSS. and furniture, &c. valued at 50,000*l.* Sir Henry Lingen's Estate (who had besieged the Castle, and burnt the Town of Brampton, &c.) was afterwards laid under sequestration, and the profits thereof ordered to make satisfaction for those great damages. Yet so honourable, so compassionate was Colonel Harley, that, after an Inventory had been taken of all the personal estate and goods, he waited on the Lady Lingen (Sir Henry being dead) and having asked *whether that was a perfect Inventory, and she had signed the same*, he presented it to her, with all his right thereto;* he died 1656. Colonel Edward Harley, his son, engaged actively on the same side with his father; but concurring in the Restoration, was made Governor of Dunkirk, and Knight of the Bath. He sat in the House of Commons for the town of Radnor, or County of Hereford, during the reigns of Charles II. and William III. and died Dec. 8, 1700, æt. 77. His celebrated son Robert, was born in Bow Street, Covent Garden, 9th Dec. 1661, and first sat in Parliament for Tregony, and afterwards for Radnor. In the reign of King William he opposed the Court. " He was a man," says Burnet, " of a noble family, and very eminently learned; much turned to politics, and of a restless ambition. He was a man of great industry and application; and knew forms, and the records of Parliament so well, that he was capable of both lengthening out, and perplexing debates. Nothing could answer his aspiring temper; so he and *Foley* joined with the Tories to create jealousies and raise an opposition." In 1701, he was chosen Speaker, on the change of Ministry. In 1704, he was appointed Secretary of State; and in 1710 he was made Chancellor of the Exchequer. On the 8th of March, 1711, he was in great danger of his life; the Marquis de Guiscard, a French papist then under examination by a Committee of the Privy Council at Whitehall, stabbing him with a pen-knife, which he took up in the clerk's room, where he waited before he

* Collins's Historical Collections of the Noble Families of Cavendish, Holles, Vere, Harley, and Ogle, fol. 1752, p. 199.

was examined. Guiscard was imprisoned, and died in Newgate on the 17th of the same month; and an Act of Parliament was passed making it felony without benefit of Clergy, to attempt the life of a Privy-Counsellor in the execution of his office; and a clause was inserted: " To justify and indemnify all persons, who in assisting in defence of Mr. Harley, Chancellor of the Exchequer, when he was stabbed by the Sieur de Guiscard, and in securing him, did give any wound or bruise to the said Sieur de Guiscard, whereby he received his death." The House of Commons voted an address to the Queen on this alarming occasion, and, upon his recovery, and attending the House, on the 26th of April, the Speaker addressed him in a respectful and congratulatory speech on his escape and recovery; to which Mr. Harley returned as respectful an answer. In 1711, Queen Anne, to reward his many eminent services, was pleased to advance him to the peerage, by the style and titles of Baron Harley of Wigmore, in the County of Hereford, Earl of Oxford and Mortimer; with remainder for want of issue male of his own body, to the heirs male of Sir Robert Harley, Kt. of the Bath, his grandfather. On the 29th of May, 1711, he was appointed Lord High Treasurer of Great Britain; and on the 15th of August he was chosen Governor of the South Sea Company, as he had been their founder and chief regulator. October 26, 1712, he was elected a Knight Companion of the most noble Order of the Garter. July 27, 1714, he resigned his staff of Lord High Treasurer, into the Queen's hand at Kensington, she dying upon the 1st of August following. On the accession of George I. he was impeached by the House of Commons, of High Treason, and high crimes and misdemeanours; and on July the 16th, 1715, was committed to the Tower of London, by the House of Lords, where he was confined till July 1, 1717,

and then, after a public trial, was unanimously
acquitted by his Peers.   He died at his house in
Albemarle Street, in 1724,* æt. 64.   Pope, in his
noble lines dedicating Parnell's Poems to this
Earl, celebrated him as possessing

> " A soul supreme, in each hard instance tried,
> Above all pain, all anger, and all pride;
> The rage of power, the blast of public breath,
> The lust of lucre, and the dread of death."

He was a great encourager of learning,† and
the greatest collector in his time of all curious
Books and Manuscripts, especially those concerning the history of his own country.

After his Lordship's decease, the following character was also given of him.   " During the time
he was prime Minister, notwithstanding such a
weight of affairs rested on him, he was easy and
disengaged in private conversation.   Intrepid by
nature, as well as by the consciousness of his own
integrity, he would have chosen rather to fall by
an impeachment, than to have been saved by an
act of grace; sagacious to view into the remotest
consequence of things, by which all difficulties
fled before him.   He was a courteous neighbour, a
firm and affectionate friend, and a kind, generous,
and placable enemy; sacrificing his just resent-
ments, not only to public good, but to common
intercession and acknowledgment.   He was a de-
spiser of money; and, what is yet more rare, an

---

* On a spare leaf of one of the MSS. in the Harleian Library,
Mr. Wanley, his Librarian, has made the following remarkable
Entry, " 21st May, 1724. To-day about ten of the clock, it pleased
Almighty God to call to his mercy from this troublesome world,
the Right Honourable Robert, Earl of Oxford, the founder of this
Library, who long had been to me a munificent Patron, and my
most kind and gracious Lord and Master."

† His Memory has been embalmed by the circle of wits, whom
he admitted to his hours of leisure and hospitality.   Pope, Swift,
Parnell, Gay, and Prior, were among his most intimate associates.
—*Collins's Biog. Peerage, augmented by Sir Egerton Brydges.*

uncorrupted Minister of State; which appeared, by not having made the least accession to his fortune."

He was succeeded by his son Edward Harley; who is remarkable for having generously completed that splendid collection of MSS. which now forms the principal treasure of the British Museum. He obtained a great estate by marrying the heiress of John Holles, Duke of Newcastle; and left all that estate, with his literary treasures, to his only child Lady Margaret Cavendish Harley, afterwards Duchess of Portland; who died in 1785. He died June 16, 1741, aged 42, at his house in Dover Street; and was buried in Westminster Abbey.

Leaving no male issue by his Lady (who survived him till Dec. 8, 1775,) his honours devolved on Edward Harley, Esq. then Knight of the Shire for the County of Hereford, son and Heir of Edward Harley, of Eywood, in the same County, Esq., one of the Auditors of the Imprest; who was next brother to Robert, first Earl of Oxford and Mortimer, according to the limitation of the patent, May 24, 1711, 10 Q. Anne.

The Hon. and Rev. John Harley, 2d son of Edward, 3d Earl of Oxford, was born Sept. 29, 1728, and appointed Dean of Windsor in Jan. 1778, and Bishop of Hereford, 1787. He was also Rector of Mary-le-bone, Middlesex; and Presteign, in Radnorshire; and died Jan. 7, 1788.

This Library contained, at the time of the death of Edward, Lord Harley, near 8000 volumes of MSS. But many of them being composed of several distinct and independent treatises, the number of Books, separately considered, may be reckoned to amount to upwards of 10,000; exclusive of several loose Papers, which have been sorted and bound up in volumes, and above 40,000 original rolls, Charters with their confirmations,

Letters Patent, Signs Manual, Privy Seals, Grants, Feoffments, Final Concords, Exchanges, Warrants, and other Deeds and Instruments of great antiquity; for the most part relating to Great Britain and Ireland.

" The Harleian Collection of MSS. was purchased by government for 10,000*l*. and deposited in the British Museum. The *Books**** were disposed of to Thomas Osborne, of Gray's Inn, Bookseller ;—to the irreparable loss, and almost indelible disgrace, of the country. It is indeed for ever to be lamented, that a collection, so extensive, so various, so magnificent, and intrinsically valuable, should have become the property of one, who, necessarily, from his situation in life, became a purchaser, only that he might be a vender, of the volumes. Osborne gave 13,000*l*. for the collection ; a sum, which must excite the astonishment of the present age, when it is informed that Lord Oxford gave 18,000*l*. for the *Binding* only, of the least part of them."—*Dibdin's Bibliomania*, p. 461.

I shall conclude this notice of the Harleian

* *Books in the Harleian Library.*

	Volumes.
Theology—Greek, Lat. French, Italian	2,000
——— English	2,500
History and Antiquity	4,000
Philosophy, Chemistry, and Medicine	3,100
Geography, Chronology, and General History	590
Voyages and Histories relating to the East and West-Indies	800
Civil, Canon, and Statute Law	1,100
Books of Sculpture, Architecture, &c.	900
Greek and Latin Classics, Grammars and Lexicons	2,400
Books printed upon Vellum, upwards of 70 fol., 40 4to., 100, 8vo.	220
English Poetry, Romances, and Novels	900
Livres Français, Italian et Hispan.	700
Parliamentary Affairs and Trials	400
Trade and Commerce	300
On different subjects under fifty different heads	4,000
Pamphlets, about	400,000
	Articles.
Prints, Sculpture, and Drawings	20,000
Portraits, 102 large folio vols., containing about	10,000

Dibdin's Director.

Library, with the following extract from the Preface to the Catalogue of the MSS. published by Order of the Trustees of the British Museum. " It would be a gross and unpardonable injustice to those who have been great benefactors to the Public, to omit the present opportunity of acknowledging, that the Harleian MSS. being placed in the British Museum as an addition to the Cottonian Library, to be consulted by the curious, and for public use to all posterity, confer an obligation on the learned, for which they stand indebted to the generous and public spirited offer made by the late Duke of Portland, and his Duchess, only daughter and heiress of Edward Earl of Oxford, and to the favour and munificence of Parliament. An event which hath not only united two very valuable Collections of ancient MSS. but happily secured to this country the most complete and extensive fund of national antiquities, that any kingdom can boast of."

HISTORICAL ACCOUNT OF THE PORTLAND FAMILY.

Henry Bentinck, Heer Van Diepenham, in Overyssel, where his family had flourished for many ages, had issue three sons; Henry, his heir; Joseph, a general officer in the service of the States-General; and William, who was created *Earl of Portland:* he had also four daughters, Eleanor, married to the Baron of Nienuren Huishen in Overyssel; Anne, married to the Baron of Van Zandenburgh in Utrecht; Sophia, wife to the Baron of Van Engelenburgh; and Joanna Maria Van Bentinck, who died unmarried, in 1705.

William Bentinck (afterwards Earl of Portland) in his youth was page of honour to William, Prince of Orange; and from thence was advanced to the place of gentleman of his bedchamber. In 1670, he accompanied him into England; and his Highness, in a visit to the University of Oxford,* being complimented with the degree of Doctor of the Civil Laws, Dec. 20, 1670; Mr. Bentinck had also the same degree then conferred on him. In 1675, on the Prince of Orange being attacked with the small-pox, which had been very fatal in his family, Sir William Temple has made this observation (Memoirs, vol. i. p. 97, 98) on Mr. Bentinck's care and assiduity:—" I cannot forbear to give Monsieur Bentinck the character due to him, of the best servant I have known in Princes' or private families. He tended his master, during the whole course of his disease, both night and day; and the Prince told me, that whether he slept or no he could not tell; but in sixteen days and nights, he never called once that he was not answered by Monsieur Bentinck, as if he had been awake. The first time the Prince was well enough to have his head opened and combed, Monsieur Bentinck, as soon as it was done, begged of his master to give him leave to go home, for he was able to hold up no longer; he did so, and fell immediately sick of the same disease, and in great extremity; but recovered just soon enough to attend the Prince into the field, where he was ever next his person."

In 1677, His Highness the Prince of Orange sent him into England, to solicit Charles II. for his marriage with the Princess Mary, eldest daughter of James Duke of York, in which negociation he was happily successful.

On the said Duke's accession to the throne, by the name of James II. Feb. 6, 1684-5, His Majesty, being apprehensive of the designs of the Duke of Monmouth, then in Holland, he ordered his envoy

* Wood's Fasti Oxon. p. 856, 857.

Skelton to get him secured by the States, and
sent prisoner into England. On His Highness
the Prince of Orange, hesitating to adopt that
severe course, he gave the Duke notice of it, and
instructed Mr. Bentinck to go privately to Brussels
to supply him with money; and to assure his
Grace, if he would make the campaign in Hun-
gary, he should be maintained with an equipage
suitable to his quality. But when, on King James's
solicitation, his Grace was obliged to leave Brussels, and thereupon had landed in England, His
Highness sent Mr. Bentinck to King James, to
offer him the assistance both of his troops and
person against the rebels; but, through a miscon-
struction put on his message, he was coldly
received; the King telling him, " He should
acquaint the Prince, that their common interest
required his staying in Holland."

In 1688, when the Prince of Orange had thoughts
of an expedition into England, he sent Mr. Bentinck, on the Elector of Brandenburgh's death, on
an Embassy to Frederick the new Elector (who,
in January, 1701, assumed the title of King of
Prussia) to lay before him the state of affairs, and
to know how much he might depend upon his
assistance; and he was so successful in his negociation, that he carried to his master a satisfactory
answer to all that was asked of him. He had a
great share in that signal revolution whereon our
present settlement is founded; in which difficult
and important transaction, he shewed all the prudence, dexterity and sagacity, of a consummate
and able statesman. He was the *person the most
entirely trusted, and constantly employed by the
Prince*,* in the necessary orders for the expedition, which was managed by him with the greatest
secrecy; and executed in an incredibly short

* Burnet's History of his own Time, vol. ii. p. 19.

time; a transport fleet of 500 vessels, having been hired in three days. His Highness embarked in a frigate of 30 guns, and Mr. Bentinck with him. When King James's army was broken and disbanded, and the King had dispatched the Earl of Feversham with a message to the Prince at Windsor, Mr. Bentinck was ordered by His Highness to arrest and secure him, for his disbanding the army without order. Also, by His Highness's commands, he wrote that letter, agreeing to His Majesty's proposal of returning to Rochester, whereby King James went over to France, and abdicated the realm.

On the accession of King William III. to the throne of these realms, in consideration of his faithful services, he was made Groom of the Stole, first Lord of the Bedchamber, and sworn of his Privy-Council on Feb. 13, 1688-9, the day he was proclaimed. And two days before the coronation, was created *Baron Cirencester*, *Viscount Woodstock*, and EARL OF PORTLAND, by letters patent, dated April 9, 1689.

His Lordship had the command of the Dutch Regiment of Horse Guards that came with the King to England; and, on His Majesty's going to Ireland, they were embarked at Highlake, and sailed thence to that kingdom, in June, 1690, and performed very gallantly at the battle of the Boyne, July 1st, where the Earl of Portland commanded as Lieutenant-General; and had a principal share in obtaining the victory; General Douglas pursuing his advice of intermixing the horse and foot for their security. On August 8th following, his Lordship had the command of those forces * which attacked the Irish that had entrenched themselves in the defiles before Limerick, and, routing them, made way for investing the place; he also attended

* History of the Royal Campaign in Ireland, p. 22, 23.

on His Majesty during that unsuccessful siege, and was further serviceable in the reduction of Ireland.

He accompanied His Majesty to Holland, and assisted in the conferences of the Congress at the Hague in the beginning of 1691. Early in the spring of 1692, he again embarked with the King for Holland; and after concerting measures for the campaign, returned to England for more forces. He arrived at Whitehall, May 2, being convoyed from the Maese, by five men of war and two fire-ships, which afterwards joined the fleet in the Downs. And soon after, his Lordship set out again to rejoin His Majesty; our Gazette announcing, that " the Earl of Portland returned to the Camp on Saturday last, having been sent with a detachment of 2000 horse, to observe the enemy, and returned to the King's Camp at Genap, July 7th, after interrupting the French detachments marching towards the Rhine." He was also in His Majesty's Camp at Grammen, Sept. 11, following. He served the campaign of the year 1693, in Holland, arriving at the Maese April 2, and shared the dangers of the unfortunate battle of Landen, July 29, where the King narrowly escaped with his life, a musket shot passing through his peruke, another through the sleeve of his coat, and a third, leaving a small contusion on his side. The Earl of Portland was likewise wounded; on which occasion the celebrated John Tillotson,* Archbishop of Canterbury, wrote him the following memorable letter:

August 1, 1693.

MY LORD,

" I cannot forbear on this great occasion to congratulate the King's safety and merciful preservation, from many deaths to which his royal

---

* Birch's Life of Abp. Tillotson, p. 280.

person was so eminently exposed in the late bloody engagement. I thank God, from my heart, who protected him in that day of danger, and likewise preserved your Lordship's life, which had been so lately restored. I hope the wound your Lordship received is not dangerous, and that it may be healed without losing the use of your hand. We have got but a very imperfect account of the issue of the whole action, and what has happened since, having received no letters of a later date than the morning after the fight, by reason of contrary winds."

His Lordship likewise attended the King the year following; and his regiment of Horse-Guards were shipped in the river Thames, and sailed for Flanders, April 14, 1694, where he also made the campaign of that year.

In 1695, he embarked with the King at Gravesend, May 12th, and was at the famous siege of Namur, and, on a general assault ready to be made, he was sent with Count Horn, by the Elector of Bavaria, to offer honourable terms to Count Guiscard the governor, in case he would surrender, and spare the lives of so many brave men on both sides; but they were to require an answer in half an hour. However, the Earl of Portland finding the French trifle, did not think it convenient to stay so long; and that city surrendered August 4th, after a month's siege.

On his return to England, as a reward for his bravery, he had a grant of the Lordships of Denbigh, Bromfield, and Yale, with other lands in the principality of Wales, which being part of the demesnes thereof, the House of Commons, on January 22, 1695-6, addressed the King to put a stop to the passing that grant. Upon which His Majesty, in answer, was pleased thus to express himself:—

GENTLEMEN,

"I have a kindness for my Lord Portland, which he has deserved of me by long and faithful services; but I should not have given him these lands, if I had imagined the House of Commons could have been concerned: I will therefore recall the grant, and find some other way of shewing my favour to him."

And soon after His Majesty conferred on him a grant of the Royal House of Theobalds, with the demesnes thereunto belonging, in the County of Hertford and Middlesex; and also granted to him the office of Ranger of the Great and Little Parks at Windsor, which was, after his decease, conferred on the Duchess of Marlborough.

In that session of Parliament his Lordship shewed a noble spirit and integrity in resisting an offer made to him on the following occasion. In 1695, there was a Report of the House of Commons, that some Members of both Houses had been bribed in relation to passing an Act for establishing the East India Company; and it appeared that 50,000*l.* were pressed on the Earl of Portland to use his interest with the King that it might pass, which he absolutely refused, saying, " *he would for ever be their enemy and opposer, if they persisted in offering him the money.*"

His Lordship had, on Feb. 14, 1695-6, the first information, from Sir Thomas Prendergrass, of the intended assassination of King William; and, with much importunity, prevailed on His Majesty not to take the diversion of hunting, as he designed; whereby the King escaped the danger of that horrible conspiracy.

On Feb. 9, 1696-7, he was elected a Knight Companion of the Most Noble Order of the Garter, at a Chapter held at Kensington, and installed at Windsor on March 25th, following.

As he constantly attended King William in all the dangers and fatigues of his wars, both in Ireland and Flanders, and distinguished himself on several occasions, he was made General of the Horse in the King's Camp at Promell, June 6, 1697. And the same year had the principal management of the peace, which was first agreed between him and the Mareschal Boufflers in the field, between the two armies, Jan. 30, O. S. 1697, and in three other conferences in July following; and which was afterwards formally concluded at Ryswick, Sept. 11th. Being in January following sent Ambassador extraordinary to France, he filled that employment with equal honour to the King, the British nation, and himself: the magnificence and pomp of his public entry, on Feb. 27th following, outshining what had been ever beheld in that gaudy court since the Duke of Buckingham's embassy, when he came to demand Maria Henrietta of France in marriage for Charles the First.

About this time, Burnet mentions, that Keppel was received into favour: the Earl of Portland observed the progress of this favour with great uneasiness; and they grew to be most implacable enemies to each other, so that on occasion of a small preference that was given him in prejudice of his own post, as Groom of the Stole, he retired from the Court in disgust, and resigned all his employments. The King used all possible means to divert him from this resolution, but without success. He consented to serve the King still in his affairs, but he would not return to any post in the household. And not long after he was employed in the new negociation, set on foot for the succession to the crown of Spain.

In January, 1698-9, his Lordship was employed by King William in the management of most foreign affairs, particularly those which related to Scotland.

In 1701, he and Lord Jersey were the principal persons concerned in negociating the Partition Treaty, for which, in conjunction with others of the Ministry, they were impeached. But, " no articles were afterwards framed against the Earl of Portland, which was represented to the King as an expression of their respect for him." He was therefore acquitted.

He preserved the esteem and affection of His Majesty to his death, being the last noble person with that glorious monarch. His Majesty, breathing with great difficulty, asked his physician, " if this could last long?" To which the Doctor replied, " an hour, or an hour and a half; though you may be snatched away in the twinkling of an eye." After that, whilst the Doctor was feeling his pulse, the King took him by the hand, saying " I do not die yet, hold me fast." Having taken a little of the cordial potion administered unto him, he faintly inquired for the Earl of Portland, who immediately came to him, and placed his ear as near as he could to His Majesty's mouth; but though his lips were seen to move, his Lordship was not able to hear any distinct articulate sound; and, in a few minutes after, His Majesty, shutting his eyes, expired with two or three short gasps, March 8, 1701-2.

After which his Lordship went over to Holland, and, May 22, 1707, arrived at the Hague; and the year after, the King of Prussia coming from Cleves by water to Hounslaerdyk, which was prepared for his reception, the Earl of Portland, July 19, N. S. 1708, went thither to compliment His Majesty in the name of the States-General. On the close of the same year his Lordship returned to England, and betook himself to a retired life, living in a most exemplary way; and dying at his seat at Bulstrode, in the County of Bucks, November 23, 1709, in the sixty-first year of his age, and was buried in the vault under the great east window of Henry VIIth's Chapel, Westminster Abbey.*

His Lordship married first, Anne, daughter of Sir Edward Villiers, Knight Marshal, and sister to Edward, Earl of Jersey, at that time Maid of Honour to Mary, Princess of Orange, and by her had issue three sons, and five daughters, viz.—

William, who died in his infancy; Henry, second son, who succeeded to his father's titles; and another William, who died in Holland.

Lady Mary, eldest daughter, first married Algernon, Earl of Essex, who leaving her a widow, Jan. 10, 1709, she was secondly married in 1714, to the Hon. Conyers d'Arcy, afterwards, K. B. and only brother to Robert, Earl of Holdernesse; she died Aug. 20, 1726.

Lady Anne Margaretta, second daughter, married Monsieur Duyvenvorde, one of the principal nobles in Holland. Lady Frances Williamyna, third daughter, married William, Lord Byron, and died March 31, 1712. Lady Eleanora, fourth daughter, died unmarried. Lady Isabella, youngest daughter, married, Aug. 2, 1714, Evelyn Pierrepoint, Duke of Kingston, and died Feb. 23, 1727-8.

His Lordship, on May 16, 1700, married, secondly, Jane, sixth daughter of Sir John Temple, of East Sheen, in the County of Surrey, Bart., sister to Henry, Lord Viscount Palmerston, and widow of John, Lord Berkeley of Stratton, and by her (who was, on April 12, 1718, appointed governess to the three Princesses, eldest daughters of his late Majesty, and died March 26, 1751,) had two sons, and four daughters; William, who died Oct. 13, 1774; and Charles John, Count Bentinck, who died March 18, 1779, aged 71; Lady Sophia, married, March 24, 1728-9, to his Grace Henry de Grey, Duke of Kent; who, by

* Dart's History of St. Peter's, Westminster, vol. ii. p. 55.

her, had a daughter, Lady Sophia, married to her
cousin, John Egerton, Bishop of Durham ; Lady
Elizabeth, married, Dec. 18, 1720, to Dr. Henry
Egerton, Bishop of Hereford, brother to his Grace,
Scroop, Duke of Bridgewater : she died Nov. 8,
1765, and was buried at Bruton, in Somersetshire ;
and was grandmother, by him, to the present Earl
of Bridgewater ; Lady Harriot, married at the
Hague, Oct. 15, 1728, to James Hamilton, Viscount Limerick, of the kingdom of Ireland ; Lady
Barbara, who married Francis Godolphin, Esq.,
afterwards Lord Godolphin ; and died April 15,
1736.

Henry, second Earl, and first Duke of Portland, married June 9, 1704, the Lady Elizabeth
Noel, eldest daughter and co-heir of Wriothesley
Baptist, Earl of Gainsborough,* with whom
he had, among other possessions, the moiety of
the Lordship of Tichfield in the county of Southampton, as well as of the said mansion-house.†
And at this seat the Earl of Portland resided whilst
he was a commoner ; and by his affability and
hospitality gained the love and esteem of all about
him. He was elected one of the members of the
town of Southampton, in the parliament which
sat first on business, Oct. 23, 1707 ; and in the
succeeding parliament, which sat November 18,
1708, was returned one of the knights of the shire
for the county, as also for the town of Southampton. On July 21, 1710, he was constituted
captain and colonel of the first troop of Horse-
Guards, which the Earl of Albemarle resigned to
him on a valuable consideration. He was created
Marquis of Tichfield, in com. of Southampton,

* Son of Edward, first Earl of Gainsborough, by Lady Elizabeth, eldest daughter and co-heir of Thomas Wriothesley, fourth
and last Earl of Southampton, and Lord High Treasurer of
England.
† Formerly the seat of the Wriothesley's, Earls of Southampton.

and Duke of Portland, by letters patent, dated July 6, 1716, 2 Geo. I. and appointed one of the Lords of the Bedchamber. On Sept. 9, 1721, he was appointed Captain-General and Governor of the Island of Jamaica;* and arriving at Spanish Town in that island, Dec. 22, 1722, remained there to the time of his decease, at St. Jago de la Vega, July 4, 1726, in the forty-fifth year of his age. He was generally beloved, being of a most noble and generous temper, and of so sweet a disposition, that he made all easy about him. His remains were brought over to England by his disconsolate widow, and deposited at Tichfield, where she herself was interred, March 1736-7.

They had issue three sons and seven daughters, whereof two sons and three daughters survived them, viz. William, who succeeded to the titles; and Lord G. Bentinck, who was born Dec. 24, 1715, and baptized Jan. 23 following, His Majesty King George I. standing godfather in person; appointed captain of a company of the first regiment of foot-guards, on April 17, 1743; being on June 27, N.S. that year, in the battle of Dettingen; on March 7, 1752, appointed one of his Majesty's aid-de-camps, and to take rank as colonel of foot; constituted colonel of a regiment of foot in 1754, and died at Bath, without issue, March 2, 1759, being then a major-general and M.P. for Malmsbury in Wilts.

Their three daughters were, Lady Anne, who was married to Lieutenant-Colonel Daniel Paid, who died Jan. 1748-9, and her Ladyship dying July 4, 1749, was buried by him in Dublin. Lady Anne Isabella, married Nov. 8, 1739, to Henry Monk, Esq. of the kingdom of Ireland, by whom she had the Marchioness of Waterford, mother of the present Marquis; she died 1783. And Lady

* He was much injured in his fortune, by the South Sea Bubble.

Emilia Catherine, who was born at St. Jago de la Vega, in Jamaica, April 5, 1726, married at Christmas, 1747, to Mr. Jacob Arrant Van Wassenar, of the province of Holland (elected into the body of the nobles of that province, Feb. 18, 1755), and died Jan. 10, 1756.

WILLIAM, SECOND DUKE OF PORTLAND, who succeeded his father Henry, was born March 1, 1708-9; after three years travels in France and Italy, returned to England in 1733. In Feb. 1735 his Grace was appointed a Lord of the Bedchamber to His Majesty. His Grace was married at Maryle-bone (commonly called Oxford) Chapel, July 11, 1734, to the Lady Margaret Cavendish Harley, only daughter and heiress of Edward, second Earl of Oxford, and Earl Mortimer, by his wife the Lady Henrietta Cavendish, only daughter and heiress of John Holles, Duke of Newcastle, by the daughter and heiress of Henry Cavendish, Duke of Newcastle.* Their Graces had issue, Lady Elizabeth Cavendish Bentinck, married May 22, 1759, to Thomas, Viscount Weymouth, afterwards Marquis of Bath.

Lady Henrietta Cavendish Bentinck, who was one of the supporters of Queen Charlotte's train at her nuptials on Sept. 8, 1761, and on May 28, 1763, married George Henry, Earl of Stamford.

William Henry Cavendish Bentinck, who succeeded his father in the Dukedom.

Lady Margaret Cavendish Bentinck, who died on April 23, 1756.

Lady Frances Cavendish Bentinck, who died an infant, Feb. 28, 1742-3.

And Lord Edward Charles Cavendish Bentinck, born on March 3, 1744, married Dec. 23, 1782, at

---

* Son of the celebrated and loyal William Cavendish, Duke of Newcastle, whose seat at Welbeck, with his large estates in Nottinghamshire, Derbyshire, and in the North, &c. have thus descended to the Duke of Portland.

Mary-le-bone, to Miss Cumberland, eldest daughter
of Richard Cumberland, Esq. by whom he has
several children.   His eldest son is in holy orders;
and is a dignitary of the church, Prebendary of
Westminster, &c.   His daughter, Henrietta, married May 8, 1809, Sir William Mordaunt Milner,
Bart.   He was many years M. P. for Nottinghamshire.

At a Chapter of the most noble Order of the
Garter, held at St. James's, March 20, 1740-1, his
Grace was first Knighted by his Majesty, and immediately after was invested with the ensigns of that
noble order, and was installed at Windsor, April
21, 1741.   His Grace was also Fellow of the Royal
Society, and President of the British Lying-in
Hospital for Married Women, in Brownlow Street,
Long Acre, London; one of the Trustees of the
British Museum, and, departing this life on May
1, 1762, was buried at Tichfield.   The Duchess
survived till July 7, 1785.   She inherited the
spirit of her ancestors in her patronage of literature
and the arts.

William Henry Cavendish Bentinck, THIRD
DUKE OF PORTLAND, was born, April 14, 1738;
and at the general election in 1761, was returned
one of the Members for Weobly, in Herefordshire.

His Grace was sent, LORD LIEUTENANT, TO
IRELAND in the Marquis of Rockingham's administration, April 8, 1782; which, as the Marquis
died soon after, his Grace only held till September
15, following.   When the coalition took place
between Mr. Fox and Lord North, which drove the
Marquis's successor, Lord Lansdown, from the helm,
his Grace was, on April 5, 1783, appointed First
Lord of the Treasury.   This also he resigned Dec.
27, following, when William Pitt became Premier.
Hence he united in firm phalanx with the com-
panions of his retreat; and, with Fox, Burke,
Sheridan, Windham, and many others, formed the

most powerful Whig opposition, for many years, to the young, eloquent, powerful, and undaunted Minister, till the alarm of the French Revolution dissolved this mighty combination; and the Duke, a convert to the master mind of Burke, felt the necessity of strengthening the hands of government, and on July 11, 1794, was appointed Principal Secretary of State for the Home Department. The seals of this office he held till July 30, 1801, when Mr. Pitt having retired, his Grace was nominated PRESIDENT OF THE COUNCIL in the new Administration of Addington; and so continued till the dissolution of that ministry.

When Lord Grenville's ministry ceased, his Grace was once more appointed First Lord of the Treasury, in the spring of 1807; and held that high office till his death, which happened Oct. 30, 1809, at the age of 71.

His Grace was of easy manners, and mild and amiable disposition; not insensible of his rank, yet unassuming in the use of it; it is not improbable that his love of ease, and tendency towards indolence, made him sometimes too ductile, and the dupe of those, by whom the rectitude of his understanding would not yet suffer him to be deceived. In this respect, he was, perhaps, not unlike his brother-in-law and relation, the Duke of Devonshire.

As a statesman, his high rank and princely estates, his long familiarity with public affairs, the plainness of his understanding, and his constitutional principles, gave him many important qualifications for the high offices which he held. It would be idle flattery to assert that he possessed the vigour and brilliancy of genius, or even of eminent talents; but on his public conduct his country may look with approbation; and his posterity may feel a just pride that he so discharged the high duties he undertook for his country, that his name will stand honourably on her annals, while many of his contemporaries of equal rank and advantages will sink into the oblivion which is the price of a selfish privacy.

His Grace was married Nov. 8, 1766, to Lady Dorothy Cavendish, daughter of William, the late Duke of Devonshire, and by her, who died June 3, 1794, he had issue:—

First, William Henry Cavendish, Marquis of Tichfield, born June 24, 1768, who, for several years represented the County of Buckingham in Parliament.

Second, Lord William Henry Cavendish, born Sept. 14, 1774, late Governor of Madras, and a Major-General in the army;

Third, Lady Charlotte, born Oct. 3, 1775, married March 31, 1793, Charles Greville, Esq. son of Fulk Greville, Esq. of Wilbery in Wiltshire, and has issue.

Fourth, Lady Mary, born March 17, 1778.

Fifth, Lord Charles, a Lieutenant-Colonel in the army, and Captain in the first regiment of Foot Guards.

William Henry Cavendish Scott, Fourth and present Duke of Portland, who is Lord Lieutenant of the County of Middlesex. His Grace having been married Aug. 4, 1795, to Henrietta Scott, daughter of the late General Scott, by His Majesty's permission obtained in September of the same year, added the name of Scott to that of Bentinck, and annexed the arms of Scott to his own. His issue are :—

First, William Henry, Marquis of Tichfield, born Oct. 22, 1796.

Second, Lady Caroline, born July 6, 1799.

Third, Lord John, born Sept. 18, 1800.

Fourth, Lady Henrietta. Fifth, Lord George. Sixth, Lord Henry. Seventh, Lady Charlotte. Eighth, Lady Lucy. Ninth, Lady Mary.

Titles. William Henry Cavendish Scott Bentinck, Duke of Portland, Marquis of Tichfield, Earl of Portland, Viscount Woodstock, and Baron of Cirencester.

Creations. Baron of Cirencester, in the County of Gloucester, Viscount Woodstock, in Oxfordshire, and Earl of Portland in the County of Dorset, April 9, 1689, 1 Will. and Mary; and Marquis of Tichfield, and Duke of Portland, July 6, 1716, 2 Geo. I.*

THE OLD MANOR HOUSE.

This Mansion, attached to the Royal Park of Mary-le-bone, was originally built in the Reign of Henry VIII. and occasionally used as one of the palaces during the reigns of Mary and Elizabeth.† From a drawing of Rooker's (in the possession of Mr. White the present District Surveyor) it seems to have retained some traces of the architecture of Queen Elizabeth's time, but the greater part appears to have been rebuilt, or at least sustained considerable alteration, at a later period, perhaps by the Forsets (to whom it went by grant from Elizabeth): the South front, which had a fine bow window, was certainly added or renewed at the commencement of the last century. A considerable school was established here by Mr. De la Place about 1703, whose daughter marrying the Rev. John Fountayne, Rector of North Tidmouth in Wiltshire, he was succeeded by him in the school. This school appears to have been in great repute, many

* Collins's Biog. Peerage, augmented by Sir Egerton Brydges.
† In Peck's Desiderata Curiosa, vol. i. p. 68, is a List of Salaries paid in Queen Elizabeth's time to the Keepers, &c. of all the Royal Palaces and Castles. At Mary-le-bone they were as follows:—

	£.	s.	d.
Keeper for Maribone Park : fee	12	13	4
Keeper of the House, Covent-Garden, and the Woodes, at Maribone	10	0	0
Lieutenant of the Chase at Maribone	10	0	0

MARY LE BONE MANOR HOUSE.

(now pulled down.)

Drawn on Stone from a sketch in the possession of John Brown, Esq. A.D. 1790.

Printed by Graf & Soret

Noblemen and Gentlemen now living, having been educated there previously to their removal to the Universities. This fine and interesting mansion, which stood at the top of High Street, nearly opposite the old church, was taken down in 1791, and some livery stables were built on its site; over the western entrance to these stables was placed a clock, which had originally occupied a prominent situation in the old mansion, but which has been removed within these few years. It does not appear that the Earls of Oxford ever inhabited this mansion; but their noble Library of Books and Manuscripts were deposited in a house built for that purpose in High Street, about 120 yards south of the above mansion. Since the removal of that Library to the British Museum, this house has been nearly rebuilt, with a modern front, and occupied as a boarding school for young Ladies called Oxford House, but it is at present unoccupied.*

At the back of this House was situated that celebrated place of amusement, Mary-le-bone Gardens, of which a more particular account will be given hereafter.

The following extracts from a Letter, written by the grandson of the Rev. Mr. Fountayne, and which appeared in one of Mr. Hone's Publications, may prove gratifying to the reader; it being evidently written by a gentleman who reverts with delight to the scenes of his youthful days:—

SIR,—" A few lines upon the subject of Mary-le-

* Mr. John Brown, of Clipstone Street, an eminent builder and most respectable man, was employed by the Duke of Portland in repairing this house, and likewise in the demolition of the Manor-House, the range of stabling erected on its site, forming part of the extensive property of which he died possessed. This gentleman, who was extensively engaged in the new buildings, which rose like exhalations about that period; resided in this parish upwards of 50 years, and dying at the advanced age of 80, sincerely lamented by all who knew him, was interred in the Cemetery on the North side of Paddington Street.

bone may not be unacceptable. My grandfather,
a Rector of North Tidmouth, was, I think also
connected with the old church at the former place;
at all events he occasionally officiated at that church.
He rented the fine ancient structure nearly opposite
thereto, called Mary-le-bone Manor-House, a view
of which, with the gardens, park, and environs, as
they appeared in Queen Elizabeth's reign I have
in my possession.* The plate is dedicated to the
" Noblemen and Gentlemen educated at this Noble
Mansion;"   *   *   *   *   *

   " Having been at this school from my infancy
almost, down to about 1790, I have a perfect re-
collection of this fine and interesting house, with
its beautiful saloon and gallery, in which private
concerts were held occasionally, and the first instrumental performers attended.   My grandfather,
as I have been told, was an enthusiast in music, and
cultivated, most of all, the friendship of musical
men, especially of Handel, who visited him often,
and had a great predilection for his society.   This
leads me to relate an anecdote which I have on the
best authority.   *   *   *   *   *

   " While Mary-le-bone Gardens were flourishing,
the enchanting music of Handel, and probably of
Arne, was often heard from the orchestra there.
One evening, as my grandfather and Handel were
walking together and alone, a new piece was
struck up by the band. " Come, Mr. Fountayne,"
said Handel, " let us sit down and listen to this
piece—I want to know your opinion of it."   Down
they sat, and after some time the old parson,
turning to his companion, said, " It is not worth

* This Print taken from a Drawing made by Gasselin, in 1700,
was published, Sept 20, 1800, by J. T. Smith, of Great Portland
Street. The Rev. Bryant Burgess, Curate of the Parish, who
received part of his education at this school, possesses a coloured
copy of this Print, which, with that politeness and urbanity of
manners for which he is proverbial, he readily submitted to the
inspection of the compiler of this volume.

listening to—it's very poor stuff." " You are right, Mr. Fountayne," said Handel, " it is very poor stuff—I thought so myself, when I had finished it." The old gentleman being taken by surprise, was beginning to apologise, but Handel assured him there was no necessity; that the music was really bad, having been composed hastily, and his time for the production limited; and that the opinion given was as correct as it was honest.

" Mary-le-bone was a sweet place in the days of my youth, but now, alas! how changed! Our only walk beyond the play-ground was " Primrose Hill," and Green-berry Hill,"* across " Welling's Farm."† I remember the fine gardens and mulberry trees, and seeing Lunardi, or Blanchard, in his balloon high over them. I remember anecdotes of Dr. Arne, and many eminent men; and especially of those wonderful men, Samuel and Charles Wesley, who, when children, were stars of the first magnitude in the musical world, and lived at or near Mary-le-bone. But time and space fail me."

Your's, &c.

J. H.

Account of the Duke of Portland's Estate, taken from a plan made by Henry Pratt, in 1708.

Barrow Hills.

Denominations.	Tenant's Names.	No. of Acres. A. R. P.		
1. Upper Primrose Hill -	Mr. Thomas Baker	9	0	12
2. Primrose Hill - - -	Ditto	12	2	16
3. White House Mead -	Ditto	9	0	36
4. White House Field -	Ditto	13	0	0
5. Wheat Field - - -	Ditto	19	2	8
	Total -	63	1	32

* Barrow-Hill.　　　† Willan's Farm.

Marybone.

Denominations.	Tenant's Names.	A.	R.	P.
6. A Hay Yard - - -	Mr. Thomas Baker	0	0	16
7. Dove House Park -	Ditto	5	3	30
8. Broom Field - - -	Ditto	9	1	16
9. Ditto - - - - -	Ditto	9	1	16
10. The Nine Acres - -	Mr. John Steel	11	3	16
11. The Ten Acres - -	Ditto	9	1	8
12. The Clay Pit - -	Ditto	11	3	20
13. Prescat - - - -	Ditto	0	1	20
14. Mill Hill Field - -	Ditto	11	3	0
15. Burgess's Farm, Home Field, and Broad Field -	Ditto	33	0	0
16. Dung Field - - -	Ditto	17	3	0
17. Part of the same - -	Ditto	2	0	12
18. The Eight Acres - -	Ditto	8	3	24
19. Park Field - - -	Ditto	12	1	8
20. The Fourteen Acres -	Mr. James Long	16	1	16
21, 22. Bowling Greens,&c.	Ditto	6	3	16
23. A Garden - - - -	Ditto	0	0	16
24. Turner's Field - - -	Mr. Nowell	7	2	12
25. A House and Garden -	Mr. Canningham	0	0	32
26, 27. Ditto ditto - -	Mr. Thos. Barjour	0	3	8
28, 29. Ditto ditto -	Samuel Mitcheau	1	2	24
30, 31. Part of the Manor House Garden - - -	Mr. Jas. Sentiman	0	2	16
32. Ditto - - - - -	Mr. Peter Lettuce	0	2	16
33, 34. A House & Garden,	Mr. Allen	0	1	24
35. Four tenements, Gardens, &c. - - - -	Mr. Card	1	1	20
36. Church Field - - -	Anthony Knight	11	0	0
37. Lower Church Field -	Ditto	9	2	20
38. A House and Garden -	Ditto	0	1	8
39. Ditto ditto - - -	Thos. Mansellin	1	0	36
40. Ditto ditto - - -	Mr. Hargrave	0	0	28
41. Ditto ditto - - -	Mr. Hemmett	0	0	20
42. Ditto ditto - - -	Thomas Bradgate	0	0	28
43, 44. Bowling Green, with Houses, Gardens, &c. -	Mr. Whitfield	0	3	36
		203	0	2

Manor of Lilestone,

(commonly called Lisson Green.)

The Manor of Lilestone, containing five hides (now Lisson Green, in the Parish of Mary-le-bone), is mentioned in Domesday-Book among the lands in Ossulston Hundred given in alms: it is said to have been, in King Edward's time, the property of Edward, son of Swain, a servant of the King, who might alienate it at pleasure; when the survey was taken, it belonged to Eideva. The land, says the record, is three carucates. In demesne are four hides and a-half, on which are two ploughs, the villans have one plough. There are four villans, each holding half a virgate, three cottars of two acres and one slave; meadow equal to one plough-land; pasture for the cattle of the village; woods for 100 hogs; and 3*d.* arising from the herbage; valued in the whole at 60*s.*; in King Edward's time, at 40*s.* This manor afterwards became the property of the Priory of St. John of Jerusalem;* on the suppression of which

* Jordan Briset and Muriel his wife, persons of rank, founded this house in the year 1100, and it received consecration from *Heraclius, patriarch of Jerusalem.* This Order, at first styled itself, servant to the poor servants of the Hospital at *Jerusalem;* but their vast endowments infected them with an uncommon degree of pride. The whole Order had, in different parts of *Christendom,* nineteen thousand manors. In 1323, the revenues of the English Knights Templars were bestowed on them. This gave them such importance, that the Prior was ranked as first Baron of England, and lived in the highest state. Their luxury gave offence to the rebels of Kent and Essex in 1381. These levellers burnt their house to the ground; but it soon rose with redoubled splendour. The first Prior was *Garnerius de Napoli;* the last, Sir William Weston, who, on the suppression by Henry VIII. had a pension of a thousand pounds a year; but died of a broken heart on Ascension Day, 1540; the very day that the House was suppressed. His monument is preserved by a drawing in the possession of Dr. Combe. Its revenue at that time according to *Dugdale,* was 2385*l.* 12*s.* 8*d.—Pennant.*

it was granted, *anno* 1548, to Thomas Heneage and Lord Willoughby; who conveyed it in the same year, to Edward Duke of Somerset. On his attainder it reverted to the Crown, and was granted *anno* 1564, to Edward Downing, who conveyed it the same year to John Milner, Esq., then lessee under the Crown. After the death of his descendant John Milner, Esq., anno 1753, it passed under his will to William Lloyd, Esq.* The Manor of Lisson Green (being then the property of Capt. Lloyd of the Guards), was sold in lots, *anno* 1792. The largest lot, containing the site of the manor, was purchased by John Harcourt, Esq., M. P. who built a noble mansion, for his own residence, at the corner of Harcourt Street and the New Road; part of the Harcourt estate was subsequently sold by auction in separate lots, and the mansion abovementioned, is now occupied by that excellent Institution, the Queen's Lying-In Hospital, which was instituted in 1752, removed from St. George's Row to Bayswater, in 1791, and established here in 1810. This charity was originally under the especial patronage of Her late Majesty Queen Charlotte, and is now honoured with the patronage of Her present most gracious Majesty.

The Portman Estate.

This Estate was granted by Sir Thomas Docwra, Prior of the Knights of St. John of Jerusalem, in England, in the fourth year of Henry VIII., to John Blenerhasset and Johan his wife, for fifty years by the following description, *viz.* Great Gibbetfield, Little Gibbetfield, Hawkfield, and Brock-

---

* The account of this Manor till it came into the family of Lloyd, is taken from Lysons' Environs, and was obligingly communicated to him by William Bray, Esq. of Great Russell Street, from original Deeds.

stand, Tassel Croft, Boy's Croft, and twenty acres
Fursecroft, and two closes called Shepcott Haws,
parcel of the Manor of Lileston in the County of
Middlesex, late in the tenure of Thomas Hobson,
under the annual rent of eight pounds, payable at
their house in Clerkenwell.

In the 24th of Henry VIII. the executor of the
said John Blenerhasset granted the remainder of
this term to William Portman and his assigns.

Queen Mary, by letters, patent, dated the 11th
of June, the first year of her reign, granted the
reversion of the premises in fee, to William Morgan
and Jerome Hulley, their heirs and assigns, for
ever; who conveyed the same to Sir William
Portman, Lord Chief Justice, and Henry his son,
their heirs and assigns.

From which time this estate, which contains
about 270 acres, has continued in the Portman
family.

Portman Family.

The Portmans appear to have been a family of
note in the County of Somerset in the reign of
Edward I. at which time lived Thomas Portman,
whose grandfather bore the present arms of Portman,
on a field Or, fleur-de-lis Azure.   His lineal
descendant, William Portman, appears to have
been settled at or near Taunton 8 Hen. IV. and
gave lands to the priory of that place (where he
was buried) to pray for his soul.   The son of
William was Walter, who married the heiress of
Orchard, in whose right he acquired a very large
property in Somersetshire, and added the name of
Portman to the family seat of Orchard, at which
place his descendants from that time resided.

His great grandson, Sir William Portman, Knt.
was serjeant at law to Henry VIII. one of the
Justices of the Common Pleas, and afterwards Lord

Chief Justice of England; in which situation he distinguished himself by displaying a degree of integrity and independence very unusual among the Judges in those despotic times. He died in the year 1555, 3 Philip and Mary, and was buried in St. Dunstan's church, London, where a monument was erected to his memory.

John Portman, his grandson, was created a Baronet 25th Nov. 1612. He married Anne, daughter of Sir Henry Gifford, Kt. of Hants, and left issue four sons, viz. Sir Henry Portman, Kt. and Bart. who married Anne, only daughter of William Earl of Derby, and died without issue, 1621; Sir John and Sir Hugh, who both died unmarried; Sir William, the purchaser of the manor of Bryanston, in the county of Dorset (who married Anne, daughter and coheir of John Collis, of Borton in Somersetshire, Esq. by his wife Elizabeth, daughter and sole heir of Humphrey Wiviliscombe, Esq.); and four daughters, viz. Joanne, who married George Speke, of Whitelackington, Esq.; Anne, married to Sir Edward Seymour of Bury Pomeroy Castle, county of Devon, Bart. ancestor of the present Duke of Somerset; Elizabeth, married to John Bluett of Holcombe, in Devonshire, Esq.; and Grace, who died unmarried.

Sir William Portman, Bart. son of Sir William, was created Knight of the Bath by King Charles II. He married three wives, 1st. Elizabeth, daughter and heiress of Sir John Cutler, Bart.; 2dly. Elizabeth, daughter of Sir John Southcote, Knight; 3dly. Mary, daughter and heiress of Sir John Holman, Bart. but having no issue by either of them the title became extinct. By a release dated Feb. 26, 1689, he devised Orchard Portman, together with other estates to a great amount, to his cousin Henry Seymour, Esq. (fifth son of Sir Edward Seymour above-mentioned), who assumed the name and arms of Portman. He married, 1st.

Penelope, daughter of Sir William Haslewood of Maidwell, in Northamptonshire; 2ndly. Meliora, daughter of William Fitch, Esq. of High-Hall in this county, but dying without issue, the whole of his large property devolved, by a further limitation in the will of Sir William Portman, to William Berkeley, Esq. of Pylle, in the county of Somerset, who, by an Act of Parliament, 9 Geo. II. was enabled to take the name, and bear the arms of Portman.

The family of Berkeley took their name from the castle of Berkeley* in Gloucestershire, which, at the time of the Conquest, was possessed by Roger, a Saxon nobleman, who, following the custom introduced by the Normans, assumed the name of Berkeley; but becoming a Monk in the priory of Stanley St. Leonard in 1091, it devolved to his nephew William de Berkeley, whose grandson Roger, Lord of Berkeley and Dursley, having taken part with King Stephen against the Empress Maud, was dispossessed of his barony and lands in favour of Sir Robert Fitzharding, from whom the families of Berkeley are lineally descended.

The family of Berkeley is descended from the blood-royal of Denmark by Harding their first ancestor; from the Dukes of Normandy by Eva, wife of Robert Fitzharding; from the ancient Saxons by Alice, daughter of the Lord Berkeley of Dursley; and from the Kings of England by Isabel, daughter of Edmond Earl of Cornwall.

Sir Edward Berkeley, uncle of Sir John, and third son of Sir Henry (from whom descended the only surviving branch of the Berkeleys of Bruton), married Margaret, daughter of John Holland, Esq., whose ancestor Thomas Holland, Earl of Kent, married Joan the Fair, grand-daughter of Edward

---

* This name is derived from two Saxon words, *Berk*, a Birch-tree (with which that part of Gloucestershire abounds), and *Ley*, a pasture.

the First, and afterwards wife of Edward the Black
Prince.   He was knighted in the first year of the
reign of Charles I. 1625.   He built the mansion
house of Pylle in Somersetshire, where he resided
and possessed considerable property.   He died in
1654.

His son, Edward Berkeley of Pylle, married
Philippa, daughter of George Speke of White
Lackington, Esq. and died in 1669, leaving issue
Edward, who married Elizabeth daughter of John
Ryves, Esq. of Ranston in this county, by whom he
had two sons, Maurice and William.   Maurice
commanded a regiment of the Somerset militia at
the battle of King's Sedgmoor, when the Duke of
Monmouth was defeated.   He died without issue in
1717, and devised his estates to his brother, William
Berkeley of Pylle, Esq., who succeeded afterwards
to the fortune, and took the name of Portman as
before-mentioned.   He resided alternately at his
three seats of Orchard Portman, Pylle (at which
he died in 1737), and Brianston.   On the 8th of
January, 1708, he married Anne, only daughter of
Sir Edward Seymour of Bury Pomeroy, Bart. by
whom he had issue, Henry William Berkeley Portman, who inherited the Portman property; Edward
Berkeley, who took the Berkeley estates, and married Anne, daughter of Thomas Ryves Esq. of Ranston (by whom he had issue two daughters); and
Lætitia (who held the Berkeley estates for her life,
after the death of her brother Edward), married to
Sir John Burland, of Steyning in the county of
Somerset, one of the Barons of the Exchequer, by
whom he had one son, John Berkeley Burland.

Sir Edward Seymour, their maternal ancestor,
was Speaker of the House of Commons, and Comp-
troller of the Household to Queen Anne, and was
one of the principal instruments of the Revolution.
He was the eldest male descendant of Edward
Seymour, the first Duke of Somerset (Lord Pro-

tector of England, and uncle to Edward VI.) whose honours being settled on the issue of his second wife, continued in that branch of the family until the year 1749, when by the death of Algernon, Duke of Somerset, without issue male, the titles of Duke of Somerset, and Baron Seymour, devolved by virtue of the remainder in the original patent, on Sir Edward, whose grandson now enjoys them.

The above Sir Edward Seymour, married for his second wife, Lætitia, daughter of Alexander Popham, Esq. by whom he had issue a daughter, and Francis, created Baron Conway by Queen Anne in 1702, father of the late Marquis of Hertford.

Henry William, eldest son of William Berkeley Portman, Esq. married Anne, daughter of William Fitch, Esq. of High Hall, in Dorsetshire. He died and was buried at Bryanston in 1761, aged 52.

He was succeeded by his only son Henry William Portman, Esq. born 1738, who inherited the Portman estates from his father, and succeeded to the Berkeley property on the death of his aunt, Lady Burland. He married Anne, daughter of William Wyndham, Esq. of Dinton, in the county of Wilts, and died Jan. 16, 1796, leaving issue by this Lady two sons, viz. Henry Berkeley Portman, Esq. M. P. for the city of Wells, who died March 22, 1803, without male issue; and Edward Berkeley Portman, Esq. second son, who inherited the whole of his large estates; he married Lucy, the daughter of the Rev. W. Whitby, of Cresswell Hall, Staffordshire. By this marriage he had issue now living, four sons and three daughters, viz.—

1. Edward Berkeley Portman, Esq. the present proprietor of the Portman estates, who married, June 16, 1827, the Lady Emma Lascelles, third daughter of Henry Lascelles, second Earl of Harewood; and has issue three children.

2. Henry William Berkeley Portman, a Captain in the army.

3. Wyndham Berkeley Portman, Lieut. R. N.
4. Fitzharding Berkeley Portman.
5. Lucy Mabella, married to G. D. Wingfield, Esq.
6. Mary Ann, married to G. Drummond, Esq.
7. Harriet Ella, married to W. Dugdale, Esq.

He married 2ndly, Mary, daughter of Sir Edward Hulse, by whom he had no issue, and died at Rome, Jan. 19, 1823. His widow survived him, and is now living.

Abstract of the Title Deed of the St. John's Wood Estate.

This Estate containing 497*a*. 3*r*. 20*p*., of which 340*a*. 1*r*. 33*p*. are situated in the Parish of St. Mary-le-bone, and the remainder in Hampstead, was granted by Charles II. to Charles Henry Lord Wotton, in discharge of 1300*l*. part of the monies due to him in his said Majesty's Exchequer, &c. The said Lord Wotton on Oct. 6, 1682, devised this Estate to his Nephew Charles Stanhope, younger son of his brother, Philip Earl of Chesterfield. It was subsequently purchased in 1732, of Philip Dormer, Earl of Chesterfield, by Samuel Eyre, Esq. from whom it descended to the present proprietor, Henry Samuel Eyre, Esq. eldest son of Walpole Eyre, Esq. of Burnham, County of Bucks.

Account of the Mary-le-bone portion of this Estate, from a Survey made in 1794.

No.	Quality.		A.	R.	P.
1	Pasture	Houses, Yard, Barn, Gardens, &c.	1	1	13
2	Ditto	Little Hay Field - - - -	7	3	24
3	Meadow	Hanging Field - - - - -	7	3	12
4	Ditto	Spring Field - - - - -	0	1	19
5	Ditto	Dutch Barn Field - - - -	8	1	14
6	Ditto	The Twenty Acre Field - -	6	3	3

32 2 5

No.	Quality.		A.	R.	P.
		Brought forward -	32	2	5
7	Meadow	Great Hill Field - - - -	16	1	26
8	Ditto	Burton-way - - - - - -	18	3	1
9	Pasture	House, Garden and Lawn - - -	1	2	38
10	Meadow	Little Robin's Field - - -	7	3	20
11	Ditto	Little Blewhouse Field - -	11	3	6
12	Arable	Seven Acres - - - - -	7	2	28
13	Pasture	Middle Field - - - - -	3	2	39
14	Meadow	Blewhouse Field - - - -	5	3	37
15	Ditto	Great Robin's Field - - -	10	1	25
16	Ditto	Horn Castle - - - - - -	5	2	18
17	Ditto	Great Garden Field - - - -	30	0	38
18	Ditto	Willow Tree Field - - - -	16	1	21
19	Ditto	Great Field - - - - - -	23	1	17
20	Ditto	Brick Field - - - - - -	34	1	35
21	Pasture	Cottage and Garden - - -	0	0	25
22	Meadow	The Slipe - - - - - -	4	0	6
23	Pasture	House, Barn, Yard, Gardens,	6	3	36
24	Meadow	Barn Field - - - - - -	14	0	4
25	Ditto	Oak tree Field - - - - -	16	1	18
26	Pasture	Piece on St. John's Wood Lane	0	0	19
27	Meadow	Four Acre Field - - - - -	5	3	31
28	Ditto	Six Acre Field - - - - -	6	1	16
29	Pasture	Cottage and Garden - - - -	0	1	37
30	Meadow	The Twenty Acres - - -	25	1	17
31	Ditto	The Nine Acres - - - - -	9	0	17
32	Ditto	The Twenty-two Acre Field -	23	0	0
		Saint John's Wood Lane - -	1	2	13
		Total	340	1	33

Account of the Family of Henry Samuel Eyre, Esq.

The first notice of its settlement in Wiltshire appears in a grant of lands made by Gelfridus le Her, of Bromham, to his wife and children, and is quoted in the copy of a visitation in 1525: the date of this grant must have been about the year

1100. The name seems evidently to be Norman, and although it does not occur in the copy of the Battle Abbey Roll, the founder in all probability came over at the Conquest. As to its derivation, we may hazard a supposition that *le Her, l' Heritière,* or " *the Heir,*" might be a distinction originally given to an eldest son, in those days where the rights of primogeniture were so much observed, and afterwards continued as a family appellation ;— and it is worth notice that " L'Heritière, is a sur- name still found in France. Of the connection between this family and that of the Eyres of Derbyshire, who were settled there before the reign of Henry the Third, there are no traces to be found, although the name is now similarly spelt, and there seems to be no difference in the arms. The elder branch, the Eyres of Bromham, were living as late as the middle of the 17th Century, but it does not appear that any of them still remain. John Eyre of Woodhampton and his wife Eleanor Cooke, founded a second branch, which was again divided into two considerable families, by the two marriages of his great grandson John ; the issue of the first, continued on the family estate, with great consideration and respectability, representing their native County in Parliament, and many places within it, and increasing their fortunes and connec- tions, by many opulent and honourable marriages ; but their lines appear to have both ended in females before the period of the Restoration, and it has not yet been discovered into what names they carried their wealth. From the issue of the second mar- riage, all the present branches derive their source. Their patriarch Robert Eyre, settled at Salisbury, as a merchant, and the title deeds of his house there, containing the conveyance from Sir Henry Long in the 33d of Hen. VIII. are still among the papers preserved at Newhouse. He lies buried at St. Thomas's Church, with a long line of descendants.

Two sons of his son, Thomas Eyre, again founded two considerable families; from the elder proceed in a direct line that of Newhouse, and Henry Samuel Eyre, Esq. the present proprietor of the St. John's Wood Estate: from the 2d descend the Eyres of Brickworth. Their founder, Giles Eyre, was a noted republican in the time of Charles, his house at Brickworth was besieged and pillaged, and himself fined and imprisoned, but he weathered the storm, and saw himself afterwards, with seven sons, seated as Members for Wilts, and places within it, in all the Parliaments of the Commonwealth; he died shortly before the Restoration, and his monument sets forth in no very temperate language, the long catalogue of his sufferings. One of his younger sons, John, went over to Ireland with his countryman Ludlow, and there founded an Irish branch, which was so considerable as to be raised to a peerage in the late reign, but they have not been traced beyond the year 1680. Sir Giles Eyre the grandson of the first Giles, was one of the Judges of the Court of King's Bench at the same period as his second Cousin Sir Samuel Eyre, Knt. who died 1699. Some curious correspondence between these two eminent lawyers is still in possession of the family. The male line of the Brickworth branch is represented by Mr. Eyre of Botley; but Henry Samuel Eyre, Esq. eldest son of the late Walpole Eyre, of Burnham, in the County of Bucks, being the nearest male descendant of the Newhouse stock, is the proper representative of the family.

LINEAGE.

Robert Eyre of Sarum, 33d Henry VIII. M. P. for New Sarum, 1557, and Mayor, 1559, married Joane, widow of George Turney, and had issue, by her, an only son Thomas; who married Elizabeth, daughter of ———— Rogers, Esq. of Poole, in the County of Dorset, and had issue:—1. Robert, eldest son, Counsellor at law ; 2. Giles, second son, who was founder of the Brickworth branch of the family ; and four other sons and three daughters. He died Sept. 10, 1628. Robert, married Anne, daughter of John Still, Bishop of Bath and Wells, and had issue one son and two daughters. His son Robert, married Anne, daughter of Samuel Aldersey, Esq. of London, by whom he had issue one son and three daughters. He died 1667. His son, Sir Samuel Eyre, Knt. of Newhouse, married Martha Lucy, third daughter and co-heiress of Francis Lucy, Esq. he died in 1669, being at that time one of the Judges of the Court of King's Bench. The issue of this marriage, was :—

1. Sir Robert Eyre of Newhouse, Knt. Lord Chief Justice of the Court of Common Pleas, who died 1735.

2. Francis.

3. Henry Samuel Eyre, Merchant of London, the purchaser of the St. John's Wood Estate, who died a bachelor.

4. Kingsmill Eyre, Esq. of Chelsea College, who married Elizabeth, daughter of ——— Atkinson, Esq.

5. Martha Eyre.

6. Lucy Eyre.

The issue of Kingsmill Eyre, Esq. were two sons, and one daughter, viz :—

1. Samuel Eyre, Esq. of Newhouse, who married Stewart Russell, daughter of John Russell, Esq. Consul General at Lisbon, and Envoy to the Barbary Powers. He died in 1795.

2. Walpole Eyre, Esq. of Burnham, in the County of Bucks, who married Sarah Johnson.

3. Elizabeth Eyre, who married Polydore Plumtre, Esq. fourth son of John Plumtre, of the County of Notts. M. P. for Nottingham.

The issue of the above Walpole Eyre, Esq. of Burnham, is ;—1. Henry Samuel Eyre, Esq. the present proprietor of the estate at St. John's Wood, in the County of Middlesex.

2. John Thomas Eyre, Esq. who married Harriet Margaret Ainslie, and has issue two sons and one daughter.

3. Walpole Eyre, Esq. of Montagu Place, Bryanston Square, who married Elizabeth A. Johnson, and has issue, two sons and three daughters, viz:—

1. Henry Samuel Eyre, born 1816.
2. Frederick Edwin Eyre, born 1817.
3. Elizabeth Annabella Eyre, born 1820.
4. Alathea Sarah Henrietta Eyre, born 1822.
5. Emma Harriet Eyre, born 1824.

The singular coincidence of the descendants of two distinct branches of this family, marrying with the immediate descendants of the family of the Hero of the Nile, and Trafalgar: have occurred in the following manner:—

Frances Elizabeth Eyre, sole daughter and heiress of John Maurice Eyre, Esq. of Langford House, a descendant of the Brickworth branch; married Thomas Bolton, Esq. only surviving son of Thomas Bolton of Burnham, in the County of Norfolk, Esq. by Susannah, *eldest sister* of Horatio, Lord Viscount Nelson, K. B. &c. &c. &c. and has issue one son, viz. Horatio Bolton, born 1823.

Harriet Eyre, grand-daughter of Samuel Eyre, Esq. of Newhouse, a (distinct branch) married George Matcham, Esq. of Hoadlands, in the County of Sussex, eldest son of George Matcham Esq. of Ashfield, in the same County, by Catherine *youngest sister* of the late Horatio, Admiral Lord Viscount Nelson, K. B. &c. &c. &c. The issue of this marriage is also one son, viz. Horatio Nelson Eyre Matcham, born 1819.

D

Land, the property of Harrow School.

John Lyon, a wealthy yeoman at Preston, who founded Harrow School, left 40 acres of land in this Parish, which he had purchased of William Sherington, citizen of London; the rents and profits of which were directed to be expended in repairing the roads from Edgeware and Harrow to London; from Gore Lane to Hyde House, and between Preston and Deadman's Hill. He also bequeathed a smaller quantity of land at Kilburn to be expended for the same purpose. One of these estates (which, both together, did not produce 50 years ago, 100*l.* per annum) is now let at about 120*l.*; the other produced about 700*l.* per annum twenty years ago, but it has since been let on building leases at double that rent. The rents of these estates are received by the trustees of the Harrow road.

ORIGIN OF PAROCHIAL DIVISIONS.

The origin of parochial divisions is justly considered as one of the most obscure and unsettled points of English topography; being too unimportant to be mentioned in general history, and too ancient to be preserved in any episcopal registers. *Camden* tells us England was divided into parishes by Honorius, Archbishop of Canterbury, about the year 636. *Hume* says, " that though parishes had been instituted by Honorius, the clergy had never been able to get possession of the tithes for more than two centuries after, viz. in the reign of Ethelwolf, who having summoned the states of the whole kingdom; with their consent, conferred this perpetual and important donation on the church." That ingenious and learned Antiquarian, Mr. Park, in his *History of Hampstead*, p. 203, thus treats this

subject: " Those who would carry back the origin
of parishes in England to a much more distant
period than they really commenced in point of fact,
would appear to have confounded the common idea
conveyed in modern language by the word *parish*,
with the totally distinct state of things which existed
under the ancient diocesan *parochiæ;* where a far
extended district was supplied by an itinerant, not
a resident ministry; where the endowment, instead
of being individually appropriated, constituted one
common fund; and where the mother church, or
ealdan mynsterre, stood alone, the solitary seat of
the Episcopalian, whose choir was the rendezvous
of the dispersed clergy, there resorting to receive
their instructions, report their progress, divide their
oblations, and perform the more solemn ceremonials
of their religion.

Of such ecclesiastical divisions as these we shall
probably find traces very soon after the first reception of Christianity in England; but we must
come down a few steps lower in the scale of time
to consider the origin of Parishes *commonly* so
called. We must behold civilization gradually
though slowly advancing, and the population of the
country increased; this, consequently, produces a
requisition for a more general diffusion of the
benefits of religious worship, and more permanent
communication between the priest and his congregation. At what period of time the distribution
of the original diocese into smaller districts might
first commence, it is now perhaps impossible to
say; but we must avoid the erroneous supposition
that such a division of ecclesiastical jurisdiction
was produced at once, or with uniformity: it was
in fact the progressive work of ages; and consequently the only question within the cognizance
of chronology would be the difficult inquiry,—in
what instance the diocesan allotment was first
encroached upon by the foundation of a filial

church within the limits of the original *parochia?*
But leaving this obscure point to be adjusted by
more determined students in monkish lore, I must
observe, that however incompatible the innovation
may appear with the *original* constitution of the
Britannic Church, it was speedily connived at, and
even encouraged by the Bishops themselves. In
that early state of things, dislike of innovation,
and fear of encroachment, were not such predo-
minating principles among the rulers of the church
as now; and necessity was probably too powerful
a plea to be stifled by them. As the people began
to settle in the hitherto uncultivated parts of the
country, which were of course farther removed
from the metropolis of the district, their distance
and alienation from the " holye mynsterre," must
have been severely felt, for here alone they could
receive the baptismal, nuptial, and sepulchral ordi-
nances, partake of the eucharist, or behold those
displays of religious splendour, which, rude as
they then were, captivated the inexperienced senses
of a generation far off from refinement. Hence I
should imagine that churches distinct from the
ecclesia cathedralis were earliest tolerated in those
distant situations, which, from the convenience of
local circumstances, or other accidental attraction,
had become the resort of concentrated populations,
forming themselves into towns or burghs. But,
however, uncertain its beginning, we soon find
the new system gaining ground, and obliterating
the primitive constitution in its progress. Religious service is provided for, not only in towns
and cities, but manerial lords are invited to erect
churches upon their own demesnes, and to form
their tenants and retainers into distinct congregations. As an incitement to such pious deeds, the
ordinary in time relinquishes his ancient right of
patronage, and vests it in the founder; he allows
him to appropriate the tithes and oblations accruing

from his own territory (which before went to the common stock) for the sole support and service of the particular church and its incumbent, empowering him to present his own clerical associate or dependent to the benefice, subject only to the episcopal examination and superintendence.

" It appears obvious, that the appropriating of tithes to individual churches must have immediately required a notorious and permanent settlement of parochial boundaries; for, otherwise, perpetual litigation must have ensued. This was simply provided for by making the limit of the lord's estate the limit likewise of the priest's jurisdiction; so that each tenant rendered his ecclesiastical dues to that church whose patron claimed his temporal services. But when (in the words of Bishop Kennett) ' the country grew more populous, and persons more devout, several other churches were founded *within the extent of the former*, and then a new parochial circuit was allotted, in proportion to the new church, and the manor or estate of the founder of it.' * Here I confess I see difficulties which my acquaintance with ecclesiastical history is not sufficiently minute to obviate. If the tithes of a large portion of the original parish were to be appropriated to the new foundation, how was the incumbent of the mother church to be reconciled to the loss? How was he to be compelled to such a diminution of his circle of authority? With respect to the civil allotment of property there is no such difficulty. A barony was easily and frequently severed into lesser fees, and these again into subordinate or mesne manors, the lords of which might each claim to erect a church, and annex their own estate to it as its parish, but how they contrived to adjust the distribution of tithes, I have yet to learn."

The modern method of providing for a more

* Kennet's Parochial Antiq. p. 587.

general diffusion of the benefits of religious worship, as exhibited in the various populous parishes adjacent to the Metropolis, is, by Act of Parliament, to divide the parish into districts, and upon the erection of a church in the new district, the minister appointed is termed a District Rector, who is subservient to the head Rector, and pays a stipulated sum annually to him, out of the fees arising from the Christenings, Marriages, &c. thus providing additional accommodation for an increased population, without interfering with the ancient boundary, or political arrangement of the parish.

On the Perambulation of the Parish, commonly called " Walking the Bounds."

The Perambulation of the circuits of Parishes in Rogation Week, was a very ancient general custom,* and one of those retained by the Reformed Church; for by an injunction of Q. Elizabeth, it is ordered, " That the people shall, once a year, at the time accustomed, with the curate and substantial men of the parish, walk about the parishes, as they were accustomed, and at their

---

* Armstrong, in his History of Minorca, 8vo. Lond. 1752, p. 5, speaking of the *Terminalia,* feasts instituted by the Romans in honour of Terminus, the guardian of boundaries and land-marks, whose festival was celebrated at Rome on the 22d or 23d of February, every year, when cakes and fruits were offered to the God, and sometimes sheep and swine, says, " He was represented under the figure of an old man's head and trunk to the middle without arms, which they erected on a kind of pedestal that diminished downwards towards the base, under which they usually buried a quantity of charcoal, as they thought it to be incorruptible in the earth ; and it was criminal by their laws, and regarded as an act of impiety to this Divinity, to remove or deface any of the Termini.   Nay, they visited them at set times, as the children in *London* are accustomed to *perambulate the limits of their parish,* which they call *processioning ;* a custom probably derived to them from the Romans, who were so many ages in possession of the Island of Great Britain."—*Brand's Popular Antiquities.*

return to church, make their common prayers;
provided that the curate in the said perambulation
as heretofore in the days of Rogations, at certain
convenient places, shall admonish the people to
give God thanks in the beholding of God's benefits,
for the increase and abundance of his fruits upon
the face of the earth, with the saying of the 104th
Psalm, &c.; at which time also the said Minister
shall inculcate this and such like sentences,
' Cursed be he which translateth the bounds and
doles of his neighbour,' or such other order of
prayer as shall be hereafter appointed."* One
of our Church Homilies is also expressly composed
for this occasion.

What is related on this head in the Life of
Hooker,† author of the Ecclesiastical Polity, is
extremely interesting: " He would by no means
omit the customary time of procession, persuading
all, both rich and poor, if they desired the preservation of love and their parish rights and liberties,
to accompany him in his perambulation; and most
did so; in which perambulation he would usually
express more pleasant discourse than at other
times, and would then always drop some loving
and facetious observations, to be remembered
against the next year, especially by the boys and
young people: still inclining them and all his
parishioners, to meekness, and mutual kindnesses
and love, because love thinks not evil, but covers
a multitude of infirmities."

There does not appear to be any law existing
to enforce the observance of this custom, nor can
the ecclesiastical Judges oblige the churchwardens
to go their bounds; it is, however, still performed
once in seven years in this parish, though not
attended with all its ancient ceremonies; the last
took place in 1828.

---

* Gibson's Codex.—Faulkner's Hist. of Fulham.
† Zouch's Edit. of Walton's Lives, 8vo. York, 1807, p. 239.

RECTORY.

" The Church of Marybone (or Tybourn, as it was then called), was appropriated in the reign of King John, by William de Sancta Maria, Bishop of London, to the priory of St. Laurence de Blakemore,* in Essex, with the reservation of a competent maintenance for a Vicar, whereby it seems to have been then made presentative of a Vicar, though it became afterwards a Donative or Curacy, in the disposal of the aforesaid Priory; the said approbation was confirmed by Roger Niger in the 7th year of his consecration, and also about the same time by the Dean and Chapter of St. Paul's, Godfrey de Lucy being then Dean." †

On the suppression of that Priory, which took place in the year 1525, the King gave the Rectory to Wolsey, with licence to appropriate it to the Dean and Canons of Christchurch; who; at his request granted it to the master and scholars of his college at Ipswich.‡ When the Cardinal fell into disgrace, the King seized this Rectory as part of his property,§ and it continued in the Crown till the year 1552, when it was granted to

---

* An Hermitage, or Priory of Black Canons, built by Adam and Jordan de Samford, to the Honour of St. Laurence, before or in the beginning of King John's Reign. This was one of the small monasteries which Cardinal Wolsey procured to be dissolved, 17th Hen. VIII., in order to the endowment of his two Colleges at Oxford and Ipswich, at which time the Earl of Oxford claimed to be founder, and it was valued at 85*l.* 9*s.* 7*d. per annum,* viz. in spiritualities, 41*l.* 13*s.* 4*d.*; and in temporalities, 43*l.* 11*s.* 3*d.* Upon the attainder of the Cardinal, this Priory was granted in exchange, 23d Hen. VIII to Waltham Abbey; and after the general suppression, to John Smith, 23d. Hen. VIII.—*Tanner's Notitia Monastica.*

† Newcourt's Repertorium.

‡ *Lysons' Environs.*—From a MS account of the manor, &c. drawn up by Mr. Thomas, who was Steward to the Earls of Oxford.   § Ibid.

Thomas Reve and George Cotton, in common soccage.* It came into the Forset family, then proprietors of the Manor, before the year 1650,† and both Manor and Rectory have since passed through the same hands. The Rectory continued an impropriation until the year 1821, when according to the Provisions made by an Act of Parliament passed in the 57th year of the Reign of George III. intituled " An Act for ratifying the Purchase of the impropriate Rectory of the Parish of St. Mary-le-bone, in the County of Middlesex," the Government purchased the right of presentation of the Duke of Portland, in whose family it had been vested for nearly a century. A grant of a portion of Crown land in the neighbourhood of His Grace's seat at Welbeck, of the value of 40,000*l*., having been made, by way of exchange.

In the year 1511, the Minister's salary was only 13 shillings per annum, paid by Thomas Hobson, then a lessee under the Priory of Blake-more. In 1650, the impropriation was valued at 80*l*. per annum,‡ the Minister was then paid 15*l*. per annum;§ at that time the whole of the emoluments could be scarcely double.

List of Names of Persons who have been Ministers of the Parish Church.

Francis Barton,	-	11 July, 1582
Thomas More,	- -	5 July, 1583
John Payton,	- -	Jan. 1585
Robert Powell,	-	10 June, 1587
Griffin Edwards,	18 Dec. 1598.	He was also

* Newcourt. † Parliamentary Surveys, Lamb. MSS. Lib.
‡ MS. in possession of John White, Esq.
§ The Commissioners appointed to inquire into the State of Ecclesiastical Benefices, proposed to unite the Parishes of Mary-le-bone and Paddington, to build a church at Lisson Green for both, and to settle 100*l*. per annum on the Minister.—*Lysons'*.

Curate of the Church of Dadington, in the year
1C40.

Thomas Swadlin, D. D. He was Minister of
this Church, during the Civil War, was of St. John's
College, Oxford ; and had the living of St. Botolph,
Aldgate, where for his eloquent preaching, he was
much followed by the orthodox party ; but in the
beginning of the troubles he was seized and imprisoned, first in Gresham College, and afterwards in
Newgate, he was sequestered, plundered, and his
wife and family turned out of doors. Upon his
liberation he retired to Oxford, where he was created
Doctor of Divinity, anno 1646, about which time
and after, he obtained a subsistence by teaching in
the neighbourhood of London. Upon the Restoration of Charles II. he was reinstated in his prefer-
ment, and in 1662, he was presented to the Vicarage
of St. James's, Dover, and the Rectory of Hougham
near that place, by the favour of Dr. Juxon, Archbishop of Canterbury. About the year 1664, he
was presented to the Rectory of All-Hallows in
Stamford, Lincolnshire, by Edward, Earl of Clarendon, Lord High Chancellor of England. He
published in 1661, a volume of Sermons on the
anniversary of King Charles's death.

Edmund Price   -   -   -   1664
John Crosbie,   -   -   -   1669
William Rogers.

George Allen, 30 May, 1672. He was also
Rector of Stanford-le-Hope, and Vicar of Mucking,
in Essex, in 1700.*

Matthew Brailsford.   -   -   1711
Randolph Ford, *Curate*†   -   1711

* The above List is taken from Newcourt's Repertorium, and
the remainder from the Parish Registers.

† Harl. MSS. No. 6824, fol. 190.—" Saturday, June 24, 1724,
I was at the funeral of the Rev. Mr. Ford, Curate of Marybone.
The Rev. Mr. Thomas Riddle, who was Curate of St. Giles's in
the Fields, and since lecturer, gave the following account, that
on one certain Sunday he performed the following duties :—

Daniel Boote,	-	-	-	1754
Thomas Dyer,	-	-	-	1760
James Parent,	-	-	-	1760
Thomas Foster,	-	-	-	1765
Stephen Deguthon,	-	-	1767
J. Baker,	-	-	-	-	1768
Sambrook Russell,	-	-	1768

William Charles Dyer.

The Hon. and Rev. John Harley, Bishop of Hereford, Dean of Windsor, Rector of Presteign in Radnorshire, and Minister of this Parish. He died 1788.

Sir Richard Kaye, Bart. LL. D. died 1809.

Luke Heslop, B. D. Archdeacon of Bucks, who died 1825.

THE OLD CHURCH.

The Church of Ty-bourn, being dedicated to St. John the Evangelist, seems to have fallen into ruin and decay through some cause now unknown, and from its lonely situation, became subject to dilapidation without controul, the ornaments, bells, &c. having been repeatedly stolen. Robert Braybroke, then Bishop of London, granted a licence to the inhabitants, upon their petition, (dated Oct. 23, 1400,) to take down the said Church, which stood on or near the site of the present Court-house, and to build a new one, of stones or flints, near the place, where, by his licence, they had lately erected

In the morning, married *six* couple; then read the whole prayers, and preached; after that churched *six* women.

In the afternoon, read prayers and preached; christened *thirty-two* children, *six* at home, the rest at the font; buried *thirteen* corpses, and read the distinct service over each of them separately, and this done by nine o'clock at night.

On the first leaf of the Register-Book, under the name of Mr. Ford, his address is written in pencil, " at *the Highlander, Little Suffolk Street, Charing Cross.*"

a chapel, which chapel might in the mean time be
used. The Bishop claimed the right of laying the
first stone ; it was also stipulated that the old
churchyard was to be preserved, but the inhabitants
were allowed to inclose another adjoining to the
new edifice.*

It is uncertain at what time the old cemetery
ceased to be respected, but its site is clearly identified by the number of human bones which were
dug up while preparing the foundation for the Old
Court House in 1727, and for the New Court
House in 1822.

Upon the erection of the New Church, as abovementioned, it was dedicated to the Virgin Mary,
and stood till May 1740, when, being in a very
ruinous condition, it was taken down. The interior
of this building is shewn in one of the plates of
Hogarth's Rake's Progress. The monuments are
represented as they then existed, and some ill-spelt
lines, pointing out the vault of the Forset family,
were actually copied from the originals :—

THESE : PEWES : VNSCRVD : AND : TAN : IN : SVNDER
IN : STONE : THERS : GRAVEN : WHAT : IS : VNDER
TO : WIT : A : VALT : FOR : BVRIAL : THERE : IS
WHICH : EDWARD : FORSET : MADE : FOR : HIM : AND : HIS

The inscription denoting the church to have been
beautified when Thomas Sice and Thomas Horn
were Churchwardens, was not fabricated for the
purpose of ridicule (though it might have served
that purpose, when contrasted with the ruinous
appearance of the Church), but proves to be
genuine.†

" The Rake's Progress, a Series of Eight Plates,
appeared in 1735. Plate V. The Rake is here exhibited
embracing the happy opportunity of recruiting his wasted
fortune by a marriage with a deformed and superannuated

* Braybroke Register, f. 348, a, b.— *Lysons'*.
† Nicholls's Life of Hogarth, p. 216, 217.

female, ordinary even to a proverb, and possessed but of one eye. As this wedding was designed to be a private one, they are supposed to have retired for that purpose to the church of St. Mary-le-bone, (which at that time was denominated a small village, in the outskirts of London), but as secret as he thought to keep it, it did not fail to reach the ears of an unfortunate young woman whom he had formerly seduced, and who is here represented, entering with her child and mother, in order to forbid the solemnization. They are however opposed by the pew-opener, lest, through an interruption of the ceremony, she should lose her customary fee, and a battle consequently ensues. A manifest token of the small regard paid to these sacred places. By the decayed appearance of the walls of this building, the torn belief, and cracked commandments, our author would humourously and effectually intimate the great indifference shewn to the decency of churches in country parishes."

" The only thing further to be noticed, is that of the poor's box, whose perforation is humourously covered with a web, where a spider is supposed to have been a long time settled, not finding so good a resting place before; and it is probable she might have continued there much longer, had not the overseer, in private, searched the box, with a view of abstracting its contents. Hence are we given to understand, that dissipation so far prevails as to drive humanity from the heart ; and that so selfish are we grown, as to have no feeling for the distresses of our fellow-creatures ; a matter which, while it disgraces the christian, even degrades the man."

Adverting to this incident, as also to the cracked commandments, and the creed destroyed by the damps of the church, Mr. Ireland observes : " These three high-wrought strokes of satirical humour, were perhaps never equalled by an exertion of the pencil ; excelled they cannot be."*

This Church was replaced by another, erected on the same site, which was opened for Divine Service

* The above description of this Plate is taken from Dr. Trusler's " Hogarth Moralized," Edit. 1831, published by Mr. Major, of Fleet Street.

in April 1742.* It is an oblong square brick building, with a small bell tower at the west end, it has
a gallery on the north south and west sides, the
altar occupying the east end. Several of the monumental slabs which were in the former church, are
preserved, and transferred to the walls of the present
building, the inscription relating to the vault of the
Forset family, is preserved with great care, the
letters are raised in wood on panel, and placed in
front of a pew directly opposite the altar.† The
entrance to this church was formerly at the east
and west ends, but upon its being converted into
the Parish Chapel in 1818, by Act of Parliament,
51 Geo. III. cap. 151, § 39, some judicious alterations were made, the entrance at the east end was
blocked up, that at the west only remaining ; the
pulpit and reading desk were separated, and removed
near the east wall, and some different arrangement
made in the pews. The organ is placed in the west
gallery. This chapel is a curacy in the jurisdiction
of the diocese of London, but in the patronage of
the Rector of the parish. The present incumbent
is the Rev. Richard Henry Chapman, M. A. Rector
of Kirkby Wiske, Thirsk, Yorkshire.

The following inscriptions are on the exterior wall
at the east end, near the top of the building :—

Rebuilt in ye. year 1741.

WALTER LEE,   } Churchwardens.
JOHN DESCHAMPS, }

Converted into a Parish Chapel,
By Act of Parliament, LI. George III.
on the IV. Feb. MDCCCXVII.
The Day of Consecration of the New Church.

---

* There is a Blank left in the Register of burials, between May
7, 1740, and April 4, 1742; and the following entry is inserted—
" In this interval the Parish Church was rebuilt."

† The two first lines of this Inscription are the originals, the
two last were restored in 1816, at the expense of the Rev. Mr.
Chapman, the Minister. The Vault is now occupied by the Portland Family.

Funeral Monuments.

In the extensive range of antiquarian science, there is no one subject more truly interesting, or deeply affecting, than that of sepulchral monuments. Whether considered as evidences of the art of sculpture, as memorials of history, or as tangible records of greatness and worth, they present irresistible claims on our feelings and fancies. They awaken and animate all the best sympathies of human nature; by inspiring reverence and adoration for merit and virtue,—detestation and contempt for folly and vice. To the historian they impart facts, and convey instruction; whilst the antiquary and artist resort to them as witnesses to verify the progress of art, the fluctuation of customs, the changes of fashion, the vicissitudes of the human race. In all ages, and in all countries, they manifest the glorious ambition of man to live " beyond the grave." The Christian religion produced, amongst its great improvements and changes a complete revolution in the moral and physical habits of mankind. It was not till some centuries after the Christian Advent that interments were allowed within the walls of churches, or any thing like monumental record was adopted. The first instance we meet with of burying within a Church, is that of Archbishop Cuthbert in Canterbury Cathedral, about the middle of the eighth century. This most dangerous and injurious practice, once begun, was eagerly followed by the powerful, proud, and infatuated Christians. It became a source of great revenue to the priesthood, and is still continued, to the disgrace of Protestant as well as Catholic Churches.*

Monuments were anciently erected agreeably to the quality of the deceased, that every one might

* Britton's Architectural Antiquities, vol. v.

discern of what degree the person was when living. Noblemen had their effigies carved in stone, or engraved on brass, and this was intended to bear a likeness to the deceased person; upon the same were usually inscribed their titles, marriages, issues, and employments. Gentry, and persons of lower condition, were interred under a flat stone,* inscribed with their name and time of their decease; and these particulars were sometimes engraved on a brass plate.† It was not till after the Reformation that monumental slabs began to be placed against the walls of Churches. The following monuments are at present existing in the old Church in High Street. Biographical notices of the more eminent persons will appear under a separate head.

Monumental Inscriptions.

East Wall.

Here lyeth interred the body of Sir EDMVND DOVCE, of Brovghton, in the Covnty of Sovth : Kᵀ· who was Cvp-Bearer to Ann of Denmark, Queene to Kynge James, and to Henryetta Maria of France, 40 yeares a constant Servant in his place, never maryed.   At the writinge hereof he was aged three score and three yeares in Anno Dni. 1644.
Mors mihi lucrum.

Arms.—Or, a fesse checky Az. and Arg. between three greyhounds courant Sable.

---

* *Brand*, says, in his *Popular Antiquities*,—"The custom of laying flat stones in our Churches and Churchyards over the graves of better sort of persons, on which are inscribed Epitaphs containing the name, age, character, &c. of the deceased, has been transmitted from very ancient times, as appears from the writings of Cicero and others."—*Cicero de Legibus*, xi.
"Lapidea mensa terra operitur humato corpore hominis qui aliquo sit numero, quæ contineat laudem et nomen mortui incisum, mos retinetur."—*Moresini Papatus, &c.* p. 86.
† *Camden's Remains*, p. 308.

The following inscriptions are on a black marble slab in two compartments.

In this Vault Neere this Monvment lyeth the Body of ELIZABETH ROBERTS, the Wife of Thomas Roberts, Esq. Son and Heire of Sir Walter Roberts of Glassenbury, in the Covnty of Kent, Kᵀ· & Barronett, by whom she had issue two Sons & one Davghter. She was the onely Davghter & Heire of Sᴿ· Mathew Howland of Stratton in the Covnty of Svrry, Kᵀ· by Dame Frances, Davghter of Edward Forsett, Esq. Lord of this Mannor; She secondly Maried Hvmphrey Scott of Havckhvrst in the Covnty of Kent, Esq. by whom she had 3 Sons & two Davghters. She liv'd desir'd and dyed Lamented on the Leaventh of December, Aᵒ· Dni. 1658.

Left Compartment.

In the Vavlt neere this Monvment lyeth interred the body of Dame FRANCEES HOWLAND, the mother of yᵉ· said Elizabeth Scot & Relict of Sᴿ· Mathew Howland of Stretham in the Covnty of Svrrey, Kᵀ· one of yᵉ· Davghters of Edward Forcett of Maribone in yᵉ· Covnty of Midde. Esq. who departed this life at Stepney, the third day of May in the yeare of ovr Lord, 1668, and about the Seventy-Seaventh yeare of her age.

For whose piovs memory the Lady Howland
her Loving Mother erected this Monvment
and intendɜs to be heere also bvried.

Arms.—1. Arg. three bars Sab. in chief, three lions rampant of the second.—Howland, impaling, Or, a lion rampant Sab. over all a bend gobony Arg. and gules.— Forset. 2. Az. on a chevron, Arg. three mullets Sable, impaling Howland. 3. Arg. a cross croslet, fitchée Sable.—Scott, quartering, Az. three conger's heads erased Or.—Conghurst and impaling Howland.

Beneath this place resteth the Body of
DEBORAH CHAMBERS,
Wife of Richard Chambers, of the City of Yorke,
Merchant, and Daughter of Edward Mesenden, Esq.
who died Oct. 30, 1680, Aged 63 years.

Arms.—Or, a fesse Az. between three conies Sable, impaling ; Or, a cross engrailed G. in the first quarter a
Cornish chough, proper.—Messenden.

Near this place lies the Remains of
Lieutenant-General RICHARD PRESCOTT,
of the 7th Regt. of Royal Fusileers,
Obiit 19th October, 1788, Ætat. 68 years.

Sacred to the Memory of
ELIZABETH, Wife of Captain TOWRY, R. N.
Obiit 19th Dec. 1806, Æt. 28.
Exemplary as a Daughter, a Wife, a Mother, and a
Christian !
Reflection dwells with melancholy Pleasure on the gentle
Virtues which adorned her Life;
While Feeling embalms her beloved Memory
with a Husband's Tears.

In a Vault of this Church are deposited the Remains of
General Sir GEORGE BECKWITH, G. C. B.
Second son of Major Gen. John Beckwith, of Bluerly in
the County of York, and of Janet, Daughter of the
Rev. Dr. George Wishart, Dean of the Chapel
Royal Edinburgh.
Who departed this life, March the 20th, 1823,
in the 70th year of his age.
Also Brig. Gen. Ferdinand Amelia Fairfax Beckwith,
(Their third son)
Who died Oct. 14, 1805, aged 40.
Also Jessie Philadelphia Beckwith, (Eldest child of their
fifth son, Maj. Gen. Sir Thomas Sidney Beckwith,
K. C. B. and of Clementina, daughter of Thomas
Loughnan, Esq.) who died July 8, 1822.
Aged 19 years.

In Memory of
Mrs. ELIZABETH HODGINS CARGILL,
of Nottingham Place, whose Remains are deposited in
the ground adjoining this Chapel.
She died March 19, A. D. 1821, aged 80 years.

North Wall.

Near this place lyeth y$^{e\cdot}$ body of GRACE LEE, late wife
of Thomas Lee, of this Parish, (*yeoman*) who died
March y$^{e\cdot}$ 24th 1724, aged 56 years. Also the body
of y$^{e\cdot}$ abovemention'd Thomas Lee, who died May y$^{e\cdot}$
27th 1726, aged 55 years. *They were tender* parents,
kind Neighbours, and *serviceable* Parishioners.

Underneath lie the Remains of
JAMES GIBBS, Esq.
Whose skill in Architecture, appears by his Printed
Works as well as the Buildings directed by him.
Among other Legacys and Charitys, he left One Hun-
dred Pounds towards Enlarging this Church.
He died August 5, 1754, aged 71.[*]

To the Memory of WILLIAM LONG, Esq.
This Monument is erected by his brother, Rear Admiral
Long, A. D. 1762.

Arms.—Sab. semèe of cross croslets and a lion rampant,
Argent.

---

[*] Posterity is indebted for the preservation of this Inscription to
Sampson Hodgkinson, Esq an ardent lover of antiquities, and
Sidesman of the parish Church, who at his own expense, had these
letters repainted in 1816 ; but no satisfactory account of the expenditure of the bequest mentioned on the monument, can be discovered in the Vestry Minutes. The above gentleman, who has
resided in the parish from his infancy, possesses a fund of genuine
entertaining biographical anecdote, an excellent collection of mine-
rals, and a curious and splendid library, which in the most kind
and obliging manner is rendered accessible to those who require
local information.

To the Memory
of WILLIAM THOMAS, Esq.
who dyed the the 30th of Nov. 1764, aged 88 years.
Also Mrs. Mary Thomas, Relict of the above, who dyed
April 7, 1768, aged 77 years. Also Mrs. Margaret
Morgan, Sister to William Thomas, Esq. who
died March 26, 1794, aged 82 years.
Also Mrs. Anne Thomas, Sister to William Thomas, Esq.
died July 9, 1781, aged 86 years.

To the Memory of ELIZABETH,
Wife of Edward Thornhill of Sunbury in this County,
was the only daughter of Francis Tredgold, (late of
this Parish) by his wife Mary; she died on the 17th
day of May, 1766, in the 26th year of her age, and
lies interred in her Father's vault in this Churchyard.
Francis Tredgold, the only child of the above Edward
and Elizabeth Thornhill, who died Oct. 11th 1762,
aged 13 months, is buried in the same Vault.

Near this place lyeth the Body of Mrs. ANN LLOYD,
Widow of William Lloyd, late of the Parish of St.
James's Westminster, Gentleman; and also Relict of
the late Mr. Humfrey Wanle, Library Keeper to the
Rt. Hon. Robert and Edward, Earls of Oxford, &c.
she Dyed March the 9th 1767, aged 70 years.

To the Memory of
The Rev. EDMUND HODSHON,
Late Rector of Spennithorne, in the North Riding of
the County of York,
Who departed this life, the 29th of July, 1778,
Ætat 42.

Arms.—Per chevron engrailed Or. and Az. 3 martlets
counterchanged.

Beneath this Monument
Rest the Remains of RALPH SMYTH, Esq.
Late of Field Town in the County of Westmeath in the
Kingdom of Ireland, who departed this life
at his House in Charles Street, Cavendish Square, on
February the 23d, 1782, aged 65.

Here lies the body
of LADY MARY WEST,
Wife of the Hon. George West, and Daughter of the
Fourth Earl of Stamford.
She died March the 1st, 1783, aged 43.

Arms.—Arg. a fesse dauncettée Sab. impaling, Barry of
six Arg. and Az. in chief three torteauxes—Grey.

Near this place lies interred
ANNE FOSTER,
who died January 10, 1786, aged 92 years.
Also Alice, the wife of John Yarker, Esq. who died
November 24, 1812, aged 85 years.
Also John Yarker, Esq. of Leyburn, in the County of
York, who died July 17, 1813, aged 84 years.
Also Anne Yarker, only daughter of the above John and
Alice Yarker, who died October 29, 1818,
aged 62 years.

Sacred to the Memory of the late
Sir GEORGE COLLIER, Knt. Vice Admiral of the Blue,
who departed this Life, April 6, 1795, aged 65 years,
the principal part of which was devoted to the
Service of his Country.

Sacred to the Memory of
CHARLES BRIETZCKE, Esq. late of the Secretary
of States Office, who died June 5, A. D. 1795, Æt. 57.
Also to the memory of his second son,
Lieutenant Charles Ware Brietzcke, of H.M.S. Hannibal,
who survived his father but a few months, having
fallen a victim to the ravages of the Yellow Fever in the
West Indies, Oct. A. D. 1795, Ætat 20.

To the Memory
of BARBARA, Countess of Scarborough,
who died 22d day of July, A. D. 1797, aged 62 years.
The well-merited affection of her Children,
Has placed this Monument in pious Sorrow, and
grateful Veneration.

Sacred to the Memory
of SAMUEL ESTWICK, Esq. whose Remains are
deposited in his Family Vault, in the Ground belonging
to this Church.
He was born the 22d of Jan. 1770, Married, the 15th of
July, 1793, the Hon. Cassandra Julia Hawke, eldest
daughter of The Right Hon. Lord Hawke; and
died the 23d of February, 1797.

Near this place are deposited the Remains of
ELIZABETH STANLEY,
Sister and heir at law to the late Sir William Stanley
of Hooton, in the County of Cheshire, Bart.
and Wife of Charles Haggerston Constable Stanley,
of Upper Seymour Street, Esq.
who has erected this Monument to her Memory,
She died the 23d of June, 1797, aged 47.

Sacred to the memory
of Mrs. JANETTE TAHOURDIN,
Wife of Peter Tahourdin, of Argyle street, Gent. who
died suddenly on the 12th day of June, 1800,
in the 35th year of her age.

In the Vault No. 3, are deposited the Remains of
ELIZABETH SMITH,
wife of Adam Smith, Esq. of the Island of Jamaica; who
died after having given birth to a Son,
on the XXX day of November, MDCCC. aged XXIX.

Near this place lieth interred GRACE,
the Wife of Lieut.-Colonel Frederick Philipse Robinson,
who died the 27th of May 1806, aged 36 years,
also two of their children.

Near this place lie the Remains of
JOSEPH JONES, Esq.
Many years a Banker in the City of London,
He died at his house in Cavendish Square, on the
XXVIIth Day of November, MDCCCXI.
Aged LXXIII years.

Near this place lie the Remains of
WILLIAM ORAM, Esq. of this Parish, who departed
this life the xxist of November, MDCCCXIII.
Aged LIV.

To the Memory of ELIZABETH,
Wife of Thomas Hart Davies of Madras, in the East
Indies, Esq., who died on the 29th day of May, 18.7,
Aged 44 years.

West Wall.

Jacet
JOHANNES CROSBIE,
Westmorlandiensis

Ortoniæ ⎱ ⎰ Prog-
Candaliæ ⎰⎱ Discipli- ⎱
Oxoniæ ⎱⎰ Alum- ⎰ natus
Londoni ⎰ ⎱ Patroci-

Artium Magister ⎱ $op.\Theta o\delta o\xi\textcircled{}$.
Ecclesiæ Minister ⎰

Ortus Aprilis 13, 1591
Sepultus, 30 Junij, 1669,
Ætatis suæ 72.

In Memory of
ELIZABETH, their beloved Daughter,
Taken from them in the Eleventh year of her age,
Her afflicted Parents, Charles and Judith Mellish,
Have placed this marble,
A pledge of their affection for a dutiful child,
Born April 27, 1771. Died March 28, 1782.
Buried under the first and second pew opposite.

Sacred to the memory of MARY CURTIS,
Wife of John Curtis, Esq. of Manchester Square,
Obiit Nov. 20, 1794, Ætat. 33.

Near this place are deposited the Remains of
SIGNOR GIVSEPPE BARETTI,
A native of Piedmont in Italy, Secretary for Foreign
Correspondence to the Royal Academy of Arts, of
London ; Author of several esteemed Works in his own
and the Languages of France and of England.

Near this place are deposited the Remains of
JOHN BROOMHEAD, Esq.
who died the 21st of January, 1794, aged 58 years.
Also of John Broomhead, his son,
who died the 19th of April, 1807, aged 37 years.
This tribute of respect is erected to their memory by
filial duty and affection.

Near this place lye the Remains of
PETER OLIVER, M. D.
Son of the Hon. Andrew Oliver, late of Boston,
New England,
who died April 6, 1795, aged 45 years.

In memory of
A life devoted to the Stvdy of Mvsical Science, and
shorten'd by Vnremitted application and anxiety in the
attainment of its object,
This marble is inscribed with the Name of
STEPHEN STORACE,
whose professional talents commanded pvblick applavse,
whose private virtves ensvr'd domestic affection.
He died March 16, 1796, aged 34, and is interred vnder
this Chvrch.

Silent his lyre, or wak'd to Heav'nly strains,
Clos'd his short scene of cheqver'd joys and pains,
Belov'd and gratefvl as the notes he svng,
His name still trembles on Affection's tongve,
Still in ovr bosoms holds its wonted part,
And strikes the chords, which vibrate to the heart.
P. H.

This marble is pvt vp by a tender mother, and
an affectionate sister.

In Memory of
JOHN PURLING, Esq. late of this Parish,
who departed this Life on the 23d day of August, 1800,
in the 74th year of his age,
and lies interred in one of the Vaults belonging
to this Church.

To the Memory of
Colonel JOHN TOTTINGHAM,
who died June 3, 1802,
aged 63 years.

In a Vault near this place are deposited the Remains of
WILLIAM AUTHER CROSBIE, Esq.
late of this Parish,
who departed this Life, February the 19th, 1804,
aged 50 years.

Sacred to the Memory
of STEPHEN HAVEN, Esq.
who departed this Life, the 17th of March, 1805, aged 44,
He was a Native of Ireland,
But passed the greater part of his life in America and the
Bahamas, in which last place he filled many Offices of
Trust and Honour, and was universally respected.
In his private Character
He was eminently distinguished for his Philanthropy
and Benevolence to the Friendless of every description.
He has left a Widow and three Children
to lament the loss of an affectionate Parent and
kind Protector.

Sacred to the Memory of
MARTHA, Widow of the late John Dymoke, Esq.
The Honourable the King's Champion,
of Scrivelsby Court, in the County of Lincoln,
who died August 9, 1811, aged 77,
Her remains are deposited in the private Dormitory
of this Church.

E

Sacred to the Memory of
ABRAHAM HOLDEN TURNER, Esq.
Late of this Parish, who died the 28th of December, 1811,
in the 53d year of his age.

Sacred to the Memory of
Mr. EDMOND TURVILLE TURNER,
Son of the above Abraham Holden Turner,
Died the 27th of October, 1815,
aged 16 years.

On this wall was formerly a monument of lead, gilt, with figures in alto-relievo, to the memory of some children of Thomas Taylor of Popes, in Hertfordshire, by Sarah, Daughter of John Wells, of Marybone, 1689, &c. But, on the alteration of the Church in 1816, this monument was *stolen ;* and it is difficult to find words adequate to express the indignation excited in the minds of the lovers of antiquity, at the commission of such an act of sacrilege. It is also equally surprising, that no proper investigation was set on foot to discover the real delinquent.

South Wall.

Near this Place is interred the Body of
THOMAS TAYLOR,
Late of *Kensington* in the County of *Middlesex*, Esq.
who departed this life, the 17th Nov. 1716, aged 80.
Also is here interred the body of
Mrs. Sarah Taylor, Wife of the said Thomas Taylor,
who changed this life for a better,
the 7th Oct. 1746, aged 80.
Preserve me O God for in thee have I put my Trust.
Psalm xvi. ver. 1.
Open me the Gates of Righteousness that I may
Go into into them and Give Thanks unto the Lord.
Psalm cxviii. ver. 19.

Arms.—Arg. on a Chief Or, two boar's heads erased, Az. (a mullet for difference), impaling, Or, a lion rampant Azure.

Near this place are interred the Remains of
Mrs. SARAH KIMBER,
who was born at Dover, A. D. 1720, and died
Oct. 13, 1768.

What ! tho' no pompous Titles grace her Name,
Nor Wealth, nor Honours, dignify her Fame :
A mild and Cheerful Temper, lively sense,
True friendship, and humane benevolence ;
These Graces of the Mind, by time improv'd,
Made her, wherever she was known, belov'd.

Near this place lieth the body of
CHARLOTTE MEYNELL,
Youngest Daughter of the late Godfrey Meynell, Esq.
of Derbyshire deceased, and Frances his wife,
She died the 2d of September 1769, aged 12 years.

Torn from her weeping Friends ere yet in Bloom
She fell too early Victim for the Tomb,
On Earth her Prudence, Innocence of thought,
Good Nature, Piety, avail'd her Nought,
Omnipotence unwilling seem'd to spare
The Virgin longer to a Mother's care,
But call'd her forth such Virtues to employ
In happy Mansions of eternal Joy,
Her tender Mother holds her Mem'ry dear,
And pays the last sad Tribute of a Tear.

Sacred to the memory of
GILBERT FANE FLEMING, Esq.
who was interred in this Church, Dec. XXVIII.
MDCCLXXVI.
This monument is here placed by his ever affectionate
and most truly grateful wife,
Lady Camilla Fleming.

To the memory of
WASTEL BRISCOE, Esq.
who departed this Life, the 10th day of November, 1796,
Aged 85.

E 2

To the Memory of
JOHN ALLEN, Esq.
Son of the Rev. George Allen, sometime Minister
of this Parish.
He was Apothecary to the Households of King George
the First, Second and Third ;
and having employed a long life, and ample Fortune,
in Acts of Benevolence and Charity,
Liberal to others, Frugal only to himself. He was
released from his Labours, and called to his Reward
March 17, 1774, in the Ninety-first year of his age.
By his Will he gave large Benefactions
To his Relations, Friends and Servants. To Poor
Clergymen's Widows and Children. To Poor Housekeepers, and the Charity Children of this Parish,
of St. Paul Covent-Garden, and of St. James's
Westminster. To St. George's Hospital,
of which he was a Governor from the first institution,
and to the Company of Apothecaries,
of which he was a most respected member,
Providence seems to have protracted the Life of this
excellent man, as an example to shew
how useful a private person may be with a mind
so dispos'd.

Near this place lies interred the body of
DANIEL M'GILCHRIST, Esq.
Late of the Island of Jamaica, who died at his house
in Portland Place, on the 6th of March 1783,
aged 64 years.
On the 14th of July 1772, he was married to Ann,
fourth daughter of the Hon. Thomas Fearon
of Clarendon in the said Island,
who erected this monument in grateful remembrance
of him.

JOANNI MONTAGU,
Armigero Antiqua Montacutorum
Ac
Trevororum Stirpe
Orto Viro Pio Probo Benevolo.
Arms. Montagu and Morthermer quarterly, not blazoned.

In a Vault in the Neighbouring Churchyard
lie the Remains of
MRS. ELIZABETH PARK,
Wife of James Park, Esq. late of Sloane Street, Chelsea.
She died on the 3d day of May, A. D. 1793.
aged 68 years.

Sacred
to the Memory of
GRAINGER MUIR, Esq.
Colonel in the Service of the East India Company.
He went to India, Anno 1747.   He was a Captain, and
led the advanced guard at the Battle of Plassey.
He commanded the army employed against the Maratta
Chief Madajee Scindia, and by his jvdiciovs condvct
Negotiated a Peace with that Chief in 1781,
and thereby laid the Fovndation of the General Peace
conclvded with the Maratta States in 1782.
With a delicate sense of Honor, he had all the ardour of
his profession as a Soldier,
He was amiable in his manners, Generovs in his
Dispositions, Affectionate and steady in his Friendships.
He retvrn'd to England in 1785,
and departed this Life the 3d of August, 1786,
aged 52 years.

Sacred to the Memory of
CAROLINE WATSON,
Engraver to Her Majesty, who died 9th June 1814,
Aged 54.
If Taste and Feeling, that with goodness dwell,
And teach the modest Artist to excel;
If Gratitude, whose voice to Heaven ascends,
And seems celestial to surviving Friends;
If charms so pure a lasting Record claim,
Preserve, Thou faithful Stone! a spotless Name!
Meek CAROLINE *! receive due Praise from Earth*
For Graceful Talents join'd to genuine worth!
GOD *gave thee gifts, such as to few may fall,*
Thy Heart, to Him who gave, devoted all.
W. HAYLEY.
Erected by John Eardley Wilmot.

Here lies the body of
EDWARD ELTON, Esq.
formerly of Clifton, in the County of Gloucester, and
Late of *Greenway*, in the County of *Devon*,
and of *Gloucester Place*, *New Road*, in this Parish,
Obiit xx Die Septembris, MCCCXI,
Ætat LXIX.

Sacred to the memory of
MRS. MARY ANN PRICE,
of this Parish, who departed this Life,
on the 12th day of April, 1820,
Aged 30 years.

In a Vault belonging to this Church
(In the full assurance of a blessed Resurrection)
are deposited the respected Remains of
Mrs. BETTENSON STAUNTON,
Eldest daughter and Coheiress of Thomas Staunton, Esq.
of Sibton Park, in the County of Suffolk,
And Annadowne Castle, Ireland,
and grand-daughter of Gilbert, Viscount Barnard, of
Raby Castle,
who departed this Life February 12, 1811, Ætat 74.
In the blameless life of this excellent Woman was
Pourtrayed the beautiful character of a sincere Christian :
She was religious without Austerity ;
Pious without Enthusiasm; Charitable without
Ostentation; Patient and resigned under great Sufferings,
Firm in Faith and pure in Heart;
" *Of such is the Kingdom of Heaven.*"
This votive Tablet, sacred to the memory of one so
Justly loved and so deeply lamented, Is affectionately
Reared by the Gratitude and Weeping Friendship
Of her faithful and adopted Child,
Anna Maria Bentley.
In the same Vault rest the Remains of her half sister,
Elizabeth Catherine, wife of James Cumberland Bentley,
Esq. who died March 10, 1810, Ætat 62.

Here lie the mortal Remains of
MRS. MARY MARSHALL,
Wife of Capt. Josiah Marshall,
Born 3d October, 1781.   Died 17th January, 1808.

In Memory of
Mrs. MARY ARNOLD,
Who departed this Life, the 23d day of August, 1807,
Aged 65 years.
By active Exertions in the Service of her Friends and
Neighbours, and of all in Poverty or Distress, she
rendered her Life extensively useful; for when unable
to afford assistance or relief herself, she cheerfully
condescended to solicit the aid of others.
" Go and do thou likewise."

In a Vault in this Church are deposited the Remains of
ANN HEWITT,
The Child of William Kellitt, and Deborah Hewitt,
Of St. Elizabeth, Jamaica, who departed this Life on the
14th of November, 1806,
Having on that day completed her Seventh year.

As with despair thy Parents saw disease,
With'ring a form by Nature made to please,
Hope glanced to Britain with reviving smile
And promis'd health in Britain's happier Isle.
Alas ! this Marble, but records how vain,
Their anxious hopes, and speaks their heartfelt pain.
They long will mourn, yet happy who like you,
In life's pure morn shall bid the world adieu.

*The following Inscriptions are on Flat Stones on the
Floor of the Church.*

Here lies the Body of
HUMPHREY WANLEY,
Library Keeper to the Right Hon. Robert and Edward
Earls of Oxford, &c.
Who died on the 6th day of July, MDCCXXVI.
In the 55th year of his age.

Here lies the body of
RICHARD LLOYD, Esq.
Son of Sir Richard Lloyd, Judge of the Admiralty,
and Brother of Sir Nathaniel Lloyd,
1742.

Here lies the body of ROBERT FRANCES,
Late of this Parish,
Who departed this Life on the 22d of Feb. 1766.

Here are deposited the Remains of
MR. WILLIAM O'BRIEN,
Who died November the 7th 1766, aged 44 years.

In Memory of
HENRIETTA MARIA,
Second daughter of Sir Charles Asgill, Bart.
Who died April 1790, aged 22.

In Memory of
DANIEL M'GILCHRISTE,
of this Parish,
Died March the 16th, 1783, aged 64.

To the Memory of
JOSIAS CALMADY, Esq. of the County of Devon,
Who died in 1756, aged 95.

Here lies interred the body of
The Right Hon. LADY ABIGAIL HAY,
Fourth Daughter of the Right Hon. George Earl of
Kinnoul, who departed this Life, July 7, 1785,
aged 60.

There is a long Latin inscription on a flat stone, in the
western entrance, to the Memory of

EDWARD GWYNN, Esq.
Of the Family of Gwynn, of North Wales,
Deputy Custos Brevium of the Court of Common Pleas,
Died 1649, aged 75.

The following Inscriptions are in the Churchyard.

Samuel Ellis, - - -	1678
Claudius de Crespigny, Esq. a French Refugee,	1695
Maria de Vierville, his wife, -	1708
Betsey, wife of Philip Champion Crespigny,	1772
Mr. Robert Knight, - -	1719

As i was, so are yea
and as i am
So shall yea be.

Frances, Wife of John Stanesby, aged 70, -	1720
Elizabeth Barefoot of St. Martin's in the Fields,	1721
John Aubrey Hill, - -	1729
Anna Head, - - - -	1740

On entering the Churchyard by the gate on the South side, a large altar tomb will be observed on the left hand, erected to the memory of the Family of Deschamps, one of whom, viz. John Deschamps, was Churchwarden of this Parish in 1741.*

John Liddiard, - - -	1741
John Dowyer, Carver, - -	1741
Captain James Desmarette, - -	1743
John Towers, Esq. - -	1744
Joan, Wife of Edmund Stouel, aged 77, -	1745
Frances Pennington, - -	1745
George Hume, Cordwainer to Geo. II. -	1748
Mrs. Frances Wagg, - - -	1749
Ormond Tomson, Esq. Capt. R. N. -	1753
Elizabeth Adams, - -	1752
Elizabeth Hurley, - - -	1765
Mrs. Ann Nugent, - -	1766
Rev. Nicholas Robert, a native of France, -	1766
Lieut. Peter Foubert, - -	1766
John Riddell, Surgeon, - -	1767

* The Reader will scarcely be able to repress a smile when he is informed, that this *Churchwarden's* memory is perpetuated by contributions from various tenants of this abode of frail mortality ; a number of old tombstones having been cut up and used for the foundation of this Tomb : parts of several different inscriptions are still legible.

James Ferguson, F. R. S. " who blessed with a fine
natural genius, by unwearied application (without
a master), attained the sciences of Astronomy
and Mechanics, which he taught with singular
success and reputation.   He was modest, sober,
humble, and religious, and his works will immor-
talize his memory, when this small monument is
no more.   He died Nov. 16, 1776, aged 66."

Isabel, his wife, - - -	1773
James their eldest son, aged 24, -	1772
Christopher Nettleton, aged 56 - -	1775
Rev. Francis Lawrence Cowley, -	1777
Mary, Wife of Richard Shadwell, Esq. -	1777
Adam Smith, - - -	1778
Joseph Burgess, Gent. - -	1779
Frances, Relict of the Rev. George Arrowsmith,	1786
William Kingsbury, Gent. of Bungay, -	1788
The Rev. Charles Wesley, aged 80, -	1788
Mrs. Eleanor Williams, - -	1791
Elizabeth Baroness O'Brady, - -	1791
William Martin, - - -	1794
Thomas Browne, - - -	1794
Frances Blair, - - -	1800
Scipio Lowry, - - -	1801
John Cable, - - -	1803
Louisa Loveday, - - -	1806
Elizabeth Loveday, - -	1807
Ann, First wife of William Child, -	1807
Maria, Second wife of the above William Child,	1808
Henry Matthews, - -	1810

Diana Gertrude Wilson, Daughter and only Child
of Sir Giffin Wilson of Stratford Place, and
Woodburn House, Bucks, one of the Masters of
the High Court of Chancery, who died the 11th of
June 1827, in the 22d year of her age.   Also
Harriet, Lady Wilson, Mother of the above,
and the Wife of the above Sir Giffin Wilson,
and youngest daughter of the late Lieut. Gen.
George Hotham, of Binfield, Berks, who died on
the 30th of April, 1828, aged 52 years.

Valentine Howell, Principal Watch-House Keeper 24 years. This Stone is erected as a tribute of respect, by the Serjeants and Watchmen of this Parish, Feb. 13, 1829.

Mrs. Christian Brown, (the Mother of Nicholas Brown, Esq. Commissioner of His Majesty's Victualling Office) who died Dec. 15, 1799, aged 75. Also the Remains of the said Nicholas Brown, who died on the 10th day of June 1830, aged 70 years.

In the Crypt or Vault underneath the Church are Deposited the Remains of several Members of the Portland Family, including

WILLIAM HENRY CAVENDISH BENTINCK,
The late Duke,
Who departed this Life, October 30, 1809, aged 71.

The population of this parish having progressively increased during a period of 50 years, in consequence of the extension of building; it became a matter of serious necessity to do something in aid of the accommodation demanded for the services of the established religion. The Church, erected when a few straggling houses constituted the whole of the habitations in the Parish, was insignificantly small, and totally inadequate to the wants of the parishioners; it was, however, situated not very far distant from the centre of the parish. Its insufficiency had been a topic of general remark, and various designs and proposals had been made

for the erection of a structure correspondent with
the number and wealth of the inhabitants. About
the year 1770, the late Mr. Portman, offered to
present the Parish with a piece of ground on the
North side of Paddington street, gratuitously, on
condition they should build a church on it, but if
they did not build it, they were to pay him 3000*l.*;
and the late Sir William Chambers, at the desire of
the Select Vestry, made a design for the building,
which possessed great merit; but after much deli-
beration and controversy, it was determined that
their funds at that particular juncture, would not
warrant the expenditure of so large a sum as would
be required for this purpose; the design was
therefore abandoned, and the 3000*l.* paid to Mr.
Portman for his land, which was consecrated for
the purposes of burial, in 1772. The late Duke
of Portland about the same time liberally offered
5000*l.* towards building a Church on the site of
Upper Harley Street, and this offer was also lost
to the Parish. The increase of Chapels in the
Parish; some erected with the consent of the
Duke of Portland (the patron), others without it,
more or less varying from the forms of the Church
of England, seemed imperiously to call upon the
Vestry to use some exertions to provide more
efficient religious accommodation; but the various
opinions which agitated the individuals composing
that body, defeated every attempt at magnificence
of design, while the necessity of providing a burial
ground (situated at St. John's Wood), which
had been purchased of Henry Samuel Eyre, Esq.
pursuant to an Act passed 46 Geo. III., and
enclosing it, erecting a minister's and sexton's
houses, and a chapel on the spot, absorbed a large
portion of the money raised by way of Church rate.
The following Letter which appeared in the Gentleman's Magazine for July, 1807, at a time when
the population amounted to above 70.000, will

exhibit the real necessity which existed for the erection of a *New Parochial Edifice.*

TO THE EDITOR.

July, 1807.

SIR,—" I was lately called upon to visit a parish church towards the North-west end of the town. It is a very small edifice, much smaller than chapels of ease generally are; I believe I may say it is the smallest place of worship attached to the Church of England, in the metropolis. Small, however, as it is, it is the only church belonging to the largest and most opulent parish in this capital, or in any part of His Majesty's dominions— a parish which, on the lowest computation, contains 70,000 souls. There is no font for baptism, no room for depositing the dead bodies on tressels, after the usual way, no aisle to contain them. They are placed in the most indecent manner on the pews. At the time I visited this scandal to our church and nation, there were no fewer than five corpses placed in the manner described; eight children, with their sponsors, &c. to be christened; and five women to be churched; all within these contracted dimensions. A common basin was set upon the communion-table for the baptisms, and the children ranged round the altar; but the godfathers and godmothers in pews, in so confused and disorderly a manner, that it was impossible for the minister to see many of them, or address and require them to make the responses, which the Rubrick directs. Not to mention the danger of the dead and the living being thus confined together, and the peculiarly delicate situation of women immediately after child-birth; all reverence for the sacrament of baptism; all solemn and awful reflections from hearing one of the finest services ever composed, and on an occasion the most interesting to the heart that can be imagined, are entirely done away, and the mind filled with horror and disgust.

A Constant Reader."

The following article also appeared in the British Review, May, 1813, art. 21, p. 375.—" It is indeed affecting, when we view the metropolis from a neighbouring eminence, to observe that portion of it inhabited by the greatest number of legislators, the greatest number of the wealthy and the well-educated, that part which is inhabited by those who hold the highest offices in church and state, wearing the appearance of a quarter appropriated to persons under sentence of excommunication: the city rich in ecclesiastical structures; the west end of the town presenting a tiresome length of street, with scarcely a single edifice appropriated to religion ascending from amidst the vast mass of inhabitation."

In the arrangement of the Crown land in Mary-le-bone Park, the late Mr. White (architect to the Duke of Portland) had previously suggested a site for a spacious and dignified parochial edifice; the necessity of which had in 1810 appeared so urgent, that Mr. Nash, in the plan made by him, described a building of that nature; and chose as a situation, the centre of a circus to be constructed at the end of Portland Place; and the Vestry having received a communication * from the Secretary to the Trea-

Treasury Chambers, Aug. 23, 1811.

* Sir,—I have received Mr. Perceval's directions, in consequence of the communication you had with him, this morning, to acquaint you, that it is his intention to recommend to His Royal Highness the Prince Regent, to make a gift to the Parish of St. Mary-le-bone of a piece of land, in Harley Field, of sufficient extent to build a chapel of as large dimensions as may be deemed necessary for the accommodation of the Parish in that part of it.

I have the honour to be, Sir,
Your very faithful humble Servant,
GEORGE HARRISON.

To the Rev. Dr. Heslop.

sury, and believing that there was an intention to confer upon them this site, together with five acres of land to surround their projected building, applied for and obtained an Act of Parliament for the diversion of the New Road; no sooner however were their efforts attended with success, but difficulties were interposed and new portions of land pointed out. An Act was however passed in the Session of 1810-11, intituled " An Act to enable the Vestrymen of the Parish of St. Mary-le-bone, in the County of Middlesex, to build a new Parish Church, and two or more Chapels; and for other purposes thereto," by which all the former acts were repealed, and new powers given to the Vestrymen and their successors (who derive their authority from an Act of the 35th of Geo. III.) to purchase lands not exceeding ten acres, for the above purposes ; and in which there was a Clause, " providing that no sum shall be given for any one site for the said Church or Chapels exceeding 6000*l.* About the end of 1812, Mr. White, Jun. the District Surveyor of the Parish, presented the Vestry with a design for a double church, upon a new principle, having for its object the accommodating a large number of persons, and at the same time admitting a magnificence of exterior ; which design was meant as an accompaniment to his father's plan for the improvement of Mary-le-bone Park.

Shortly after the delivery of the design above mentioned, the Vestry offered premiums by public advertisement to architects, as they had done in the year 1770, for plans and elevations of a parish church : but about a fortnight previous to the time of receiving such plans and elevations from the artists, they gave public notice that the designs were not to be proceeded with ; it should appear, on account of the difficulties which had arisen in obtaining the ground which the Lords of the Treasury had proposed to grant them. A triangular

piece of ground was, however, granted to the Parish
by the Treasury, on the south side of the New Road
near Nottingham Place, and the Vestry proceeded
to erect a Chapel capable of containing a considerable number of persons; the foundation was laid on
the 5th of July, 1813, and the fabric was proceeded
with nearly to its completion. At that period,
however, the work was stopped, and the Vestry
came to a resolution to convert the intended chapel
into a parochial church. This occasioned a considerable alteration to be made in the original
design, and particularly in regard to the exterior
of the building. The principal front, next the
New Road, underwent a very important change,
a more extended portico and a steeple were substituted for the former design (which consisted of
an Ionic portico of four columns, surmounted by a
group of figures and a cupola); and other alterations
were made in order to give the edifice an appearance
more analogous to the character of a Church.

Drawn from Nature & on Stone by Edw.ᵈ Hassel. Printed by Graf & Soret

NEW ST MARY-LE-BONE CHURCH.

London, Published by John Smith, 49, Long-acre 1833.

THE PARISH CHURCH.

This church is one of the handsomest structures of the kind in the metropolis. It was designed by the late Thomas Hardwicke, Esq. who in this, and other of his works, has proved himself a worthy disciple of his master, Sir William Chambers. The north front, which is extremely rich and elegant, is seen from York Gate, Regent's Park, the church being situated on the south side of the New Road. This front consists of a handsome winged portico of the Roman Corinthian order, surmounted by a tower. The portico is composed of eight columns, six in the front and two in flank, raised on a flight of steps, and sustaining an entablature and pediment, the architecture after the Pantheon ; within the portico are three lintelled entrances, surmounted by cornices and two arched windows ; above the central doorway is a panel, bearing the following inscription :—

This Church was erected at the Expence of the Parishioners,
And Consecrated IV. February, MDCCCXVII.
THE REV. ARCHDEACON HESLOP, D. D. Minister.
THE DUKE OF PORTLAND
SIR JAMES GRAHAM, Bart. } Churchwardens.
GEORGE ALLEN
JOHN RUSSELL } Sidesmen.

Above this is a long panel designed for sculpture, which has never been set up ;* the ceiling of the portico is panelled, each panel containing an expanded flower. The wings have no windows on their northern front, the angles are guarded by pilasters, and the flanks are enriched with two

* It is to be regretted, that the appropriate bas-relief, which was proposed to represent the Entry of Our Saviour into Jerusalem, should not have been placed in this panel ; as an ornament of that kind well executed, would have added much to the grandeur of this front.

columns. The entablature continued from the portico, and surmounted by an attic and balustrade constitutes the finish to the entire building. The tower is in three stories ; the first is rusticated, and forms a plinth to the elevation, it is finished with a cornice, and has a dial in each face ;* it supports a circular story, which has a peristyle of twelve Corinthian columns, sustaining an entablature, upon which rises the third story, a circular temple raised on a stylobate of three steps, and pierced with arched openings ; to the piers between the arches, are attached eight caryatidal statues of angels, supporting an entablature and cornice which is broken in the intervals between the statues. The elevation is crowned with a spherical dome, and finished with a small pedestal, sustaining a vane. The east and west sides of the church are uniform ; they are made into two stories by a plain course ; each story has five windows, the lower are slightly arched, the upper lofty, with arched heads, besides one window in the returns of the wings. The south front consists of a centre, flanked by two wings, which project diagonally from the building, being formed at the angles, which are cut off. The wings contain windows corresponding with the church, in their sides and the eastern niche a doorway, and has in its front, wings ; they are guarded at the angles by pilasters, and the central division has a Venetian window.

The Interior is approached from the north front by a circular vestibule, formed in the basement story of the tower, and two lobbies at the sides of it, which contain stairs to the galleries, and by an entrance in the south-eastern wing. The sides and north end are occupied by two spacious tier of

---

* A curious error has been made by the artist who painted the dial plate, which faces the south, the Numerals indicating the hour of *Nine*, being transposed, two *Elevens* are consequently exhibited.

galleries, with panelled fronts, supported by slender
iron columns, having reeded shafts, and leaved
capitals ; to those of the lower tier are also attached
modillions ; the shafts are bronzed, and the capitals
gilt.   The altar, which is at the south end of the
church, has a mahogany screen, enriched with four
Ionic pilasters, between which are the usual inscriptions, and a painting of the Holy Family by West,
presented by the artist to the parish ; a gallery
above, contains seats for the charity children, and
the organ. As originally constructed, there was an
arched opening in the centre of the instrument,
occupied by a transparency on canvas, a copy of
one of the painted windows in St. George's Chapel,
Windsor, from the design of Mr. West ; the subject, " the Angel appearing to the Shepherds ;" the
principal figure in the angelic group had the face
of a child, with the thigh of a giant.   The greatest
absurdity, however, consisted in the erection of
private galleries at the sides of the organ, which
were fitted with chairs, and fire-places, and in their
openings to the church, so exactly resembled the
private boxes which look upon the proscenium of
our theatres, that the spectator might almost suppose he was in a building which originally had that
destination.

    In the summer of 1826, some judicious altera-
tions took place; the organ was reduced to the
customary form and size, the transparency being
removed; the galleries were made to sweep round
to the instrument, thus causing the destruction of
the private boxes, the space formerly occupied by
which, being filled with seats for the children of the
National School; the theatrical appearance is in
consequence removed, and the building partakes
more of the sacred character to which it is appropriated.   The ceiling is curved at the sides, the
horizontal portion made into panels by bundles of
rods bound together with ribbons ; in the centre is

a large expanded flower. The pulpit and desks are constructed of mahogany, and are situated on opposite sides of the area of the building. The former is elegantly carved; it rests on a single pillar, which spreads at the capital, and is finished with a group of cherubim heads. In front of the upper northern gallery, are the royal arms and supporters of George IV. neatly carved in oak. The font, which is placed beneath the northern gallery, is a handsome circular basin, of veined marble, standing upon a pillar of the same material. The portico and tower, together with the cornices, attic, &c. are stone; the walls are brick, covered with stucco. The cella or body of the church, is 86 feet 6 inches in length, and 60 feet in breadth. Its exterior height, to the coping of the balustrades, is 52 feet 5 inches: its breadth to the middle of the flanking columns is 96 feet. The expence of the building, furnishing, &c. was nearly 80,000*l.* the congregation accommodated, including the charity children, is between three and four thousand persons.

The present Rector is the Rev. J. Hume Spry, D. D. a Prebendary of Canterbury, who was instituted by the Crown in 1825, on the death of Luke Heslop the late Rector.*

Curates :—The Rev. Bryant Burgess, M. A.

The Rev. John Moore, M. A.

Clerk and Sexton, Mr. William George Paux,†

---

* The following anecdote of the liberality of the present Rector has come to the knowledge of the compiler of this volume. There being no Rectory House, The Rev. Dr. Spry, at the commencement of the year 1832, offered to purchase a splendid mansion situated in York Terrace, on the Crown estate (which had then lately become vacant), and to present it to the Parish, to be used as the residence of all future Rectors, provided the Crown would concede the ground rent. The Government, however, did not consider itself justified in acceding to this proposal.

† This gentleman is the first Parish Clerk who has personally officiated, during the last 70 years, the situation having been generally presented to the Duke of Portland's Steward, whose duty was done by Deputy.

appointed by the Crown the 19th of August, 1826, on the resignation of Reynier Tyler, Esq., who was one of the Poor Knights of Windsor, and had been originally appointed to that office by His Grace the Duke of Portland.

Against the side walls are sculptured memorials on tablets of white marble, many of which are neatly, and even classically designed ; having the arms beautifully emblazoned.

List of Persons, to whose Memory Tablets are erected in this Church.

North Wall.

Richard Cosway, Esq. R. A. Principal Painter to
    H. R. H. George Prince of Wales,   -   1821

William Fairlie, Esq. formerly of Calcutta,   -   1825

The Rev. Doctor John Vardill, Regius Professor of
    Divinity in King's College, New York,   -   1811

Urban Vigors, Esq. Lieut.-Gen. in the Hon. East
    India Company's Service,   -   1815

Thomas Warre, Esq.   -   -   - 1824

Claud Russell, Esq. formerly Member of Council
    of Fort St. George in the East Indies,   -   1820

Charles Clarius Fitzgerald, -   -   1822

East wall.

Benjamin Oakley, Jun.   -   -   1815
He was interred in the Church of Tooting Graveney, in Surrey, and removed thence (by a Faculty from the Bishop of Winchester), and deposited in the Family Vault beneath this monument, 15th Feb. 1817.

Colonel Hugh Henry Mitchell of the 51st Regt. of
Foot, who married 3d July, 1804, Lady Harriet
Isabella Elizabeth Somerset, Daughter of Henry
5th Duke of Beaufort, and died April 20th,   1817

Margaret, Countess of Clonmell, Relict of John,
Earl of Clonmell, Lord Chief Justice of Ireland, 1829

Robert Powney, Esq.   -   -   1817

John Bebb, Esq. of Gloucester Place,   -   1830

Joseph Fernandez Madrid, Envoy Extraordinary
and Minister Plenipotentiary from the Republic
of Columbia to His Britannic Majesty   1830

Major Arthur Balfour, of the East-India Company's
Bengal Service,   -   -   1817

Clementina, Wife of Vice Admiral Sir Pulteney
Malcolm, K. C. B. and Daughter of the Hon.
Fullerton Elphinstone,   -   -   1830

Isabella Mary Fairlie, died 23d January, 1830, also
John Fairlie, her infant son, died January 3,   1829

Benjamin Howton, Esq. upwards of 60 years a resident of this Parish,   -   -   1819

Anna Maria, Wife of George Carrington, of Mis-
senden Abbey, in the County of Bucks,   -   1829

Edmund Alexander Howard, Esq. of York Place,   1827

Lieut. Gen. William St. Leger, who served his
Country many years in America, Europe and
Asia,   -   -   -   1818

Lieut. Gen. Robert Nicholson of the Hon. East
India Company's Service at Bombay,   -   1821

William Gordon, who died Nov. 1, 1809, and
Charles Mackinnon, who died April 14, 1824,
both sons of the late Stephen Haven, Esq. and
Lydia his wife.

Rachel, wife of Col. I. B. Taylor,   -   1814

Augusta Elizabeth, Wife of John Kirkland, Jun.
Esq. of Baker Street, Portman Square, and eldest
daughter of Major General J. A. Vesey,   -   1824

Charlotte Frances, Fourth daughter of Maj. Gen. J. A. Vesey, who died 3d July, 1824, and Margaret, youngest daughter of John Kirkland, Esq. of Glasgow, who died 26th Feb. 1823.

Dona Maria Brigida de Faria e Lacerda, Wife of of Sir John Campbell, K. C. T. S., Lieut. Col. in the British and Maj. Gen. in the Portuguese Service, who died Jan. 22, 1821. Also John David Campbell, son of the above, who died 28th May, 1824, aged 3 years and 9 months.

David Lyon, Esq. - - 1827

Colonel Thomas Matthias Weguelin, of the Hon. East India Company's Service, Bengal Establishment, 23d May, 1828. Also George St. Clair, 3d Son of the above.

West Wall.

Elizabeth Mary Booth, - - 1820

William and Martha Joachim, who were many years Resident in this Parish, and whose Remains are deposited beneath a tomb in the cemetery on the South side of Paddington Street, (without date).

Sir James Sibbald, Bart.

Edward Ravenscroft, Esq. of Portland Place, 1828

Lettice, Second Daughter of the late Thomas Patten, Esq. of Bank Hall, - 1817

John Cotton, Esq. late of the Bengal Civil Service, 1828

John M'Camon, Esq. late of Gloucester Place, 1808

Emma Catherine Bampfylde, only Child of Sir George Warwick Bampfylde, Bart. and Dame Penelope his wife, - - 1825

Lieut.-Colonel Richard Fitzgerald, of the 2d Life Guards, who fell in the 43d year of his age, in the Field of Waterloo ; and of Georgiana Isabella Simha D'Aguilar, his Widow, who died 2d Dec. 1821, aged 63.

Gilbert Hall, Esq. formerly a Surgeon in the Service
of the Hon. East India Company, at Calcutta, and
late of Manchester Street,   -   1820

Sir William Fraser, Bart. F. R. S. one of the Elder
Brethren of the Trinity House, and formerly a
Commander in the Hon. East India Company's
Naval Service,   -   -   1819

James Sutherland, Esq. formerly of Bombay,   1828

Alexander George Mackay, of Bagthorpe Hall in
the County of Norfolk,   -   -   1827

Mary Swinney, Spinster,   -   -   1826

General Robert Morse, late Inspector General of
Fortifications, Jan. 28, 1818. Also his Wife,
Sophia, daughter of Peter Godin, Esq. of South-
gate, who died Jan. 11, 1818.

Maria Mackenzie,   -   -   1821·

Mrs. Martha Udny, widow of Robert Udny, formerly of Teddington, Esq. and Sub-Governess of
Her late Royal Highness, The Princess Charlotte
of Wales. In the midst of jarring interests, she
secured the respect and affection of her Royal
Pupil, and the approbation of His Majesty. She
was born in 1761, and died 1st of Sept. 1831.

In the Vestry.

Rev. LUKE HESLOP, D. D.
Archdeacon of Bucks, and Rector of St. Mary-le-bone,
Died 23d of June, 1825, aged 86 years.

---

*In the spacious Vaults underneath this Church, are
deposited the Remains of many of the Nobility and
Gentry, among whom are the following Eminent
Persons.*

Matthew Montagu, Baron Rokeby of Armagh in the
Kingdom of Ireland, and a Baronet of Great Britain,
who died Sept. 1, 1831.

Augusta, Countess of Glasgow, Daughter of James Hay, 14th Earl of Errol. Her Ladyship was married on the 4th of March, 1788, to George Boyle, Earl of Glasgow, and died on the 23d of July, 1822.

The Hon. Augustus Phipps, Brother to the Earl of Mulgrave.

A Child of the Earl of Munster.

Lord Viscount Kelburne.

James Sutherland, 5th Baron Duffus, in the County of Elgin, in the Peerage of Scotland, and a Baronet of Nova Scotia. The title was restored to His Lordship by Act of Parliament, in 1826, the Peerage having been forfeited by the attainder of Kenneth, 3d Lord, in 1715. His Lordship died on the 30th of Jan. 1827, when his honours devolved on his distant kinsman, Benjamin Dunbar, the present Lord.

John Henry Upton, Viscount Templetown.

The Viscountess Templetown. This Lady was daughter of John Montagu, 5th Earl of Sandwich, and was married Oct. 7, 1796, to John Henry Upton, Baron Templetown, who was created a Viscount, March, 1806. Her Ladyship died 4th of Oct. 1824.

The Right Hon. Sir Geo. Warrender, Bart. of Lochend, East Lothian, N. B. was born 5th Dec. 1782; and inherited the title, as the fourth Baronet, at the decease of his father, in June 1799.

Brownlow Bertie Mathew, Esq.

Algernon Percy, first Earl of Beverley. His Lordship was the 2d son of Hugh, first Duke of Northumberland (who was created Baron Louvaine of Alnwick, County of Northumberland, in the Peerage of Great Britain, with remainder to Algernon Percy, his 2d son, and the heirs male of his body). He succeeded the Duke his father in the Barony, in 1786, and was advanced to the dignity of Earl of Beverley, County of York, in 1790. His Lordship was born 21st Jan. 1750, and died 21st Oct. 1830.

General Cowell.

Dowager Lady Mary Knightley.

John Hugh, eldest son of John Gibson Lockhart, Esq.
and Grandson of Sir Walter Scott, Bart. He was a
favourite child of the late lamented Baronet, who
dedicated his " Tales of a Grandfather" to him, under
the title of Hugh Little John, Esq. He died at his
father's house in the Regent's Park, in his 11th year.

Lieut. General Malcolm Grant.

Admiral Isaac Prescott.

Two Children of Sir Robert Sheffield.

Sir Henry Chamberlain, Bart. This gentleman filled the
situations of Consul-General and Charge d'Affaires
in Brazil, and was created a Baronet 22d Feb. 1828.
He died July, 31, 1829.

Sir Murray Maxwell, Bart. Capt. R. N.

James Northcote, Esq. R. A.

Here is also the Family Vault of Catherine, Countess of
Pembroke and Montgomery; in which are deposited
the Remains of her Father, His Excellency the late
Count Simon Woronzow, who died in 1832.

In the vestibule on the east side is the following inscription:—Thomas Verley, late of this Parish, gave £50.
the Interest to be given in Bread, viz. Twelve Penny
Loaves to the Poor, every Sabbath Day for ever, 1692.

The Rectory district is bounded on the south,
by Oxford Street from Vere Street to Orchard
Street ; on the west, by and including the east sides
of Orchard Street, Portman Square, Baker Street,
and Park Road ; on the north, by and including
the south side of Primrose Hill Road ; and on the
east, in part by the parish of St. Pancras, and by
the south-east quadrant of the circle in the Regent's Park, formed by the roads running southward
and eastward from the said circle ; and continuing
southward includes the west sides of Devonshire
Place, Wimpole Street, and Vere Street.

Acts of Parliament relative to the District Churches.

By the provisions of an Act of Parliament, passed April 6, 1821, the Vestrymen were empowered to agree with the Commissioners acting under the Acts 58 Geo. III. c. 45, and 59 Geo. III. c. 134, both Acts for " Building and promoting the building of additional Churches in populous Parishes," and they accordingly agreed with the said Commissioners to procure sites for four District Churches, and to pay the sum of 20,000*l.* towards building such Churches; and the Lords of the Treasury having granted a site for the building of a District Church, on the east side of Regent Street, the said Vestry purchased a site in Wyndham Place, of Edward Berkeley Portman, Esq.; they also purchased another site situate at the corner of Stafford Street, and Great James Street, all in the said parish of St. Mary-le-bone. By this Act, they also agreed to provide another site in the eastern part of the parish, to be approved of by the Lords Commissioners, and the Lord Bishop of the diocese. It was also enacted that the Parish should be under the jurisdiction and Visitation of the Lord Bishop of London, and of the Archdeacon of Middlesex for the time being (the same having been hitherto extra-episcopal). It was also provided that the Parish of St. Mary-le-bone should remain one entire and undivided Parish, for all civil and other purposes, save and except as regarding Ecclesiastical purposes. It was likewise stipulated that five thousand pounds should be paid to the Commissioners within twelve months after the foundation of each District Church should be laid. The Commissioners with the consent of the Bishop, were to assign a particular District to each and every one of the District Churches, which was to be confirmed by his Majesty in Council, and such division or District to be under the immediate care of the respective District Minister, with respect to his Ecclesiastical duties, excepting the burial fees, which are made payable to the Vestrymen of the said Parish, in like manner as burial fees at the Parish Church. All tithes, and other emoluments to continue and belong to the Incumbent of the Parish Church, as if no such division of District had taken place, or as if this Act had not passed. The Vestrymen, with consent of the Bishop, to fix pew rents. Each District Minister to appoint clerk and pew-openers to his own Church, and to remove the same as he may think fit, subject to the approbation of the Patron. Commissioners, with consent of the Bishop of London, to assign proportion of pew-rents to the Minister of each District Church. To appoint salary to clerk. If stipend to Minister does not amount to 500*l.* then Vestrymen to make up the same to that sum. Distinct account of pews to be kept. Right of Presentation to District Churches vested in the Crown. Each District Minister to pay yearly 200*l.* to the Rev. Luke Heslop, D. D. the present Minister of the Parish, as long as he shall continue to be the Incumbent, and after his death the said payment to cease, and from thenceforth the sum of 100*l.* per annum to be paid by each District Minister to the Incumbent Rector to be thereafter appointed. The District Ministers are also prohibited from publishing Banns, or the Solemnization of Marriages and Baptisms, the same being directed to be performed at the Parish Church, and the fees for the same to be paid to the Incumbent Rector. The Parish from the date of passing this Act to be deemed a Rectory, and the Incumbent Minister thereof shall be deemed a Rector.

By an Act passed July 5, 1825, the Four District Churches were to be named severally, St.

Mary's ; All Souls ; Christ Church, and Trinity, in the Parish of St. Mary-le-bone ; the District assigned to each Church was to be called a District Rectory, and the Incumbent Ministers respectively to be styled District Rectors. They were also empowered to publish Banns, Marry, and Baptize in their several Districts, and to perform all other parochial functions of a Minister, in the same manner, as the Incumbent Rector of St. Mary-le-bone, and also to take all fees for the same respectively, save and except with respect to burials.

By an Act passed, June 14, 1827, the Vestrymen were empowered to alter the boundary of the Parish, so as to include the whole piece of ground purchased for the site of Trinity Church, of the Vestrymen of the parish of St. Pancras. His Majesty having granted two slips of ground on the east and west sides of the Church, for improving the appearance of the same, the said land to be vested in the Vestrymen of the said parish, and their successors, for ever. By this Act it was also declared lawful for the Commissioners of Woods, Forests and Land Revenues, for and on behalf of His Majesty, to appoint from time to time one Churchwarden of the said Parish, a Sidesman, and likewise one of the Beadles.

ST. MARY'S CHURCH.

The site of this church, which is situated in Wyndham Place, was purchased of Edward Berkeley Portman, Esq. The church was built from the designs of Sir Robert Smirke, and was consecrated January 7, 1824. The principal front, contrary to the usual arrangement, is the southern; in the centre of which is the portico and tower. In its plan the building consists of a nave, or body, with side aisles, a portion of the design at the angles being taken out of the plan to form vestries and lobbies, whereby the body is made longer than the aisles.

The tower is circular in plan; the elevation is made into three stories; the basement has a doorway with a lintelled architrave, and above it three round-headed windows. A portico consisting of six Ionic columns and two antæ, sustaining an entablature and attic, the latter ornamented with arched panels instead of a balustrade, sweeps round that portion of the tower which projects from the main building. Above the parapet the circular tower is continued, and forms a stylobate to the second story, which has eight semi-columns, of the early Corinthian Order, attached to it, with windows having arched heads in the spaces between; the cornice is finished with a parapet set round with Grecian tiles, and upon this story is a pedestal, still continuing the same form, having four circular apertures for the clock dials, and finished with a cornice sustaining a circular temple pierced with eight arched openings, the piers between which are ornamented with antæ, supporting an entablature, cornice, and parapet, the latter set round with Grecian tiles, and crowned with a conical dome, on the vertex of which is a gilt cross. The remaining part of this side of the church is formed into two stories by a string course, and finished by a cornice

Drawn from Nature & on Stone by Edw.ᵈ Hassell.

Printed by Graf & Soret.

ST MARY'S CHURCH.

and parapet continued from the portico; the lower
story contains, on each side the portico, three square
windows with stone architraves, and the upper story
the same number of lofty arched windows with
architraves of stone round the heads, resting, by
way of impost, on a string course. Within the
portico there is also an entrance, with a window
above it in the wall of the church on each of the
towers. The west front is in like manner made
into two stories, and also vertically into three divisions, the lateral ones containing windows, and
finishing with cornices and parapets as before; the
central division has three doorways, with lintelled
heads in its basement, and three arched windows
above. This division is surmounted with a pediment to conceal the ridged roof. The north side of
the church only differs from the south in having
three more windows in each story in the space
which is occupied by the tower and portico on the
side already described. The east front is in three
divisions, the side ones similar to the western; the
central division retires behind the line of the front,
and has a square window divided into three compartments by antæ, and finished with a pediment. The
church is built of brick, except the tower, cornices,
and other particulars before enumerated. The
height of this church, from the base to the top of
the tower, is 135 feet; elevation of the body of the
church, 42 feet 6 inches; length of the exterior,
128 feet; height of the pillars of the portico,
33 feet.

THE INTERIOR

is made into a nave and side aisles. On each side
the former are square piers, supporting galleries,
the fronts of which are composed of a cornice and
attic, which being continued round the whole
church, divide the elevation into two stories. Upon
the upper member of the attic are placed at intervals flat square plinths, from which rise six fluted

columns, intended for Grecian Doric, on each side
of the church, sustaining an anomalous entablature,
on which rests the ceiling. The nave is arched in
a small segment of a circle; the ceiling of the aisles
is horizontal; the surface of both is divided into
square panels. A western gallery extends across
the church to the depth of two of the intercolumniations. The altar has a handsome screen of scagliola
in imitation of various marbles; it is composed of
an ornamented wall, finished by a cornice and attic,
and flanked by piers. The central portion, imitating
Sienna marble (upon which, most strange to say,
the commandments have *not* been inscribed), is enriched with a square panel of porphyry, surrounded
by gold mouldings above the altar, between two
long perpendicular panels of the same materials.
The piers have Ionic antæ, of porphyry, with
gold capitals; the architrave and cornice, and the
attic above the piers, are statuary marble with gold
mouldings, the latter portions charged with crosses
in irradiations of gold, and sustain vases supported
on grouped modillions. The centre of the attic,
which is Sienna, has a narrow horizontal panel
enriched with honeysuckles in circles splendidly
gilt. Above this is the east window; the antæ are
veined marble, and sustain an entablature and
parapet of the same material. The window is filled
with stained glass: the subject, the Ascension of our
Lord; of which, whether for accuracy of drawing,
propriety of colouring, or felicity of effect, the less
that is said, the better.* The commandments are
inserted in gold letters, on a white ground, on that
portion of the wall not occupied by the screen,
and the north and south sides of the recess in
which the altar is situated. The decorations of the
altar are judicious and appropriate; while the altar

* This *morbid* specimen of modern stained glass, was erected
by means of a private subscription at 5*l.* 5*s.* per head. It is said
to have cost 250*l.*

itself, in extent of railing, is capable of accommodating perhaps the largest number of communicants
of any church in London: not fewer than twenty-
six being able commodiously to kneel together. But
the great defect, not only of the altar in particular,
but of the whole church, is, the want of even Milton's "dim, religious light." A cloudy or foggy
day, in the latter months of autumn—to say nothing
of the season of winter—almost shrouds it in dark-
ness. The pulpit and reading-desk are exactly
similar: helping not only to wound the eye by their
stiff and offensive uniformity—and depriving very
many of the auditors of the gratification of both
hearing and seeing—but to propagate that into-
lerable error in *acoustics*, of inducing the sound,
or voice, to spring from a corner, instead of from
the centre of parallel lines. The font is situated
in the front of the altar-rails: it is a handsome
circular basin, of white marble, standing on a pillar
of the same material; its situation is, however,
a very incorrect one. The organ is placed at the
back of the spacious western gallery, in a handsome case.

The estimate was 20,000*l.* and the number
accommodated, according to the Reports of the
Commissioners, is 1828 persons, which, however, is
considerably less than the actual number.

It would have been desirable, if possible, to have
procured a site for this church in a more central
part of the District than that which has been assigned to it. In short, it should almost seem as if
the greatest possible pains had been taken to select
a site, in all respects the most inconvenient for the
majority of the congregation: it being surrounded
by streets of worse than a second rate description.*

---

* The reader will smile to learn that some of the most *classical*
and *picturesque* names are affixed to streets, of the description
above alluded to: to wit, *Cato Street* (memorable for an event
which will be found described in the subsequent pages) now

If it be said, that the accommodation of the *poor* has been principally consulted, the answer is, the poor are always *sure* to fill the free seats allotted to them, wherever the service of the Church of England is decently and impressively performed. The tower and cupola of this church form a tolerably picturesque termination to the view from Cumberland Gate, Hyde Park.

The present Rector is the Rev. Thomas Frognall Dibdin, D. D. Chaplain in ordinary to his Majesty,* who was instituted on the consecration of the church in 1824.

Curate, the Rev. William Henry Charlton, M. A.

Assistant Curate, William Henry Millington, M. A.

Clerk, Mr. Joseph Langdon.

The District assigned to this church is bounded on the south by Oxford Street, from Orchard Street to Edgware Road; on the west, by the Edgware Road; on the north, by and including the south side of the New Road, from Edgware Road to York Place; and on the east by and including the west side of Orchard Street, Baker Street, and York Place.

called *Horace Street ; Virgil Place, Homer Row, Nelson Place, Paradise Row, Pomona Place, and Britannia Gardens !!*

* The numerous splendid works that have emanated from the pen of this accomplished gentleman and scholar, are so highly appreciated by the learned, and the curious in black letter lore, that no extensive library can be said to be complete without possessing them ; and when from death, or other circumstances, any valuable collection containing these works is brought to the hammer, they produce more competition than those of any living author.

The Western National School.

Supported by Voluntary Contributions.

The west front of the St. Mary-le-bone Western National School House is seen in the annexed view of the church. This building was erected in the year 1824, the late James Tillard, Esq. a private gentleman of Canterbury,* advancing 4000*l.* for that purpose, on condition of receiving an annuity of 200*l.* during his life ; and dying in 1828, he bequeathed the above sum to the Charity. The elevation of the principal front of this spacious and handsome edifice, is in a corresponding style with the church. Here are two extensive school-rooms, capable of accommodating 600 children, viz. 350 Boys, and 250 Girls ; 100 of whom are clothed, viz. 50 Girls and 50 Boys, at the expense of the Charity. The children are received indiscriminately from the Districts of St. Mary and Christ Church.

Patron.
Edward Berkeley Portman, Esq. M. P.
Patronesses.
Her Grace The Dow. Duchess of Roxburgh.
The Rt. Hon. The Dow. Countess of Castle Stuart.
The Rt. Hon. The Dow. Countess Manvers.
The Rt. Hon. The Countess Mount-Norris.
The Rt. Hon. The Dowager Lady Elcho.
Mrs. Portman.
President.
The Right Honourable Lord Kenyon.
Treasurers.
Sir Claude Scott, Bart. and Co.

---

* The above gentleman also advanced, by way of loan, the sum of £20,000. to the Parish, to assist in erecting the four District Churches, which he also bequeathed to the Parish on his death in 1828, together with the Interest which he had already received.

Honorary Surgeon.
J. C. Cox, Esq. 33, Montagu Square.
Schoolmaster and Secretary.—Mr. James Martin.
Schoolmistress.—Mrs. Felton.
Collector.
Mr. Joseph Langdon, 44, Upper York Street.

Donations and Subscriptions are received by the Treasurers, Sir Claude Scott, Bart. and Co., Cavendish Square ; also by Messrs. Hoitt, Booksellers, Upper Berkeley Street ; and Mr. J. Langdon, the Collector.

Rules and Regulations.

The children are instructed conformably to the system of the Central National School in Baldwin's Gardens.

The children attend Divine Service every Sunday morning and afternoon; and a select number in the evening.

Prayers from the Liturgy of the Church of England are read daily to the children.

Each child is admitted on the recommendation of a Trustee.

Any person giving 10*l.* or upwards, at one payment, is constituted a Trustee for Life.

Every person subscribing 1*l.* annually, to be an Annual Trustee.

A Trustee for Life may recommend any number of children, and an Annual Trustee three.

No child to be admitted under the age of six years; nor continued in the school after the age of fourteen.

No child to be admitted who has not had the small pox, or been vaccinated.

Ten Managing Trustees to be elected by ballot, at a General Annual Meeting, which is held in the month of March.

The Patron, Patronesses, President, Vice-Presidents, and Auditors, shall, together with the ten elected Managing Trustees, have the entire direction of this Charity, until the return of the Annual Election; subject to the control of a General Meeting of the Trustees.

A General Meeting may be called at any time, on a requisition signed by ten of the Trustees.

A Monthly Meeting of the Patron, Patronesses, Trustees, &c. is held at the School house, on the first Thursday in every month, at 11 o'clock in the forenoon, for the admission of children, and for general business. Three of whom to form a quorum.

Two Visitors are appointed monthly at such Meeting, who shall have the management of the School confided to them for that month.

An Annual Public Examination to take place in the month of May; when all Trustees are earnestly requested to attend.

Every Lady subscribing, may vote by proxy, to be signed by the Lady, and delivered by a Trustee.

The Ladies Visitors superintend the work and discipline of the Girls' School, in conjunction with the Monthly Visitors, but no alterations are made in the Rules and Regulations, without the sanction of the Monthly Board.

Applications are continually making for Children to be placed in services of different descriptions, and it is gratifying to be informed that those children who have left the Schools, are conducting themselves in a manner satisfactory to their employers, and creditable to the School.

ALL SOULS CHURCH.

The Ground on which this Church is built, was granted to the Parish by the Commissioners for building the New Street. The first stone was laid on the 18th of Nov. 1822, and it was consecrated on the 25th of Nov. 1824.

With the exception of the steeple and portico, the exterior shews a plain stone building, lighted by two tier of windows, and finished with a ballustrated parapet. The former portions are, then, the only parts particularly to be described. The steeple consists of two portions, a circular tower and a cone; the first rests on a flight of steps, and is occupied to a considerable portion of its height by a peristyle of twelve Ionic columns, sustaining the entablature of the order. The capitals are highly enriched; from the volutes depend festoons of foliage, and between them, attached to the abacus, is a cherubim with expanded wings: the effect, however, is not pleasing, the exuberance of the ornament giving to the capital an appearance of clumsiness. Above the entablature of this peristyle the tower is continued plain to the remainder of its height, broken only by the dials. The base of the cone, which is situated within the circular tower, is surrounded with a peristyle of fourteen Corinthian columns sustaining an entablature and ballustrades; the remainder of the cone is unbroken; the surface is fluted, and to render the point the more acute, it is finished with metal. It surely would have produced a better effect if the spire had terminated in the usual way with a cross: as it is, the whole structure has so novel an appearance, that to those who have been accustomed to the old style of church-towers, the present suffers greatly by comparison; its novelty surprises, but does not

Drawn from Nature & on Stone by Edw.ᵈ Hassel.   Printed by Graf & Soret.

produce delight. The pointed spire transplanted from the country village, and made a finish to a shewy street of modern houses, is so out of character, that whatever may be the merit of originality displayed by Mr. Nash, his design is less pleasing than if it had assimilated more closely to the older style of church-spires, of the school of Sir C. Wren and his followers. The approaches are by two doorways in the principal front, and by another beneath the lower peristyle, which leads into a circular vestibule, lighted by two windows. The interior is very pleasing; it is formed more closely on the model of the older Churches in the Italian style than the generality of the new ones are. The west, north, and south sides, and a portion of the east end, have galleries attached to them, resting on octagonal piers; the residue of the east end is occupied by the altar. Above the fronts of the galleries rises a colonnade of Corinthian columns sustaining an architrave and cornice, on the latter of which rests the ceiling of the Church. The south and north sides have each eight columns; two others are situated on the eastern gallery, and two more to correspond on the western. The ceiling of the centre division of the Church is elliptical, flattened in the centre, the whole surface of the cove being enriched with octagonal sunk panels. The fronts of the galleries are panelled, and are broken at intervals by the plinths of the columns, on which are sculptured chaplets in relief.

The altar is very handsomely ornamented. An extensive crimson curtain, tastefully arranged in festoons, is drawn up sufficiently to display Mr. Westall's painting of "Christ crowned with Thorns," exhibited at Somerset House in 1822. Immediately beneath this is the altar-table, the whole composition being far superior to the general arrangement of the altar in Churches. The pulpit and desk are placed against the piers sustaining the extreme ends of the galleries at the east; the former is bracket-shaped, but is not remarkable for beauty or ornament. The font is situated, contrary to custom, near the altar-rails; it consists of a circular basin of marble, sustained on a pillar of the same form and material. At the west end is a semi-circular recess, which contains the organ and its gallery. The instrument is contained in a handsome case, the design of which consists of a pediment between two circular towers, finishing in cupolas; on the apex of the former a gilt cross. The ceiling of this portion is fluted and radiated. Whatever may be the faults resulting from the liberties which have been taken with the general style of ecclesiastical building on the exterior, they are fully atoned for by the light and elegant arrangement of the inside, and the church-like appearance which is given to it by the adherence to the old fashioned arrangement. The superior grandeur which results from the division of the interior by colonnades into nave and aisles, is so apparent, that it is almost to be wished that such an arrangement was enforced in all the new Churches, by the same authority which in other respects has controlled the formation of them. The congregation accommodated is 1761.

The Reverend George Chandler, D C. L. Dean of Chichester, is the present Rector, who was instituted in 1825, on the removal of Dr. Spry to the Rectory of the Parish.

Curates:—The Rev. Wm. Lucius Coghlan, M. A.
          The Rev. Henry Latham, M. A.

Clerk, Mr. John Paux.

All Souls District is bounded on the south, by Oxford Street, from Tottenham Court Road to Vere Street; on the west, by and including the east sides of Vere Street and Wimpole Street, to Great Mary-le-bone Street; and on the north, by and including the south sides of Great Mary-le-bone Street, (east of Wimpole Street,) New Cavendish Street, and Upper Mary-le-bone Street.

EASTERN NATIONAL SCHOOL.

This School was instituted in 1824, for receiving children of the indigent inhabitants of the All Souls and Trinity Districts. The school-house is a commodious building, situated in Riding House Lane, adjoining the east end of All Souls Church, and was erected by subscription ; here is sufficient accommodation for 500 children, but the number at present educated amounts only to 417, viz. 257 Boys, and 160 Girls, of whom 44 Boys and 30 Girls are clothed at the expense of the Charity.

Patron.
The Right Honourable and Right Reverend the Lord Bishop of London.

Patronesses.
Her Grace The Duchess of Portland.
The Most Noble The Marchioness of Lothian.
The Most Noble The Marchioness of Cornwallis.
The Right Hon. Viscountess Duncannon.
The Right Hon. Lady Robert Seymour.
The Right Hon. Lady Skelmersdale.
Mrs. Saxby Penfold.   Mrs. Spry.

President.
The Rt. Rev. The Lord Bishop of Bath and Wells.

Treasurers.
The Very Rev. The Dean of Chichester.
The Rev. Dr. Penfold.

Bankers.
Sir Claude Scott, Bart. and Co. No. 1, Cavendish Square.

Honorary Surgeon.—John Propert, Esq.

Schoolmaster and Secretary.—Mr. Pain.

Schoolmistress.—Mrs. Pethrie.

Collector.—Mr. Byers, 7, Foley Street.

Donations and Subscriptions are received by the Treasurers; by the Bankers, Sir Claude Scott, Bart. and Co. No. 1, Cavendish-square; and by Mr. John Byers, the Collector.

The School is conducted strictly on the System of the National Society as exemplified in the Central National School in Baldwin's Gardens, Gray's Inn, and no books are used in the School except those on the list of the Society for promoting Christian Knowledge.

The Laws and Regulations of the School are precisely similar to those of the Western National School, with the exception that a quarterly examination of the children takes place in the months of March, September, and December; and a public examination in the month of June, of which due notice is given.

The Girls' School is under the superintendence of the Ladies Patronesses, with other Ladies not exceeding ten in number, who are selected by the Committee of Management from the families of the Trustees, with their consent and approbation; and the Ladies thus appointed constitute a Committee of Visitors, who superintend the work and discipline of the Girl's School, but are not permitted to make any alteration in the Rules and Regulations, until the sanction of the Committee of Trustees has been obtained.

Drawn from Nature & on Stone by Edw.ᵈ Hassell.   Printed by Graf & Soret.

CHRIST CHURCH.

London, Published by John Smith, 49, Long- acre 1833.

CHRIST CHURCH.

The site of this church was purchased of Thomas Wilson, Esq. It was built from the designs of the late Phillip Hardwick, Esq. and was consecrated in 1825. The portico and principal front are at the east end. The western end of the church abuts against the houses on the north side of it. The building is in two separate portions, the first, which is entirely of stone, comprises the entrance and tower; the second portion consists of the body of the church, and is wholly appropriated to the congregation; this is built of brick, with stone dressings. There is an entrance from the portico, to the basement story of the tower, which is formed into a circular vestibule, crowned with a dome, in the centre of which is an opening, encircled with a gallery and ballusters. On the south and north sides are openings to other vestibules of the same form, covered also with domes, having circular lantern lights on their centres. In these are the stairs to the galleries, and the entrances to the body of the church. To the lateral vestibules are also entrances from the north and south sides of the building, each of which is flanked with a pair of Ionic columns, finished with the appropriate entablature, without pediments; the north and south fronts have each a series of five long windows, with arched heads, and are furnished with parapets and balustrades. The portico and pediment are of the Ionic Order, and above and behind the pediment rises a plain square tower. Above this tower, whose monotony is broken only by the clock, is a square portico of four columns on each face, and the steeple is finished by a campanile and cupola which supports a ball and cross. Although the portico and principal front are at the east end, the altar retains its proper situation, this arrangement was occasioned by necessity; it is the same at Bishopsgate church, but the effects of the alterations are here met with far greater ingenuity than in that church.

INTERIOR.

The architecture is of the Corinthian Order, and, together with the Ionic of the exterior, is formed after the Italian examples. The nave and aisles are separated by six lofty columns, and two pilasters on each side supporting the entablature of the Order. The ceiling is arched, and is pierced by windows corresponding with the intercolumniations. The ceiling of the nave is arched, and formed by ribs into six principal divisions, each filled with an oval panel, the borders of which, as well as the ribs, are ornamented with scroll mouldings. The ceiling of the aisles is flat, and unornamented. Galleries are erected in the aisles, as well as across the west end of the nave, and are supported by pilasters. The fronts are coloured in imitation of oak paneling, resting on an architrave of stucco. The altar is simply ornamented; the screen occupies the whole of the eastern wall, and is situated in a recess between the lateral vestibules, which have already been described. The sides of the recess have large niches, and the eastern wall is divided into three compartments by pilasters sustaining the entablature. The commandments, creed, and paternoster, are inscribed in these divisions upon long arched pannels. Upon the entablature are two small statues of angels seated, and holding a ribbon, inscribed, GLORY TO GOD IN THE HIGHEST, and between them is an urn with wreaths of foliage. The ceiling of the chancel is ornamented with sunk panels, each containing an expanded flower of a circular and angular form alternately. In the body of the church, at a short distance from the altarrails, the pulpit and reading and clerk's desks, are placed on opposite sides. The two former are copies of each other; their form is octagonal, resting upon a terminal column. The furniture of the altar, pulpit, &c. is crimson velvet, and a glory encircling I. H S. inscribed on the front of each; two handsomely carved chairs, with a mitre on the back of each stand within the rails. A neat organ is erected in the western gallery. The fittings up of the interior for the accommodation of the congregation are neat and convenient, and the building is well adapted for hearing the service The excellent arrangement of the entrances preserves that quietness so essential to a church, and adds to the beauty of the whole design.

There are catacombs underneath this church, in which the remains of a few persons are deposited, but no tablets are as yet erected in the church.

The present Rector is the Rev. Robert Walpole, B. D. who was instituted in 1828, on the removal of the Rev. G. Saxby Penfold, to Trinity.

Curate :—The Rev. William Joseph Hutching, M. A.

Clerk, Mr. William Harrison.

The Christ Church District, is bounded on the west, by the Edgware Road ; on the north by the Parishes of St. John, Hampstead, and St. Pancras ; on the south east, by and including the north side of the Primrose Hill Road ; on the east, by and including the west side of Park road, and west side of Upper Baker street ; and on the south, by and including the north side of the New Road from Upper Baker Street to Edgware Road.

TRINITY CHURCH.

Part of the ground for building this Church was exchanged by the Vestry of this Parish with that of St. Pancras, the boundary of the Parish having been altered to facilitate this arrangement, the Treasury having granted two slips of ground to aid their object. This Church was designed by Sir John Soane, R. A., and consecrated in 1828.

In common with the parish or rectory Church, on the opposite side of the road, the usual Church arrangement has been departed from; in this instance, the principal front faces the south instead of the west, and the altar is at the north end of the building.

The principal front is made into a centre with side divisions; the first portion consists of a portico of four Ionic columns, imitated from the Temple on the Ilyssus at Athens; they are raised on a flight of steps of equal height with the plinth on which the entire building is elevated, and are surmounted by their entablature. The frieze displays the Grecian fret; behind the portico are entrances to the Church, and collateral to it are two plain divisions, containing lofty arched windows, divided in height by a transverse stone; the central portion is built or faced with stone, these smaller divisions, with their returns at the flanks of the building, are built with brick, and form a disagreeable contrast with the stone work of the front and flanks. Such small portions of brick-work rather show a peculiar taste, than indicate an attention to economy, for no one can conceive that in an edifice, where the funds allowed of a number of expensive columns, any necessity could exist for leaving a small portion only of the corners of the building destitute of a stone covering.

In the side divisions, the cornice only of the

Drawn from Nature & on Stone by Edw.ᵈ Hassell

Printed by Graf & Soret

T R I N I T Y   C H U R C H .

London. Published by John Smith, 49 Long-acre 1833.

entablature is applied, and the entire elevation is surmounted by a blocking course and *ballustrade*.

Above the portico rises a tower in two stories, the first or belfry, is square in plan: in each face is an arched window, with a circular perforation above for the dial, over which the Grecian fret is again introduced. At the sides of the windows, and near the angles of the tower, are insulated columns of the "Tivoli Corinthian" Order, standing on pedestals; the story is crowned with an entablature, the blocking course over each column is finished with a very beautiful cinerary urn, or pyramidal sarcophagus.* The second story is circular, a peristyle of six columns, of the same order as the tower of the Winds at Athens; the columns are raised on a stylobate, and crowned with an entablature, over which is a blocking course, broken by Grecian tiles at intervals, corresponding with the columns. A cupola, sustaining a large vane instead of a cross, crowns this story; the cella is pierced with windows between each alternate pair of columns.

---

* The history of the construction, or rather of the finishing of this *first story*, furnishes an additional proof, if any were wanting, of the parsimony, or rather meanness of public bodies, in the prosecution of public works. Sir John Soane, the architect, (whose public spirit and private collection of ancient and modern art, place him at the head of modern Virtuosi), was at first compelled, from the very limited estimate allowed for the building, to adopt the plan of pilasters, instead of the bold and beautiful columns as they now stand. The drawing exhibiting this first plan was left for public inspection at the Court-house; and the effect, as might have been expected, was meagre and poverty-stricken. In consequence, the Rev. Dr. Penfold, the first and present Rector, set on foot a subscription, (which was readily carried into effect, to the amount of £.1200.) for the production of an enlarged and more ornamented tower. The result was, the tower, or rather the first story of it, as we now behold it; and it is no vague or unmerited compliment to the architect, to say, that a more beautiful piece of ecclesiastical architecture, is not to be seen in the whole range of modern churches. Had the funds at the disposal of Sir John Soane, been on a scale befitting the liberality of a large and opulent parish, the second story of this tower would have been on a scale of proportionate magnitude with the first.

The eastern flank of the church, assimilates in general design with the front already described; it is made into a central and lateral divisions, the former consists of six half columns of the Ionic Order, between two pairs of antæ, forming seven divisions, having lofty arched windows in each intercolumniation, divided into two heights by a transom; the lateral divisions have similar windows to the central. An entablature crowns the columns, with the favourite fret in the frieze. Above the side divisions, in common with the west front, the cornice only is retained; and a ballustrade forms the finish to the elevation. The central portion, like the principal front, is faced with stone. The small collateral divisions at each angle, as before observed, are brick. The northern elevation is recessed in the centre, with a corridor connecting the projecting wings, in the style of Walworth Church. Above this are three windows, and the elevation is finished with an acroterium.

The interior of this church is generally admired for the tasteful nature and general pleasing character of its decorations. In breadth it is made into a nave and aisles by columns and arches. A small division is made at the north and south ends of the church by arches, crossing the whole building at right angles with the former ones, and which rest upon piers rising from the floor. The smaller arches above the galleries are semi-circular; the larger ones crossing the nave are segments of large circles. The division to the north forms the chancel, the south one contains the organ gallery. An arch of the like form is also constructed at the north end above the altar windows. The spandrils of all these arches are pierced with circles, giving an air of great lightness and elegance to the whole composition. The side aisles are occupied by galleries, sustained on an architrave supported by *unfluted* Grecian Doric columns. The fronts are panelled.

From the architrave four octangular pillars without capitals, are carried up, and sustain five semi-circular arches springing immediately from the pillars, without the intervention of imposts, and occupying the space between the piers at the north and south ends; the divisions northward of the piers are covered by plain circular arches. A gallery crosses the south end of the church, in which is erected the organ. On each side of this instrument is an additional gallery for the charity children.

The ceiling, part of which is pleasingly broken into portions by the various divisions of the church, is quite flat, and formed into large panels; that portion which belongs to the central division is surrounded with a frieze of foliage disposed in a continued scroll. Each panel in the centre row is enriched with a flower, as are all the panels in the aisles and chancel.

The altar-screen is a beautiful composition, in three divisions. The centre contains the decalogue on dark red panels, and is bounded by two pilasters sustaining an architrave, cornice, and pediment, having cherubim applied as acrotèria; beneath the architrave is a dove in white marble, with expanded wings, surrounded with a golden irradiation. The lateral divisions contain the Creed and Paternoster on corresponding panels, and the whole is flanked at the sides with two columns, and finished with an architrave and cornice enriched with scroll work, and broken above the columns, where the cornice is decorated with acroteria and cherubim. The body of the screen, and the pilasters and columns, are painted in imitation of Sienna marble; the capitals, frieze, and other enrichments of white veined marble. In the wall above the altar are three arched windows glazed with ground glass, which on that account greatly detract from the appearance of the building.

The pulpit and reading desk are executed in

oak, and rest upon columns on opposite sides of the nave.   The font, consisting of a circular basin of marble, sustained on a pillar of the same material, is placed in front of the altar-rails.   The basement story of the church is occupied by spacious and well ventilated catacombs, but the number of persons at present deposited in them is very limited.

The congregation accommodated is 2003. The estimate was 21,829*l*. 10*s*.

The present Rector is the Rev. George Saxby Penfold, D.D. Rector of King's Swinford, Staffordshire, who was instituted on the consecration of the church, in 1828.

Curates :—The Rev. Fred. Hamilton, M. A.
            The Rev. William James Early Bennett, M. A.

Clerk, Mr. Henry Charles Bell.

Trinity District is bounded on the north and north-west, by and including the Quadrant of the Circle in the Regent's Park, and the Roads running southward and eastward from the said circle; on the east, by the Parish of St. Pancras; on the south, by and including the north sides of Upper Mary-le-bone Street, New Cavendish Street and Great Marylebone Street (eastward of Wimpole Street); on the west, by and including the east sides of Devonshire Place, Upper Wimpole Street, and Wimpole Street, north of Great Mary-le-bone Street.

Oxford Chapel, now St. Peter's.

Previously to the erection of the New Churches, this Chapel was considered one of the most beautiful structures in the metropolis. It is situated in Vere Street, Oxford Street, and was erected about 1724; Marriages, Christenings, &c. were performed here while the Parish Church was rebuilding in 1741: his Grace the Duke of Portland was also married at this Chapel in 1734. The building is of brick, strengthened with rustic quoins of stone. The principal entrance at the west end is approached by a flight of steps, leading to a porch of the Doric order; the entablature supports a triangular pediment which contained on the tympanum, a coat of arms carved in stone; these arms appear to have belonged to a descendant of Aubrey De Vere, the last Earl of Oxford of that family. They were however taken down in the year 1832, when the Chapel was repaired, and it was then named St. Peter's. The steeple springs from the centre of the roof, at this end, and consists of three stages, viz. a square tower of brick, above which is an octagon tower, open on all the sides, and crowned with a dome, from which springs a second, and smaller octagon tower, like the first, which supports a ball and vane. At the east end is a Venetian window, above which is a triangular pediment. A modillion cornice of stone is continued all round the building, and at each corner was a handsome stone vase, but these latter ornaments have been removed within these few years. This Chapel passed to the Crown at the same time with the Rectory.

The Minister of this Chapel is the Rev. Edward Scobell, M. A. lately appointed by the Crown, on the death of the Rev. J. Percival.

PORTLAND CHAPEL, NOW ST. PAUL'S.

This Chapel is situated in Portland Street, and is a handsome brick building, decorated with stone dressings, and having a stone steeple at the west end: it was erected in 1766, on the site of Mary-le-bone basin, which was formerly a reservoir of water, for the supply of that part of the metropolis, but had been disused for many years. By some unaccountable neglect, this Chapel was omitted to be consecrated, at the time of its erection, and Divine Service was performed in it until the latter end of the year 1831, when (it having in common with the Rectory of the Parish passed into the hands of the Crown), the important ceremony of consecration was performed, and it was dedicated to St. Paul.

The present Minister is the Rev. John Crofts, M. A.

There is nothing remarkable in the architecture of the other Chapels of this Parish, they having been erected at various periods, as the population increased, and more accommodation for religious worship was required.

BENTINCK CHAPEL,

Which is proprietary, and situated in Chapel Street, New Road, was erected in 1772, and opened by the Rev. — Hunt, father of the talented Editor of the Examiner. The Rev. Basil Woodd was Minister of this Chapel for a period of 45 years, dying on the 12th of April, 1831. Her Royal Highness the late Duchess of York frequently attended Divine Service at this Chapel.

The present Minister and proprietor is the Rev. Henry Hinxman, M. A.

WELBECK CHAPEL, NOW ST. JAMES'S,

Is situated in Westmoreland Street, Mary-le-bone Street, was erected in 1774, and was then called Tichfield Chapel. This Chapel also passed to the Crown with the Rectory, and has since been named St. James's.

The present Minister is the Rev. Thomas White, M. A.

Assistant Minister, the Rev. Philip Jennings, D. D.

PORTMAN CHAPEL,

Is the property of the Minister, the Rev. J. Harris, and was erected in 1779, it is situate in Baker Street, a short distance from Portman Square.

QUEBEC CHAPEL,

Situated in Quebec Street, was built in 1788. This Chapel is the property of B. Simmonds, Esq. His Majesty's 2d Regiment of Life Guards attended Divine Service at this Chapel on Sundays during the time they occupied the Barracks in King Street : part of the service is chaunted after the cathedral style at this Chapel.

The present Minister is the Rev. Alfred Williams, M. A.

BRUNSWICK CHAPEL,

Was resigned to the Crown, on the appointment of the Minister, the Rev. Dr. Penfold, to the Rectory of Christchurch. This Chapel, erected in 1795, and situated in Upper Berkeley Street, is remarkable for the number of persons of high rank and consequence which form the congregation. The present Minister is the Rev. St. Vincent Love Hammick, appointed by the Crown, on the death of the late Rev. William Fawssett, D. D.

MARGARET STREET CHAPEL,

The property of Henry Drummond, Esq. This building is situated in Margaret Street, Cavendish Square; was first converted into a Chapel in 1789. The present Minister, is the Rev. William Dodsworth, M. A.

There are several Dissenting Chapels also in this Parish, the principal of which are: the Scotch Chapel in Wells Street, 45 years under the Ministry of the late Dr. Waugh. Hinde Street Chapel, belonging to a congregation of the Wesleyan persuasion. Paddington Chapel, situated in Homer Place, New Road, under the Ministry of the Rev. J. Stratton, who professes the doctrine of the Independents. Shouldham Street Chapel, under the Ministry of Mr. George, a Baptist. Blandford Street Chapel, a Baptist Meeting. Providence Chapel, under the Ministry of Mr. Huntingdon, frequented by a congregation styling themselves Independents, situated in Little Titchfield Street, was burnt down on the 18th of July, 1810;* Aenon Chapel, New Church Street, Edgware Road ; Wesleyan Chapel, Salisbury Street; and a Chapel lately estabished by Mr. Irving, in Newman Street, in a room which was formerly the gallery of the late Benjamin West, P. R. A. Also a Roman Catholic Chapel in Spanish Place, and another in Little George Street, dedicated to Notre Dame de l'Invocation.

* It is said that when this Chapel was burnt down, the Minister observed, that " *Providence* having allowed the Chapel to be destroyed, *Providence* might rebuild it, for *he* would *not*"—and in consequence, the site is occupied by a timber yard.

CEMETERY ON THE SOUTH SIDE OF PADDINGTON
STREET. *Consecrated in* 1733.

It is computed that more than 80,000 persons
are interred in this cemetery; the monumental
inscriptions are so numerous, that it becomes necessary only to select the following list of persons
to whom memorials have been erected.

Susan Coy, - - - 1733
Mr. John Phillips, - - 1733
Flora Pond, wife to Ambrose Pond of Rickmersworth, in
the County of Hertford, Gent. - 1738
Major Isaac De L'Aigle - - 1739
Frances Rothery (sister of Dr. William Nicolson, Arch-
bishop of Cashel, and mother of Joseph Rothery,
Archdeacon of Derry), - - 1740
Matthew Gossett, Esq. a Gentleman-Pensioner, " well-
known for his skill in some of the Polite Arts." 1740
Mr. James Hamilton, - - 1749
George Rawlinson, First Master Cook to his most be-
loved and revered Royal Master, George III. in whose
Household he passed half a Century.
John Reynolds, Master-painter of the Ordnance, 1752
John Lawson, Esq. - - - 1753
The Hon. Enoch Hall, Esq. Chief Justice of North
Carolina - - - 1756
Here is a splendid Mausoleum, erected by the Hon.
Richard Fitzpatrick, to the memory of his beloved
wife, the Hon. Susanna Fitzpatrick, who died March
28, 1759, Ætat 30. The following inscriptions also
appear on the west and north sides :—The mortal
Remains of Anne, Baroness de Robeck, youngest
daughter of the Hon. Richard Fitzpatrick, who departed
this Life, Oct. 22, 1829, aged 80 years, were depo-
sited in this mausoleum, by her disconsolate Son, the
Baron de Robeck, on the 13th Nov, 1829. This
Mausoleum was completely repaired by John Michael
Henry Fock, Baron de Robeck, Grandson of the
Hon. Richard Fitzpatrick, An. Dom. 1830.

John Castles ("late of the GREAT GROTTO, whose
   great ingenuity in shell-work gained him universal
   applause.")   -   -   -   1757
Thomas Buck, Gent. of Whitehill, Co. of Kent, 1761
Francis Moore, Esq.   -   -   1761
Rev. Thomas Morice,   -   -   1762
Mary Du Bisson, Spinster, aged 61,   -   1762
Barak Longmate,   -   -   1764
Dame Anne Milbanke, Relict of Sir Ralph Milbanke,
   Bart. of Halnaby in the County of York,   1765
Mr. Duncan Grant, late of H. M. S. Marlborough 1765
Archibald Bower, Esq. Author of the History of the
   Popes,   -   -   -   1766
Anne, Relict of Capt. Geo. Edwards, R. N.   -   1767
Sir Andrew Chadwick, Knt.   -   -   1776
William Guthrie, Esq.   -   -   1770
Frances Rivett, Widow of John Rivett, Esq. of Checkers
   in the County of Bucks, and daughter of John Rus-
   sell, Esq. late Governor of Bengal. She was Bed-
   chamber Woman to her R. H. Princess Amelia, 1775
George Mercer, Esq. one of the Justices of the Peace of
   the County of Middlesex,   -   -   1776
Robert Adams, Esq. of Cavendish Square,   -   1778
Benjamin Rujolas, Gent.   -   -   1779
George Lee, Esq.   -   -   -   1782
Dame Margaret Chadwick,   -   -   1783
Rev. Joseph Hooley, Vicar of Breedon and Ratby, and
   Rector of Newtown Linford, all in the County of
   Leicester,   -   -   -   1783
Rev. J. Carpenter, Rector of Bignor, and Vicar of Pag-
   ham, in Sussex,   -   1785
Gideon Gossett, Esq.   -   -   1785
Mr. Thomas Jackson, Gent.   -   1786
Sir Alexander Allan, Bart. -   -   1787
Robert Auchmuty, Esq. Judge of the Admiralty of the
   Four New England Provinces   -   -   1788
Mr. Thomas Chaplin, of the Sec. of State's Office, 1788
Constant Decharme, Merchant,   -   1788
Francis Marden, Esq. of the Hon. East India Company's
   Service at Bombay,   -   -   1789
Hester, Wife of Capt. George Martin,   -   1790

Mrs. Hester Fitzmaurice, sister of Lord Westcote, and
    Relict of John Fitzmaurice, Esq.   -   1790
Silvester Rossi, -   -   -   1790
Jessentour Rozea, Jun. Esq.   -   -   1791
Matthew Stourton, Esq.   -   -   1792
Sir Thomas Mills, Knt.   -   -   1793
Rev. Joseph Davenport,   -   -   1794
Henry Lloyd, Esq. of Boston, in North America, 1795
Capt. William Henry Brisbane, of the Royal Navy, Son
    of Admiral Brisbane, " He was raised to the rank of
    Captain, by his gallant conduct, when first Lieutenant
    of H. M. S. Romney, in an action with the Sybylle,
    a French ship of war, of equal force, which she cap-
    tured."   -   1795
Jane Simondson, a faithful Servant for 19 years in the
    family of John Martin Leake, Esq.   -   1796
Mrs. Anne Leland, Wife of Lt. Gen. John Leland, 1797
Doctor John Breynton,   -   -   1799
Francis Wheatley, Esq. R. A.   -   -   1801
Sir Charles Ventris Field, Knt.   -   1803
Mr. John Burgess,   -   -   -   1803
Admiral Sir Richard King, Bart.   -   1806
Samuel Greig, Esq. Late Captain in and Commissioner
    for the Navy of His Majesty the Emperor of all the
    Russias, and officiating Consul General for his said
    Majesty, in Great Britain   -   -   1807
Henry Stuart S. S., B. 28th Sept. 1793, D. 9th July,
    1794. Also Charles Henry Stuart, S. S., B. 17th
    March, D. 1st Oct. 1802. Sons of J. Ferdinand
    Smyth Stuart, *Great Grandson of King Charles II.*
    rest here. " Most beautiful smiling innocents, Alas !
    How fallen ! How changed !" And Spencer Perceval
    Stuart, S. S., B. June 14th. D. Aug. 4, 1807.
Joseph Bonomi, Esq.   -   -   1803
Anna Maria De Bathe, 1796, and Sir James Michael de
    Bathe, Bart. her husband, -   -   1808
Dr. Ainslie of Dover Street, Piccadilly.
Mr. James Belcher, who died regretted by all who knew
    him, July 30, aged 30 years,   1811
James Hume, many years in the house of Cox and
    Greenwood, Charing Cross   -   1813

Ralph Wilde, Esq. Capt. in the 89th Regt. and Major
  in the Portuguese Infantry, killed at the battle of
  Salamanca,   -   -   -   1812
John Thomas Malling, son of the late Major John
  Joseph Maling, of the Royal African Corps,   1816
Alexander Farquharson, Esq.   -   -   1818
Edward Jones, Bard to H. M. Geo. IV.   -   1824
Maria Georgiana, daughter of Henry Frankland, late of
  the 37th Regiment,   -   -   1824
Miss Micaela Lauriana Tilt (eldest daughter of Lieut.
  Col. Andrew Tilt of His Majesty's 37th Regiment 1825
Miss Mary Anne Pickersgill, only daughter of the late
  Lieut. Joshua Pickersgill, Dept. Assistant Quarter
  Master General to the Bengal Army,   -   1825
Alexander Esplin, of Langholm, Dumfriesshire,   1825
Westgate Copping, Esq.   -   -   1825
Louisa Elizabeth, daughter of the Rev. W. Barlow, 1826
John Meek, Esq. formerly of Jamaica,   -   1826
Selina Innes, Relict of the late William Innes, of the
  Island of Jamaica, Esq. and daughter of the late Sir
  William Chambers, Knt. Comptroller-General of His
  late Majesty's Works,   -   -   1827

The following lines (which are scarcely legible) are
inscribed on a stone erected in 1777, to the Memory of

GEORGE CANNING, Esq.

Father of the late Right Hon. George Canning,
Principal Secretary of State for Foreign Affairs, during
the late Reign.

Thy virtue and my love no words can tell,
Therefore a little while my George farewell;
For faith and love like ours, Heaven has in store
Its last best gift—to meet and part no more.*

* This stone and its inscription are fast mouldering to dust. A
trifling sum would restore it to its pristine beauty : and when one
considers the character, worth and wealth, of many Individuals
connected with the name of CANNING, one is more than surprised,
that this tribute to the memory of the Father of one of the most
eminent Orators and Statesmen, that ever graced the annals of this,
or of any other Country, should be suffered to sink into oblivion.

Caroline Malie, wife of Thomas Malie, M. D. Surgeon
to His Majesty's 1st Regiment of Dragoon Guards.
Lieut. Aaron Young, of the Royal Marines, - 1827
Rev. Joseph Davidson, Fellow of King's College, Cam-
bridge, - - - 1828
Anne Green, who died at Boulogne, - 1830
Mrs. Letitia Paux, - - 1830
Alexander Peter Allan, Esq. late of Basseterre, in the
Island of St. Kitts, - - 1830
Samuel Copping, Esq. - - 1830
Ellen Stanley Crozier, daughter of Henry Robert Cro-
zier, Esq. and Caroline Stanley, - 1831
Capt. Felix Thompson, 2d West-India Regiment, 1831

CEMETERY ON THE NORTH SIDE OF PADDINGTON STREET.

This ground was purchased of the late Mr.
Portman for 3000*l*. and consecrated in 1772. It
is smaller than that on the south side, and contains
a large number of tombs, some of which are of the
most splendid description. Memorials are erected
to the following persons.

Philip Deare, Esq. - - 1774
Anthony Pelham, Esq. M. D. - - 1776
Mrs. Frances Gwynn, Relict of the late Colonel Leonard
Gwynn, - - - 1776
Lady Charlotte Wentworth, 3d daughter of Thomas,
Marquis of Rockingham (and likewise that of Elizabeth
Wombersley).
"The Rich and the Poor, meet together,
The Lord is the Maker of them all."
Elizabeth Wombersley lived 55 years in the service of
the said Lady Charlotte Wentworth, and died in her
family.
Ann Nasso, wife of Marco Nasso, Esq. of Rathbone
Place, - 1779
Mary Horne, widow of Captain Edward Horne, R. N. 1781
Benjamin Charles Collins, Esq. of Salisbury in the County
of Wilts, - - - - 1785

Family Vault, " The within Burial Place is the property of Wade Toby Caulfield, Esq. and his Family for ever."

Joseph Tullie, Esq. of Yorkshire, Receiver-General of the Duchy of Lancaster, and Deputy-Usher of the Exchequer, - - - - 1774

Edward Cauldwell, Esq. Captain in the Navy (who married Anna Maria, only child of Thomas Clark, Gent. of Westminster, - - 1780

Mary, widow of Captain Edward Thorne, of the Royal Navy, - - - 1781

Mr. Henry Sutton, son of Sir Richard Sutton, Bart. 1782

John Jefferson, Esq. late Master of His Majesty's Ship Sandwich, - - - - 1782

Dame Leonora Rush, daughter of Brigadier-General Sutton, and Relict of Sir John Rush, Kt. - 1785

David Aquiton La Rose, - - - 1786

Malcolm Macpherson, Esq. - - 1787

Jonathan Court, Esq. Commander of a Ship in the service of the East-India Company, - 1787

Frances Purling, wife of Matthew Purling, Esq. 1787

Malcolm Macpherson, Esq. - - 1787

William Newson, Esq. R. N. - - 1787

Alice, wife of William Baillie, Esq. - - 1788

Henry Bradley, Esq. - - - 1789

Mr. John Christopher Zumpe, Gent. 1790.
" When Life is past and Death is come,
Then well is he, that well has done.

Catherine, Wife of the Rev. William Affleck, 1791; also, the Rev. William Affleck, late Rector of North Luffenham, County of Rutland, and Vicar of Potton in Bedfordshire, 1806; also, Elizabeth, Baroness Fyffe, daughter of the above, 1827; also, of Colonel Gilbert Affleck, son of the above, 1831.

Mrs. Mary Newey, wife of Mr. James Newey, of the Custom House, - - - - 1794

Stephen Riou, Esq. who died, March 12, 1780; in the same grave is interred the body of his wife Dorothy Riou, who died Jan. 1, 1801; Captain Edward Riou, of H. M.S. Amazon, who so nobly distinguished himself at Copenhagen on the 2d of April, 1801, under Lord Nelson (was their second son:) and who was killed there by a cannon shot in the 38th year of his age. In commemoration of whose Services the Parliament of the United Kingdom voted a Monument to be erected in St. Paul's Cathedral.

Also, the Remains of Colonel Philip Riou, who died, Oct. 21, 1817, after an honourable Service of more than 40 years in the Royal Artillery.

Matthew Purling, Esq.   -   -   - 1791
Susanna Tipping, Spinster, died, Nov. 1791, aged 65
    years.
Anne, Wife of Major-General William Martin, and
    daughter of James Gordon, Esq. of Boston,   1793
Mr. Henry Smith, of this Parish, who was suddenly
    bereft of life on his Birth Day, by a fall from his horse
    on the 23d of October, 1794, aged 29.
Captain John Bower,   -   -   - 1794
Robert Grews, Esq.   -   - 1794
Mary, Wife of the Rev. B. Lawrence, and daughter of
    Robert Grews, Esq.   -   -   - 1796
Caroline, daughter of Sir Cecil Bisshopp, Bart.   1797
Mr. Thomas Singer, 1797; also, Mr. William Singer,
    son of the above, who was unfortunately drowned as
    he was bathing in the river Ouse, in Yorkshire, June 7,
    1798, aged 19 years.
The Family Vault of Lieutenant-General Sir Alan Came-
    ron, K. C. B. purchased,   -   -   - 1797
Robert Catherwood, Esq. late of East Florida,   - 1797
Alexander Elmsley, Esq.   -   -   - 1797
Captain Robert Winch,   -   - 1798
Mrs. Ann Brettell, wife of George Brettell, of Baker Street,
    Esq.   -   -   -   -   - 1799
William Allsop, Esq.   -   -   - 1800
Harriet Creyke, 2d daughter of Ralph Creyke, Jun. Esq.
    of Rawcliffe House, Yorkshire.
William Douglas, Esq. of Somerset Place,   - 1800
Miss Jane Simpson of Bradley, in the Co. of Durham, 1801
Duncan, Mᶜ Andrew, Esq.   -   1802
Lady Ann Sheridan, of Portland Place,   1802
Henry Cornelisen, Esq.   -   - 1803
Anne, Wife of the Rev. B. Lawrence, Curate of this
    Parish,   -   -   -   - 1803
Miss Henrietta Hellen Abernethie, daughter of the late
    Dr. Abernethie, Physician in Banff,   -   - 1804
Lieutenant-Colonel Robert Hunter, of His Majesty's 3d
    Regiment of Foot Guards,   -   - 1804
The Rev. Robert Sumner, M. A. Vicar of Kenilworth and
    Stoneleigh, in Warwickshire, 1802; also, Robert
    Sumner, son of the above, of Corpus Christi College,
    Cambridge, 1804.
Charlotte, wife of William Boscawen, Esq.   - 1804
Mrs. Rose Pearson, 1804, also, Mr. William Penrucker,
    of this Parish, who was killed by a cannon ball, in an
    action with the enemy off Boulogne, Sept. 6, 1804, in
    the 29th year of his age.
Mr. Michael Hoyle,   -   - 1805

Mrs. Anna Clarke, widow of Captain Clarke, R. N. who
died at Barbadoes, 1776, she died,   -   -   1805
Philip Rogers Bearcroft, Esq. Commissary of Accounts
to the Leeward Islands, and one of the Commissioners
for investigating the Accounts of Army Expenditure in
the West Indies, during the last war,   -   1805
John Sumner, Esq. late of Bengal,   -   -   1808
James Durnford, Esq. 1803; also, the Hon. Mrs. Amelia
M'Veagh,   -   -   -   -   1808
Juliana Wright, daughter of the late S. Wright, Esq. 1808
Mr. Joshua Brown, resident in this Parish 50 years, 1808
Robert Gregory, Esq. formerly Chairman of the Court of
Directors of the H. E. I. C. and M. P. for Rochester, 1810
Mrs. Johanna Hart, wife of Mr. Thomas Hart, of the
Royal Navy,   -   -   -   -   1810
William Johnston, Esq. late of Up. Berkeley Street   1810
Mrs. Mary Stephens, Relict of General Stephens, 1810,
also, her son Lieutenant-Colonel Edward Stephens, of
the 3d Regiment of Guards,   -   -   1811
Mrs. Sarah Agar, wife of James Agar, Esq. of Welbeck
Street,   -   -   -   -   1811
Francis Maria Drought, daughter of the Hon. Thomas
Wallen, President of the Council of the Island of
Jamaica, and wife of Thomas Drought, Esq.   -   1811
Miss Jane Vick, daughter of William Vick, Esq.   1812
Miss Mary Clotilda Perkins, daughter of Captain Perkins,
R. N.   -   -   -   1812
John Schweitzer, Esq.   -   -   -   1812
Robert Curry, Esq. late of His Majesty's Navy,   1812
Mrs. Mary Fowler, Relict of the Rev. Bernard Fowler,
late Rector of Wormley, Herts,   -   -   1812
The family Vault of John White, Esq. who died,   1813
Josiah Tatnall, Esq. formerly of His Majesty's Council
for the Bahama Islands,   -   -   -   1813
William Robinson, late Deputy Clerk of this Parish, 1814
Thomas Greenwell, Esq.   -   -   1814
Jane Greenwell, wife of the above,   -   -   1832
Edward Jones, Esq.   -   -   -   1815
Mrs. Elizabeth Stewart, wife of Lieutent-General James
Stewart, 1807; also, General James Stewart, 1815.
Mary Ann, wife of the Rev. Okey Belfour, Minister of
St. John's Chapel in this Parish,   -   1816
The Rev. Charles Coleman, of Ratharnham, County of
Dublin,   -   -   -   -   1817
James Bruce, Esq. Lieutenant-Governor of Dominica,
1808; also, his brother-in-law, Captain John Thomson,
of the Coldstream Guards, 1808; also, William
Thomson, Esq. of Spring Garden, Musselburgh, near
Edinburgh,   -   -   -   1817

Mr. John Jones, late Vestry Clerk of this Parish, which
situation he filled for nearly 37 years, with credit to
himself, and advantage to the Parish, 1818

Mr. John Keeble, 25 years Pastor of the Church Meeting,
in Blandford Street, 1824; also, Mrs. Elizabeth Keeble,
1822.

Sarah Windowe, wife of Henry Windowe, Esq. of Pains-
wick Lodge, County of Gloucester, - 1826

Family Grave of Mr. Joseph Lee, To the Memory of
Charlotte Dew, upwards of 60 years, a good and
faithful Servant in the Family of Sir Simeon Stuart,
Bart. - - - 1828

Anne Gouldsmith, wife of Richard Gouldsmith, Esq.
1825, and Richard Gouldsmith, Esq. husband of the
above, - - - - - 1832

Master George Desanges, son of Elizabeth and Louis
Desanges, Esq. of Stratford Place, - - 1832

I must not quit the solemn boundaries of this cemetery,
without paying "the passing tribute of a sigh" to the
memory of one whose ashes repose within it, but of
whose name there is yet no visible record.—It is of Mr.
THOMAS TURNER, for 34 years principal Corrector
of the justly celebrated Shakspeare Press, of whom I
would now be understood to speak. The individual in
question was not less distinguished for his amiable and
obliging manners, than for his *professional* attainments.
Mr. Turner was not the merely cold, mechanical corrector of typographical errors, but the suggester of
valuable hints, and the furnisher of substantial information. To an extensive knowledge of ancient and modern
literature, he added an intimate acquaintance with the
Oriental languages; his reading was various and solid,
his taste accurate and refined; and in general attainments, for the successful execution of the important
office consigned to his care, he was undoubtedly *excelled*
by none: many testimonies of admiration for his talents,
exist from authors of his day, who attained no small
celebrity by their works, and of whom, many were
deeply indebted to him for his Editorial assistance, and
it is no slight testimony to his reputation, to add, that
to *his* pen, the late Mr. Gifford (the Editor of the
Quarterly Review, and perhaps the shrewdest philological critic this country ever produced) confessed himself indebted for many a happy emendation.

————————" Qui prægravat artes
Infra se positas extinctus amabitur idem."

HOR.

St. John's Wood Chapel.

This is a substantial unpretending chapel of the
Ionic order, designed by the late Thomas Hardwick, Esq. It is divided into two stories, with
square windows to give light to the pews under the
galleries, and with lofty semi-circular headed windows to light the galleries and body of the edifice.
The portico is tetrastyle, and has a dial or clock-
face in the tympanum of the pediment. Above
this is a cubical tower, with steps, which forms a
pedestal to a handsome lantern of the Roman Doric
order. Apertures between the columns give light
to the belfry, which is covered by a hemispherical
cupola, ball, and vane.

The interior has a very novel and pleasing appearance, the pillars and pews being painted white,
and having mahogany mouldings on the tops. The
pulpit and reading desk are on opposite sides of the
building ; the altar is at the north end, the usual
inscriptions are painted in gold letters on a black
ground: above these inscriptions is a small semi-
circular stained glass window, producing a very
pretty effect as seen from the entrance to the
chapel. It is singular, that although the interior
of this chapel has never been painted since it was
consecrated in 1814, it appears as fresh and clean
as at the first day, which can only be accounted
for, by the purity of the atmosphere, and absence
of surrounding buildings.

The present Minister is the Rev. Thomas
Wharton, M. A., Master of the Clergy Orphan
School.

Clerk, Mr. John Emperor.

The monumental tablets placed against the walls
of this chapel, are most beautiful specimens of
modern sculpture, by the most celebrated professors of the age : here may be seen the productions

of Chantrey, Behnes, Wyatt, Hardenberg, Rouw,
Austin, Blore, C. H. Smith, Lupton, Sams, &c.
and it is to be regretted, by all lovers of the Fine
Arts, that the sum charged for permission to erect
a monument in this chapel is so enormous, that it
amounts almost to a prohibition.

In the Vaults underneath this chapel are deposited the Remains of many eminent persons; among
whom is Mrs. West, the wife of the late Benjamin
West, P. R. A. who promised, a short time before
his death, to paint an altar-piece for presentation
to this chapel, but his dissolution frustrated the
carrying of his kind intention into effect.

List of Monuments in the Chapel.

North End.

Charles Reynolds, Lieutenant-General in the Service of
the East India Company. He served in India from the
year 1772, till 1807, with eminent advantage to the
Public and honour to himself. He filled the office of
Surveyor-General under the Presidency of Bombay;
and has left, for the information of the World, a Map of
Hindustaun, constructed from actual survey by himself
and assistants; a lasting monument of his professional
fame! He died at Cheltenham on the 24th of June,
1819.

Sacred to the Memory of an affectionate friend and kind
father, John Tunno, Esq. of Devonshire Place, died
May 15, 1819, aged 73 years. (A beautiful Monument
by W. Behnes, Sculptor. Bust of the deceased on a
Pillar, with a mourning figure of a young man, size of
life).

Lieutenant-General Charles Morgan, many year's Senior
Officer on the Bengal Establishment, in the Service of
the East India Company; he died March 21, 1819,
(Splendid Monument by F. Hardenberg).

Sarah Capel, daughter of John and Eleanor Capel, of Russell Square, 1822. (Splendid Monument by Chantrey).

Maria Anna, the wife of Thomas Hayward Budd, of Bedford Row, London, Esq. who died on the 25th of April 1819; also, the Body of Thomas Hayward Budd, Esq. who died July 14, 1820. (A beautiful Monument by R. J. Wyatt).

" She is not dead but sleepeth."

William Ruddiman, Esq. M. D. formerly of Madras, who died January, 20, 1826.

Mrs. Eliza Kyd, wife of Lieutenant-General Alexander Kyd, who died Jan. 22, 1819; also, Lieutenant-General Kyd, of the Hon. East-India Company's Service, Chief Engineer, Bengal Establishment, who died Nov. 25, 1826.

West Side.

Sophronia Rebecca, Relict of the late Lieutenant-General G. Stibbert, who died Oct. 18, 1815.

Robert Woodmass, Esq. late of Montagu Square, who died Jan. 28, 1820.

Charles Augustus Godfrey Pieschell, Esq. who died April 6, 1821, aged 70 years. His liberal contributions during his life to the numerous Charitable Institutions of this Country, his munificent bequests at his death for their support, and the Establishment of an Asylum in his native city of Magdeburgh, in Germany, for the Education of Poor Boys and Girls, are lasting Records of his Benevolence.

Isabella, wife of Patrick Bartlet, Esq. of Nottingham Place, who died Feb. 8, 1821.

" Of such is the Kingdom of Heaven."

Charles Binney, Esq. formerly of Madras, who died Feb. 2, 1822.

Augustus Frederick Pieschell, Esq. late of Wandsworth Common, and of Ballards in the County of Surrey; who died Dec. 15, 1822. This tablet is placed next to that erected to the memory of his departed relative, by the wishes of his surviving mother, brothers and sisters, at Magdeburgh, in Germany.

South End.

Jane Arbuthnot, daughter of the late Robert Arbuthnot, Esq. Secretary to the Board of Trustees, for the Improvement of Manufactures in Scotland; and of Mary Urquhart, of Craigston, his wife. She died in Wimpole Street, Feb. 2, 1819.

Miss Mary Alston, who died July 4, 1825.

Susannah Maria, wife of the late Lieutenant-Colonel Flint, of the 25th Regiment of Foot, who died Feb. 18, 1825

In Memory of John Farqhar, Esq. of Fonthill Abbey, in the County of Wilts, and of this Parish, who departed this life July 6, 1826, aged 76 years. (Handsome Monument with medallion head, likeness of the deceased, by P. Rouw Sculptor).

Lieutenant-General George Deare: he commanded the Corps of Artillery on the Bengal Establishment for many years, and served as a Major-General on the Staff of the Army of that Presidency. He died March 5, 1828.

East Side.

George Cherry, Esq. late of Nottingham Place, in this Parish, and for many years, Chairman of the Victualling Board; who died Feb. 12, 1815.

Anna Maria Lushington, eldest daughter of William Lushington, and Anna Maria his wife; she died with the hooping-cough, at the early age of seven years, on Sept. 24, 1816.

Peter Cherry, Esq. of Gloucester Place, New Road, who died Jan. 10, 1818; also, his wife Elizabeth, who survived him only six months.

Martha Maria, Relict of the late George Frederick Cherry, Esq. the Hon. East India Company's Senior Judge of the Court of Appeal at Benares; she departed this life, Jan. 21, 1819.

John Williams, Esq. many years a Resident in the Island of Newfoundland, who died in this Parish, Jan. 26, 1819.
　　" Be thou faithful unto Death,
　　　And I will give thee a crown of life."

Charlotte Stratton, Spinster, daughter of the late William Stratton, Esq. Member of Council at Bombay; who departed this life on the 11th day of October, 1819, aged 43 years; also, in Memory of her Mother, Jane Stratton, who died May 15, 1830, in her 80th year.

About 40,000 persons lie interred in the cemetery belonging to this chapel. But from the comparatively small number of memorials erected, the casual visitor would not suppose there were one-half the number.

List of Persons to whom Memorials have been erected.

Sally, wife of Thomas Tomlins, who died July 9, 1815; also, the abovenamed Thomas Tomlins, who died August, 1824.
In Memory of Edward Foxhall, Esq. who died Oct. 29, 1815.
David Pike Watts, Esq. late of Portland Place. A name recorded by the founder himself of the Madras system of Education, as the first person, who actually introduced that system into practice in England. He died July 20, 1816, aged 62 years. This tomb was erected by his only surviving child Mary Watts Russell, and his son-in-law Jesse Watts Russell. (Marble Tomb by Chantrey).
Isabella, wife of Mr. John Sowerby, who died Feb. 27, 1820.
George Mowbray, Esq. who died May 16, 1825.
John Stewart, Esq. July 21, 1826.
William Raymond, Esq. Lieutenant-General in His Majesty's Service, who died June 9, 1830.

Jonathan Fiske, - - - - 1823
Mrs. Charlotte Faulkner, - - - 1822
This Ground was bought by Mr. John Finlayson of Upper
  Baker Street, to deposit under this stone the mortal
  remains of Mr. Richard Brothers, who resided and died
  in Mr. Finlayson's House, on January 25, 1824.
Mary, wife of William Porden, Esq. Architect, - 1819
Mrs. Sarah Pratt, - - - - - 1820
John Lack, Esq. - - - - 1824
The Rev. Francis Thomas Hanson, Rector of Wydford,
  Herts, and of Quidenham, Norfolk, - 1824
Eleonora Franklin, wife of Captain John Franklin of the
  Royal Navy, - - - 1825
Margaret, wife of James Walker, Esq. Collector of His
  Majesty's Customs, at Berbice, - - 1828
Philip Raine, Esq. of Gainford, in the County of Dur-
  ham, - - - - - - 1824
Captain John Meade, of the 36th Regiment, 1827
Amelius Peach Sparkes, infant son of the late George
  Sparkes, Esq. of Elmfield House, Devon, - 1826
Samuel Cleverly, Esq. M. D. - - - 1824
Mr. Thomas Hogg, - - - - 1825
Walter Sumpter, Esq. - - - 1823
The Rev. Alexander Hewatt, D. D. - - 1824
Dr. Robert Gordon, late Physician to His Majesty's
  Forces, and Deputy Inspector of Hospitals, 1822
Mr. Henry Hawkins, Lieutenant of the Royal Navy, 1821
Captain John Lutman, late of the Royal Veteran Battalion,
  and formerly of the 81st Regiment; who after painfully
  lingering from a severe wound received on the 16th of
  January, 1809, in the Battle of Corunna, when serving
  in the latter Corps, died Jan. 20, 1821.
Matthew Evan Thomas, Architect. A Student of the
  Royal Academy of London, and a Member of the
  Academy of Rome and Florence, - - 1830
Margaret, 4th daughter of Donald M'Leod, Esq. 1822
William Greene, Esq. Surgeon, R. N. - 1822
Maria Candidade Britto, Native of Fundao, in the King-
  dom of Portugal, - - - - 1824
Thomas Tredgold, Esq. Civil Engineer, - 1829
Sarah Watson, wife of Thomas Watson, M. D. - 1830
Gregorio Franchi Chivalier; of the Portuguese Order of
  Christ, who died in London, - - 1828
Francis Beaty, Esq. Purser in the Royal Navy, - 1822
Miss Mary S. Mackenzie, daughter of Alexander Mac-
  kenzie, Esq. Banker in Inverness, - - 1820
James Farley Pratt, Esq. son of George Pratt, Esq. of
  the Island of Antigua, - - 1819

Francis Skelton, M. D.   -   -   - 1827
Mrs. Mary Ann Fitz Gerald, Spinster, who died Sept. 4,
    1816, aged 60, she was eldest daughter of the late
    Colonel Anster Fitz Gerald of the Desmond Branch of
    the family.
Captain Frederick Ernest De Pirch, of the 73d Regiment
    and son of the late Lieutenant-General De Pirch, of
    Stargard, in Pomerania. He died March 26, 1815.
Baron De Beaufort,   -   -   - 1814
Martha, wife of Donald Ross, late of the Colony of
    Berbice,   -   -   -   - 1820
John Francis William Rocquelin, a Native of Eu in
    France,   -   -   - 1819
Lionel Booth, of Saxmundham, Suffolk,   - 1815

On the West Side of this Cemetery, opposite No. 44
on the wall, and 26 feet from it, is a flat stone, underneath
which are deposited the Remains of Joanna Southcott, the
pretended Prophetess, with the following inscription:

In Memory of
Joanna Southcott,
who departed this life, Dec. 27, 1814, aged 65 years.
" While through all thy wondrous days,
Heaven and Earth enraptur'd gaz'd.
While vain Sages think they know,
Secrets, Thou Alone canst show.
Time alone will tell what hour,
Thou'lt appear in " Greater " Power.
                                        Sabineus.

On a black marble Tablet, let into the wall opposite to
the above spot, is the following inscription in gilt letters,
in addition to the above.

" Behold the time shall come, that these Tokens which
I have told Thee, shall come to pass, and the Bride shall
Appear, and She coming forth, shall be seen, that now is
withdrawn from the Earth."
                        2d of Esdras, Chap. 7th, ver. 26th.
" For the Vision is yet for an appointed time, but at
the end it shall speak, and Not Lie, though it tarry, Wait
for it; Because it will Surely Come, it will not tarry."
                        Habakkuk, Chap. 2, ver. 3d.
" And whosoever is delivered from the Foresaid evils,
shall see My Wonders. 2d of Esdras, Chap. 7, ver. 27th.
                        (See her Writings.)
This Tablet was Erected
By the sincere Friends of the above,
Anno Domini, 1828.

Dr. Samuel T. Bridger, late of the Hon. East India Company's Service, - - - - 1821
Janet Frances, Infant daughter of Lieutenant-Colonel Colquitt, of the Grenadier Guards, - - 1818
Emma Caroline Ward, daughter of James Ward, Esq. R. A. - - - - 1817
Captain George Warde Paterson, of the Hon. East India Company, Madras European Regiment, - 1817
Mary Anne, wife of Charles Dupre Russell, Esq. of the Bengal Civil Service, - - - 1831
William Meredith, Esq. - - - 1831
George Cochrane, Esq. Family Vault.
Eliza, wife of David Henderson, Esq. - - 1830
Matilda, wife of Alexander John Colvin, Esq. - 1830
Susan Anne, the wife, and the infant son of George Anderson, Esq. - - - - 1830
Margaret M'Leod Macqueen, eldest daughter of Captain Roderick Macqueen, who died Sept. 2, 1829. (This is a splendid Monument, with Inscriptions upon white marble slab, and an iron canopy ornamented and raised on iron pillars).
Fanny, wife of Lieutenant Horatio Nelson Noble, 1829
Mrs. Frances Hughes, Relict of Robert Hughes, Esq. late of the East India Company's Civil Service, at the Presidency of Madras, - - - 1827
William Parry, Esq. late of Montagu Square, and of Walton Hall, in the County of Suffolk, - 1826
The Rev. Gilbert Parke, Minister of St. John's Wood Chapel, - - - - 1824
John Harwood, late of King's Lynn, in the County of Norfolk, Esq. - - - - 1824
Thomas Robertson, Esq. late of the Hon. East India Company's Naval Service, - - 1822
Sir William Young, K. G. C. B. Admiral of the Red Squadron of His Majesty's Fleet, and Vice Admiral of Great Britain, - - - 1821
The Rev. Millington Buckley; also, Mrs. Ann Buckley, Relict of the above, - - - 1829
Charlotte Barnett, fourth daughter of Benjamin Barnett, Esq. of London, Banker, 1821; also, Mrs. Avice Barnett, Relict of the above Benjamin Barnett, Esq. 1822.
Thomas Wheeler Milner, Esq. - - 1819
William Charles Hicks, Esq. 2d son of the late J. W. Hicks, Esq. of the City of Bath, - 1818
Family Vault of Sir John Coghill, Bart. Eliza Hinde, da. of Sir John Coghill, Bart. late of Coghill Hall, Yorkshire; and Wife of the Rev. Nathaniel Hinde, Rector of King's Swinford, Staffordshire - 1821

George Jones, Esq.   -   -   -   1829
Mary Richards, Relict of the Rev. Geo. Richards, of
  Longbredy, Dorset, 1815; also of Marcia, Lady of
  Major-General Sir Colquhoun Grant, K. C. B. 3d
  daughter of the above, 1818; also of Master Marcus
  Richards Grant, son of the above Gen. Sir Colqhoun
  and Lady Grant, 1818.
Robert Heathcote, Esq. 1819; Lieut. Col. George Deare
  Heathcote, of the East India Company's Bengal Mili-
  tary Establishment, son of the above.
John Manners, son of John William Calvert, M. D. 1824
Augusta Louisa, and Louisa Anne, 2 Daughters of the
  Rev. Christopher Hawkins, Rector of Kelston, in the
  Co. of Somerset,   -   -   -   1818
Lieut.-Col. Robert Monckton Grant, of the Hon. East
  India Company's Service,   -   1814
Stephen Harris, Esq. Lieut. R. N. and late Resident in the
  Province of Tipperah in Bengal,   -   1815
Mrs. Anne Truscott, widow of Richard Truscott, Esq. of
  the Royal Navy,   -   -   -   1820
Miss Eliza Okeover Heming, daughter of Capt. George
  Heming, -   -   -   1816
John Hey, D. D. Norrisian Professor of Divinity at Cam-
  bridge, from 1780 to 1795,   -   1815
Richard Egan, son of Colonel Egan, of Bombay,   1827
James Torre, Esq. of Snydale in the County of York, 1816
Mr. Robert Gillam, Secretary to the British Institution;
  to the Committee of Taste, and to the Society for Bet-
  tering the Condition of the Poor,   -   1817
John Gray, M. D. late Physician of His Majesty's Naval
  Hospital at Haslar, who died at his apartments, York
  Buildings, 1826. During the eventful period of the
  French Revolution War, Dr. Gray held various respon-
  sible offices connected with the Medical Department of
  the Navy; St. Vincent, Nelson and Collingwood, were
  his personal friends. It was at the direct request of the
  Hero of the Nile, on his return from the pursuit of the
  French to the West Indies in 1805, that he was ap-
  pointed Physician to the Fleet, which won the Battle of
  Trafalgar. His merit was fully acknowledged, yet quite
  unobtrusive; and such was the amiableness of his character, and the conciliatoriness of his manners, that
  though placed in some difficult situations, he made
  every one who knew him his Friend.
Mr. William Bell, Gent.   -   1818
John Oliver, Esq. of Hoole Hall in the County of
  Chester,   -   -   -   -   1832
John Jackson, Esq. R. A.   -   -   1831

Stanley, Infant son of Capt. William Edward Parry, R. N. and Isabella Louisa, his wife, 1828; also Isabella Maria, Infant daughter of the same parents, - 1828
George Biglands, Esq. late of Oporto, - 1831
Herbert Lawrence Welch, son of M. L. Welch, Esq. 1832
Thomas Leigh Whitter, Esq. - - 1830
Patrick Closey, Esq. - - - 1831
William M'Dowal Robinson, Esq. Royal Navy, 1829
Adolphus Moscheles, - - 1829
Miss Margaret Elin, daughter of John B. Elin, Esq. of Kingston, Jamaica, - - 1829
Mary Saunders, Spinster, aged 60, - - 1829
Lieut. Col. James Shortt, late of His Majesty's 10th Regiment of Infantry, - - - 1829
James Owen, Esq. - - - 1828
Amelia, wife of Thomas Lord, Esq. - 1828
Elizabeth Newbold Babington, widow of the late Rev. William Babington, Rector of Cossington in the Co. of Leicester, - - - 1832
Thomas Creswick Watson, of the 3d Lt. Dragoons 1831
Susanna Hume, late of the Island of Trinidad, 1830

H

CONDUITS AND WATER-WORKS.

The principal source from which the inhabitants of the City of London obtained their water in the 13th century, was from the springs rising on the high grounds on the north and western sides of the Capital, from which it was conveyed by pipes to different parts of the City.

These conduits, and the springs from which they derived their supply, were considered of great importance by the Corporation; and some of its members bestowed considerable sums in establishing and keeping them in proper condition.

About 1238-9, a large sum was raised by subscription in furtherance of a scheme for bringing water from nine conduits in and near the Village of Tyburn, which was accordingly carried into execution, and is the first instance upon record of water being conveyed to the city by pipes. In several parts of the city, conduits were erected for the reception of this water; the first of which was built in the year 1285, at the west end of Cheapside, then called West Cheap, and these conduits were found so convenient that they soon increased to nineteen in number. In 1431, the Tyburn water was laid into the Standard in Cheapside, at the expense of Sir John Wells, the late Mayor. It was customary for the Citizens to visit these conduits annually on the 18th of September, on horseback, accompanied by their ladies in waggons, when they had an allowance out of the city purse for a dinner; and it is noted by Strype, that on the 18th of September, 1562, " The Lord Mayor, Aldermen, and many worshipful persons, rode to the conduit-heads to see them, according to the old custom: then they went and hunted a hare before dinner, and killed her; and thence went to

dinner at the Banquetting House, at the head of
the conduit, where a great number were handsomely
entertained by their Chamberlain.   After dinner,
they went to hunt the fox.   There was a great cry
for a mile, and at length the hounds killed him at
the end of St. Giles's, with great hollowing and
blowing of horns at his death; and thence, the
Lord Mayor, with all his company, rode through
London, to his place in Lombard Street."

The establishment of the water-works at London
Bridge in 1512, and the subsequent introduction
of the New River in 1618, having superseded the
use of the Tyburn water, the Corporation let the
water of these conduits on a lease for forty-three
years, for the sum of 700*l.* per annum.   The Mary-
le-bone water-works were in the possession of
Hugh Merchant, lessee, in 1698, which had then
been established thirty-six years; and supplied
Covent Garden and St. Martin's Lane.   These
water-works were situated at a short distance from
the south end of Portland Place; Portland Chapel
having been built on the site of Mary-le-Bone
Basin, which was anciently a reservoir belonging
to the said water-works.   They are often mentioned
in old Newspapers as the cause of many fatal
accidents, and the scene of as many suicides.*

One of these ancient conduit-heads is still in
existence in Mary-le-bone Lane, near the corner
of Wigmore Street, and another in Oxford Street,
near North Audley Street: these conduits, which
have long been disused, all communicated with
each other by pipes under ground, and also with
the cisterns which were formerly underneath the
Lord Mayor's Banquetting House.   The water pipes
used in those times were not always embedded in
the earth as is the present custom, but inclosed

---

* There is a view of this Basin by Chatelain in the British
Museum.

within a capacious arch of brick-work, on a table
of stone, into which workmen could descend to
repair any decay or accident.   An arch of this
description was discovered some years ago in Bond
Street, leading from the conduits at Tyburn to
others in the neighbourhood of Conduit Street,
and has since been converted into a sewer.   Some
of these pipes have been discovered near Stratford
Place, so completely corroded as to present the
appearance of lace-work.

The Parish is now supplied with water, partly
by the Grand Junction Water-Works Company,
but principally by the West Middlesex Water-
Works Company, whose office is situated in the
New Road, near Mary-le-bone Church, and who
have an extensive reservoir on Barrow Hill, at
the northern extremity of the Parish.

OXFORD STREET,

originally called Tyburn Road, and subsequently named Oxford Street, is the site of the ancient military way, noticed p. 5, ante, and is described by *Pennant* as " a deep hollow road, full of sloughs; with here and there a ragged house, the lurking place of cut-throats, insomuch that I never was taken that way by night, in my hackney coach, to a worthy uncle's, who gave me lodgings at his house in George Street, but I went in dread the whole way." During the Civil Wars, in 1642, the Parliament ordered that trenches and ramparts should be made near all the highways leading to the City, and in different places about London and Westminster. These fortifications consisted of a strong earthern rampart, flanked with bastions, redoubts, &c., surrounding the whole city and its liberties, including Southwark. In Tyburn Road, in 1643, there were three forts erected, viz.—a redoubt, with two flanks, near St. Giles's Pound; a small fort at the east end of the road, and a large fort with four half bulwarks across the road opposite Wardour Street.* In a map of London, of the

* In May and June, 1643, the erecting of these fortifications was prosecuted with uncommon zeal, as appears by the following extracts from the public papers:—

" May 8.—The work in the fields to trench the city goes on amain. Many thousands of men, women, and servants go out daily to work; and this day there went out a great company of the Common Council, and divers other chief men of the city, with the greatest part of the trained bands, with spades, shovels, pick-axes, &c. May 9.—This day many thousands of citizens, their wives and families, went out to dig, and all the porters in and about the city, to the number of 2,000. May 23.—Five thousand feltmakers and cappers went to work at the trenches; near 3,000 porters, with a great company of men, women, and children. May 24.—Four or five thousand shoemakers. June 5.—Six thousand tailors."—*Perfect Diurnal.*

" It was wonderful to see how the women and children, and vast numbers of people, would come and work about digging and carrying of earth to make their new fortifications."—*Whitelock's Memorials,* p. 60.

year 1707, King Street, Golden Square, is represented as perfect to Oxford Road ; between which
and Berwick Street were fields.   Hence to St.
Giles's was covered with buildings; but from King
Street westward not a house could be seen, such
was the south side of Oxford Street : the north side
contained a few scattered buildings; but not the
least resemblance of streets, west of Tottenham
Court-road.   In a plan of the date of 1708, the
Lord Mayor's Banquetting-House is exhibited,
standing at the south end of a field called *Mill
Hill Field.* This house, which was a very commodious and handsome building, stood at the north
east corner of a bridge, called the Banquetting
House Bridge, near the spot where Stratford Place
has been subsequently built: under this mansion
were two cisterns for the reception of the water
from the neighbouring conduits, but, it having
been neglected for many years by the citizens, it
was taken down in the year 1737, and the cisterns
arched over.   In the abovementioned plan is also
shewn the Adam and Eve, which was a detached
public-house situated by the road side, in a field
called Dung Field, on or near the spot now called
Adam and Eve Court, nearly opposite Poland
Street ; in a field near this house also stood the
Boarded House, frequented by pugilists and prize-
fighters; the line of houses on the north side of
Oxford Street, appear, however, to have been completed about 1729, and it was then called Oxford
Street.   Maitland, whose work was published in
1739, says, " this street of fine houses has been
lately beautifully paved from St. Giles's to the
Banquetting-House Bridge; and the said bridge
being only about 15 feet broad, it not only proved
very incommodious to the numerous carriages,
and travellers passing that way, but it likewise
was very disgraceful to the spacious street on both
sides thereof, wherefore the Commissioners for

repairing the roads in these parts, applied to the Citizens of London for a piece of their ground to enlarge the same, which they not only generously granted, but likewise gave the sum of one hundred pounds towards defraying the expense of enlargement." The starlings or piers of this bridge remained an obstruction to the sewer, till within these few years, when the sewer underwent a thorough repair, and these obstructions were removed.

In the architecture of the buildings in this street there is nothing remarkable to describe: they are of all heights, and entirely destitute of uniformity: some of the houses have been rebuilt within the last twenty years, and have a beautiful appearance. This street, containing nearly 400 houses, is of an extensive width, and more than a mile in length, and may be now considered one of the most beautiful leading thoroughfares in the Metropolis. The long line of shops (with scarce a private house in the whole length of street), are fitted up in the most expensive style—the interiors brilliantly illuminated—and the display of a variety of costly articles of every description, calculated to please the eye and suit the taste of the most fastidious beholder, being tastefully arranged in the windows for sale; together with the brilliancy of the numerous parochial gas-lamps, render this street one of the most pleasing promenades of the West end of the Town.

Oxford Street will give rise to many melancholy reflections, when it is remembered how many unfortunate criminals have passed through it for the purpose of paying the forfeit of their lives, as a sacrifice to the offended laws of their country. The public place of Execution for criminals convicted in the County of Middlesex, having been formerly situated in this Parish, and at the west end of Oxford Street, near Tyburn Turnpike. It has been asserted, that criminals were executed on this spot as early as the reign of Henry II.* It would be idle to attempt to record the names of even one hundredth part of the criminals who have expiated their offences at this place. " In 1626, Queen Henrietta Maria was compelled by her priests to do penance under the gallows at Tyburn: what her offence was we are not told, but Charles was so disgusted at this insolence, that he soon after sent them, and all her Majesty's French servants, out of the kingdom."† On the 29th of November, 1628, John Felton, who stabbed the Duke of Buckingham, Aug. 23d of the same year, was executed here. " This Felton was a man of that stout spirit, that upon receiving an injury from a gentleman, he cut off a piece of his little finger, and sent it him with a challenge, to let him know he valued not his whole body, so he might obtain his revenge."‡ Here also at different periods in the last century, suffered the two Perreau's, brothers, and the Rev. Dr. Dodd, for forgery; Hackman, for shooting Miss Reay, as she was coming out of the theatre, and the infamous Catherine Hayes, for the murder of her husband (who had resided in this Parish) which was attended with uncommon atrocity. The latter criminal suffered the utmost severity of her sentence; being literally burnt alive, in consequence (as it was said) of the

* Sir Robert Tresilian, Chief Justice of the King's Bench, and Sir Nicholas Brembre were executed at Tyburn in the reign of Richard II. (1388), for High Treason; and a late writer says:—" In regard to Tyburn, I have taken some trouble to ascertain when it first became a place of execution, but have not been able to trace it earlier than the period when these eminent individuals suffered there; and I doubt whether any authentic record of a prior date can be adduced on this point."—*Dobie's Hist. of St. Giles' in the Fields.*
† Whitelock. In the illustrated *Pennant* in the Print-room at the British Museum, is a plate exhibiting the Queen in the act of kneeling under the gallows.
‡ Echard, p. 440, b. Peck's Desiderata Curiosa.

indignation of the populace, who would not suffer the executioner to strangle her (as was usual) before the fire was kindled.

The gallows, which was triangular, was for many years a standing fixture, on a small eminence at the corner of the Edgware Road, near the Turnpike, on the identical spot where a tool house has been since erected by the Uxbridge Road Trust; beneath this place lie the bones of Ireton, Bradshaw, and other of the regicides, which were taken from their graves after the restoration, and buried under the gallows, with every mark of indignation and contempt. In the early part of the last century, the frequency of executions on this spot, was considered so annoying, that it was proposed to select another for that purpose, and Kingsland was said to have been contemplated as a more convenient place: this proposal was, however, never acted upon; but, after the buildings had become numerous, and were still increasing, the gallows was removed (after being used) and deposited in a house which is still standing at the corner of Upper Bryanston Street and the Edgware-road: this house has at this day curious iron balconies to the windows of the first and second floors, which were used by the sheriffs when attending in their official capacity as witnesses of the executions. To pursue this powerful instrument of death to the termination of its existence, it appears that in 1783, when Tyburn ceased to be the place of execution, the gallows was purchased by a carpenter and converted into stands for beer butts, in the cellars of a public-house in the neighbourhood, viz. the Carpenter's Arms in Adams Street.

"The awful procession to Tyburn, intended to impress the multitude with sentiments of reverence for the laws of their country, produced a very contrary effect; and the eager and detestable curiosity of the populace, to witness executions, became a source of considerable emolument to certain mis-

creants, who were in the habit of erecting scaffolds
for spectators; many of these scaffolds were substantial wooden buildings, and erected at every
point from whence a glimpse of the execution could
be obtained; the prices for seats varied according
to the turpitude or quality of the criminal:—Dr.
Hensey was to have been executed for High Treason in 1758, the prices of seats for that exhibition
amounted to 2s. and 2s. 6d.; but, in the midst of
general expectation, the Doctor was *most provok-
ingly* reprieved.   As the mob descended from their
stations with unwilling steps, it occurred to them,
that, as they had been deprived of the intended
entertainment, the proprietors of the seats ought to
return the admission-money; which they demanded
in *terms vociferous,* and with *blows offensive,* and
in short, exercised their happy talent for rioting
with unbounded success.*   On this occasion a vast
number of these erections were destroyed.

The place of execution was removed to Newgate
in 1783, Ryland, executed for forgery, was the last
criminal who suffered at Tyburn.   The first criminal who was executed by a machine then newly
invented, and called the "*New Drop*" was launched
into eternity on the 9th of December in that year.
To shew the prevailing extent of crime at this
period, it is only necessary to observe, that fifteen
persons were executed June 23, 1784, and from
February to December, in 1785, no less than
ninety-six individuals suffered at Newgate by this
new machine.

CAVENDISH SQUARE.

In the year 1715,† the plan for building Cavendish Square, and several new streets on the north

* Malcolm's Lond.
† *Evening Post, March* 16, 1715.—On Wednesday last four
gentlemen were robbed and stripped in the fields between London
and Marybone.

side of Tyburn Road, was first suggested; about
two years afterwards the ground was laid out, and
the circular piece in the centre, inclosed, planted,
and surrounded by a parapet and iron railing.
The whole of the north side was taken by the celebrated James Brydges Duke of Chandos, (then Earl
of Carnarvon) who acquired a princely fortune as
pay-master of the forces in Queen Anne's Reign,
and who was afterwards called " The Grand Duke"
from the grandeur and state in which he lived.

The Duke, it is said, took this immense plot of
ground, which extended a long way back towards
the north, with the intention of building a town
residence, correspondent with that of Cannons.
Of this he completed no more than the wings, which
are sufficiently spacious to have become stately
mansions.   One, was that large mansion at the
corner of Harley Street, formerly occupied by the
Princess Amelia, aunt to George III. and afterwards
by the Earl of Hopetown, and the Messrs. Hopes
of Amsterdam; on whose quitting, it was purchased
by George Watson Taylor, Esq. who expended an
immense sum in altering and beautifying it; but
after a few years further alterations were made,
and the domestic offices belonging to the original
building, which extended some distance up Harley
Street, being taken down, six additional houses of
considerable dimensions were erected on their site.
This house is now in the occupation of Viscount
Beresford.   The other wing was the corresponding
mansion at the corner of Chandos Street, now in
the occupation of His Grace the Duke of Richmond.   The centre part is occupied by two splendid mansions with handsome stone fronts.   They
contain a rustic basement story, which supports a
range of handsome Corinthian columns, crowned
with their proper entablature.   Above these is a
triangular pediment, in which is a circular port-hole
window ornamented with a wreath, and the roof is

concealed by an attic balustrade; they were designed by James, of Greenwich, who was architect
to the Duke of Chandos. The vacancy between
one of these houses and the corner house of Harley
Street, has been lately filled up by a modern building, now the residence of Sir R. Frankland.

At this period, Harcourt House, the largest
mansion on the east side, and Bingley House, now
Harcourt House, on the west side, a noble mansion
designed by Inigo Jones, were the only other houses
in this square. The latter, which is 153 feet in
length, and 70 feet in breadth, is entirely concealed
from view by a high brick wall, which may have been
deemed necessary at the time of its erection, from
its solitary and dangerous situation. It is now the
residence of His Grace the Duke of Portland, who
has erected a handsome range of stable and domestic
offices at the back of the house, in Wimpole Street,
in the style of the mansion, from the design, and
under the superintendance of Samuel Ware, Esq.
his Grace's architect. The South Sea failure in
1720, caused a temporary suspension of building,
and it was several years before the square was
completed. The following anecdote is related in
the *European Magazine*, vol. 52.—" At one time,
during the South Sea bubble, the Duke of Chandos's
stock was worth £300,000. He went to the old
Duke of Newcastle to consult what to do? He
advised him to sell. No: he wanted half a million:
—" Why then," said the Duke, " sell £100,000.
and take your chance for the rest."—No! he kept
all, and lost all!*

The following paragraphs will serve to point out
an historical fact, and shew the curious ideas entertained of these improvements at the time. *The
Weekly Medley, of Sept.* 13, 1718, observes :—
" Round about the New Square which is building near
Tybourn-Road, there are so many other edifices, that a
whole magnificent city seems to be risen out of the

ground, that one would wonder how it should find a new set of inhabitants. It is said it will be called by the name of Hanover Square. On the opposite side of the way, towards Mary-le-bone, which seems a higher and finer situation, is marked out a very spacious and noble Square, and many streets that are to form avenues to it. This Square, we hear, is to be called Oxford-square, and that ground has been taken to build houses in it by the Right Honourable Lords, the Earl of Oxford, the Earl of Carnarvon, the Lord Harcourt, the Lord Harley, and several other Noble Peers of Great Britain. The ground sold at first for 2s. 6d. per foot, afterwards for 15s."

The following ill-natured observations also appeared in the *Weekly Medley, of Sept.* 1719 :—

" Not far from Tavistock-street, lives a man by profession a Measurer and Surveyor ; this fellow is everlastingly boasting of himself, and vapouring of his performances, and has the boldness to style himself the Prince of that calling. If towards being a Prince of a trade, it is necessary to make himself wealthy and great, by undoing all that are subject to his management, he richly deserves the name ; for you must understand, that as among authors there is a *cacoëthes scribendi*, so there is an *ædificandi cacoëthes*, or an itch of building, that prevails much among our tribe that dabble in mortar. All the raw and inexperienced workmen that lie under this evil, have been drawn by this boaster to build in and about Hanover-square, till they have built themselves quite out of doors in this part of the world, and so are obliged to cross the water, to another climate, and take up their lodgings in *Mint Square ;* where they still rear palaces in their imaginations, and metamorphose themselves into that species of men called castle-builders ; and there they and their families fill their mouths with curses against their projecting *Prince.*"

In the centre of the enclosure is an equestrian Statue of William Duke of Cumberland, by Chew, erected in 1770, at the expense of Lieutenant-General William Strode, " in gratitude for private kindness, and in honour of public virtue." There

is a burlesque representation of this statue as a
vignette to a work entitled, Critical Observations
on the Buildings and Improvements of London, by
J. Stuart, 4to. 1771.   This Statue was re-gilt in
1783, at the expense of the Princess Amelia.
Adjoining to Harcourt House, formerly resided
the celebrated Shute Barrington, Bishop of Durham.
At the south-east corner of the square is the
Banking-house of Sir Claude Scott, and Co. convenient offices having been erected on the garden
at the back for carrying on the business : the
entrance to these offices is in Margaret Street.

Cavendish Square now contains 37 houses ; those
on the south side extending from the corner of
Old Cavendish Street to the corner of Margaret
Street, being numbered in the square : the following
persons of high rank reside in this square.   The
Dukes of Portland and Richmond; Marquis of
Titchfield, Earls of Wicklow, Charleville ; Lords
George and Henry Bentinck ; Viscounts Duncannon
and Beresford ; Countess of Antrim ; Lord C.
Townshend, Lord Dufferin ; Honourable William
and Lady Louisa Duncombe; Sir George G.
Tuthill, M. D. ; Marquis of Winchester ; Sir W.
Browne Folkes ; Sir Edward C. Dering, Bart. ;
Major-General Sir Charles Dalbiac ; Lieutenant-
Colonel Reid; Sir Martin A. Shee, P. R. A. ; S.
Love Hammick, *Surgeon;* Mrs. Baillie ; Dr. A.
P. W. Philip; Edmund Macdonnel, Esq. ; Captain
and Mrs. Polhill; Charles Scott Murray, Esq. ;
Sir R. Frankland; Hon. Mrs. Marley ; Stephen
Thornton, Esq.; Thomas Hamlet, Esq. ; Dowager
Lady Astley; Walter Calvert, Esq. ; Frederick
Reade, Esq. ; Mrs. Bertie Matthew ; Richard
Parrott, Esq.; Dr. John Sims ; John Ogilvie, Esq.
Here is also, at the corner of Holles Street, a large
Hotel comprising two extensive houses, kept by
Marshall Thompson.

To induce the builders to speculate, a Chapel

and a Market was projected for the convenience of the inhabitants. The Chapel was erected in Vere Street, from the designs of Gibbs, and completed about 1724, but the Market, although erected about the same period, was not opened until the year 1731, owing to the opposition of Lord Craven, who was fearful that it would affect the profits of Carnaby Market. Edward, Earl of Oxford, however, finally obtained a grant, under the great Seal, in 1731, " authorising himself, his lady, and their heirs, to hold a Market, on Mondays, Wednesdays, and Saturdays, for the sale of flesh, fish, fowls, herbs, and all other provisions." However this Market may have answered the expectations of the projectors at the time of its erection, does not appear, but it is certain, that its trade has not kept pace in a proportionate ratio with the increase of population, and upon its being repaired a few years since, the interior was converted into a large room, and used as an office for the payment of the Outpensioners of Chelsea Hospital. The shops in this Market-place are quite of an ordinary description.

About 1729, most of the streets leading to Cavendish Square were began to be built, and the ground laid out for others : these streets were named after the families of the proprietors of the land, their titles, or country-seats, a fashion which has prevailed ever since all over the parish, viz. Henrietta Street, Vere Street,* Holles Street,

* This Street was named after the Veres Earls of Oxford.— March 12, 1703, died Aubrey de Vere, the twentieth and last Earl of Oxford of the de Veres. The changes of the eventful times in which he lived did not seem to affect him ; he was so passive under Oliver the Protector that he was not even fined ; and, when William came over, he went over to him from James II. He had been easy with the gay and frolicsome Charles II , grave with William III., and was graceful in old age at the Court of Queen Anne. After the death of Charles I , to whom he was Lord of the Bedchamber, he became Lieutenant-General of the Forces, Colonel and Captain of the Horse Guards, Justice in Eyre, Lord Lieute-

Margaret Street, Cavendish Street, Welbeck Street, Wimpole Street, Princes Street, Bolsover Street, (not now existing) Castle Street, John Street, Market Street, Harley Street, Mortimer Street, &c.

Captain Rathbone commenced the erection of Rathbone Place about 1720; he died in 1721: Wells Street was also commenced about this period.

In a Map published in 1742, the diminutive church of St. Mary-le-bone is exhibited detached from London, with two zig-zag ways leading to it, one near Vere Street, which was the then western boundary of the new buildings, and the second from Tottenham-Court-Road. Rows of houses with their backs to the fields extended from St. Giles's Pound to Oxford Market, but Tottenham-Court-Road, had only one cluster on the west side, and the spring-water house. Hence it will be observed, that Oxford Street, from Oxford Market to Vere Street on the south and west, and Marybone Street on the north, and the site of Titchfield Street on the east, formed the outline of the new buildings. The zig-zag way above-mentioned near Vere Street, still retaining its original name of Mary-le-bone Lane, was the communication between the high road and the village.

nant and Custos Rotulorum of the County of Essex. He had been a Privy Counsellor to him and each subsequent sovereign, and was Hereditary Lord Chamberlain, Senior Knight of the Garter, and Premier Earl of England. He married Anne, daughter of Paul, Viscount Bayning. He may be said to have committed polygamy by the following act : a lady, whose name is not known, was celebrated for the performance of the part of Roxana on the stage ; influenced by violent love, and unable to succeed in his purpose by other means, he prevailed on her to consent to a private marriage. It was afterwards discovered to have been celebrated by the Earl's trumpeter in the character of a priest, and witnessed by his kettle drummer. His father, the valiant Robert de Vere, Earl of Oxford, had nobly married Beatrix Van Hemins, a boor's daughter of Friezeland.—*Noble.*

HIGH STREET,

Being situated in the centre of the Parish, formerly comprised the principal part of the Village of Mary-le-bone: the Church, the Royal Palace, the Rose Tavern, and Bowling-greens, the splendid mansion built for the purpose of containing the Earl of Oxford's Library, the Rose of Normandy, and a few detached houses with gardens formed the prominent features of its early days; the eastern entrance to the Parish Church yard, and the Infant School, the National School, the Police Office, and the Parish Charity School being the principal modern additions. The houses have nothing to recommend them in point of architectural beauty, being plain brick buildings; and from their having been built at various periods are destitute of uniformity; they are however, principally occupied by respectable tradesmen.

THE ROSE OF NORMANDY.

This House, supposed to have been built about 200 years ago, and the oldest now existing in the Parish, is situated on the East side of the street; was formerly a detached building, used as the house of entertainment in connection with the Bowling-green at the back. The following description of this Bowling-green, from Mem. by Sam. Sainthill, 1659, appeared in the Gent. Mag. vol. 83, pt i. p. 524. " The outside a square brick wall, set with fruit trees, gravel walks, 204 paces long, seven broad; the circular walk 485 paces, six broad, the centre square, a Bowling-green, 112 paces one way, 88 another; all except the first, double set with quickset hedges, full grown and kept in excellent order, and indented like town walls." * The entrance to this House is by

* In a map of the Duke of Portland's estate of 1708, there are

descending a flight of steps, the street having been
raised at a later period : it has been repaired at
various times, but the original form of the exterior
has been preserved, and the staircase and ballusters
are coeval with the erection of the building : an
extensive yard at the back is laid out as skittle
grounds, and is level with the ground floor of the
house. This House is now one of the best conducted public houses in the Parish, the company
consisting of the most respectable tradesmen and
ancient inhabitants of the neighbourhood, the
worthy host, Mr. Bradley, having tenanted the
house for more than 26 years; and the obliging
hostess having been born in the Old Manor House,
described, p. 32.

MARY-LE-BONE GARDENS.

On the site which is now occupied by Beaumont
Street, Devonshire Street, and part of Devonshire
Place, was formerly a celebrated place of amuse-

two Bowling-greens exhibited, one of which was situated near the
top of High Street, and abutting on the grounds of the Old Manor
House : the other was situated at the back of this house ; the street
afterwards called Bowling-Green Lane, but now Bowling Street,
having formed its southern boundary : in connection with the first
was a noted tavern and gaming-house, called the Rose Tavern,
much frequented by persons of the first rank. It afterwards grew
into much disrepute. This is perhaps the place alluded to by
Lady Mary Wortley Montague, in this line :—

" Some Dukes at Marybone bowl time away ; "

and which is meant by Pennant, who when speaking of the Duke
of Buckingham's minute description of the house afterwards the
Queen's Palace, and his manner of living there, says ;—" He has
omitted his constant visits to the noted gaming-house, at Marybone ; the place of assemblage of all the infamous sharpers of the
time ; " to whom his Grace always gave a dinner at the conclusion
of the season ; and his parting toast, was, " May as many of us
as remain unhanged next spring, meet here again." These
Bowling-Greens were, however, afterwards incorporated in that
well-known place of entertainment, called Marybone Gardens.

ment, known by the name of Marybone Gardens.
From the circumstance of a French Chapel having
been erected upon this spot it was called by some
the French Gardens. Marybone Gardens were
opened before the year 1737, the Public having
free access; the sum of one shilling being then
first demanded for admission by Gough the proprietor, for which an equivalent was to be received
in refreshments. As these gardens became more
fashionable, various entertainments were provided.
Balls and evening concerts were given; some of
the first singers were generally engaged there,
and fire-works were frequently exhibited. The
musical department was for some time under the
direction of Dr. Arne, and the enchanting Music
of Handel and other celebrated composers was
often heard in the orchestra there. The fire-works
were under the superintendance of Signor Torré.

" In 1772, the entertainment of an evening at
Marybone Gardens, in this year consisted (after
the representation of Mount Ætna, as an addition
to the usual concerts and songs was performed)
of the common fire-works, consisting of vertical
wheels, suns, stars, globes, &c. in honour of the
King's Birth-day, June 4, 1772, who was, with
the Queen, represented in transparencies surrounded by stars. When the fire-works were
concluded, a curtain, which covered the base of
the mountain, rose and discovered Vulcan leading
the Cyclops to work at their forge; the fire
blazed, and Venus entered with Cupid at her side,
who begged them to make for her son those arrows
which are said to be the causes of love in the
human breast: they assented, and the mountain
immediately appeared in eruption, with lava
rushing down the precipices."

Dr. Kenrick, the Author of the Duellist, opened
a Course of Lectures in the Theatre for Burlettas
at Marybone Gardens, in July, 1774, which he

termed " a School of Shakspeare," where he re-
cited different parts of the works of our inimitable
dramatist, and particularly that of Sir John Fal-
staff, with much success, to crowded audiences.

The Newspapers of that month vented severe
complaints against the proprietors of these gardens,
for having demanded 5s. entrance money to a
Fête Champétre, which consisted of nothing more
than a few tawdry festoons and extra lamps; indeed
they appear to have been suggested by the conduct
of the spectators, who demolished most of the
brittle wares of the scene, and injured the stage.
A second attempt produced this description:—
" The orchestra, boxes, theatre, and every part
of the gardens were beautifully illuminated at a
vast expense, with lamps of various colours, disposed with great taste and elegance. The grass-
plat before M. Torré's building was surrounded
with two semi-circular rows of trees, and hedges,
prettily contrived, divided, and forming two walks;
and between every tree hung a double row of
lamps bending downwards: between every break
orange and lemon-trees were placed, and the whole
was hung with festoons of flowers, and other pastoral
emblems. On this place the rural entertainment
was held, consisting of singing and dancing; several
airs were well sung by Mr. Thompson, Mr. Bannister,
Miss Wewitzer, and the rest of the performers.
On the left hand of this rural scene was a stile,
and a walk which led to a temple sacred to Hymen,
which was transparent, and had a very pretty effect,
when viewed at a distance. The gardens were not
clear of company at six o'clock next morning."

The following is a description of an evening's
entertainment at these Gardens, taken from a Newspaper in which it appeared a few days after it had
taken place, and in which there are some curious
allusions to the fashion of the Ladies Head-dresses
of that date.

" On Tuesday Evening, July 28, 1776, Mary-bone Gardens exhibited a scene equally novel and agreeable; namely, a representation of the Boulevards of Paris. The boxes fronting the ball-room, which were converted into shops, had a very pleasing effect, and were occupied by persons with the following supposititious names, legible by means of transparent paintings. *Crotchet* a music-shop; a gingerbread-shop (no name), the owner in a large bag-wig and deep ruffles, *à-la-mode* de Paris; *Medley* (from Darley's) a print-shop; *New-fangle*, a milliner; a hardware shop and lottery-office in one (the price of tickets 11*l*. 14*s*.) *La Blonde*, a milliner; *Pine*, a fruiterer; *Trinket*, a toyman; *Fillagree*, ditto; Mr. *Gimcrack*, the shop unoccupied, and nothing in it but two paper kites; *Tête*, a hair-dresser. The shop-keepers seemed rather dull and awkward at their business, till the humour of the company had raised their spirits by purchasing; and then, in proportion to their trade, their diligence advanced. *Madame Pine*, Messrs. *Trinket*, and *Le Marchand de Gingerbread*, ran away with the custom from all their competitors. Mr. Tête indeed would have had a good share of trade, but that the ladies were previously provided with every article he had to sell, and superior of the kind; for if his head-dresses were as big as a peck, many of theirs could not be crammed into a bushel.

" The Ball-room was illuminated in an elegant manner with coloured lamps; and at one end of it women attended, selling orgeat, lemonade, and other cooling liquors. This was intended as a representation of the English Coffee-house at Paris.

" There was a great variety of different amusements; and amongst the rest a booth representing that of Signor Nicola at Paris, in which eight men, at the command of the supposed Signor, who was behind the scenes, exhibited a dance called the

Egyptian Pyramids, standing on the backs, arms,
and shoulders of each other, to an astonishing
height."

As the Population of the neighbourhood increased, much uneasiness arose in the minds of
the inhabitants, lest some accident should be occasioned by the fire-works, which producing frequent
complaints to the Magistrates, these Gardens were
finally suppressed in 1778, and the site let to
builders.

Extract from a Deed of Assignment made by
Thomas Lowe, conveying his property in Marybone
Gardens to certain Trustees, for the benefit of his
Creditors, on the 3d of Feb. in the 9th Geo. III.
viz. 1769.

By Indenture bearing date the 30th day of
August, 1763, made between Robert Long, of the
Parish of St. Mary-le-bone, otherwise Marybone,
Esq. and the said Thomas Lowe, the said Robert
Long, in consideration of the yearly rent, did
demise unto the said Thomas Lowe, all that
Messuage then or then before called the Rose
Tavern, situate and being in the Parish of St.
Mary-le-bone aforesaid, with the tap-house thereunto belonging, and also a Room or Building
known by the name of the French Chapel, together
with a stable or brewhouse adjoining, or near to
the same, and also all that other Messuage, situate
in the same parish, then before in the possession
of Daniel Gough, on the East side of the town
of Saint Mary-le-Bone, alias Marybone, fronting
towards the West on the Road leading to Marybone
Church, and North on a Gateway or passage
leading from the said Road into Marybone Gardens.
And also all that great Garden and the several
pieces or parcels of garden ground and walks to
the said Messuages or either of them belonging,
which had been lately used therewith by the then

late Tenants of the said Messuages in the carrying
on a Musical Entertainment at Marybone Gardens,
and also the orchestra, and all Rooms and Buildings
erected, built and set upon the said pieces and
parcels of ground or any part thereof, and also the
organ then standing in the said orchestra, and also
a harpsichord and all the musical books and music
then being on the said premises, and used in carrying on the said musical entertainment, and all
boxes, benches, tables, lamps, lamp-posts, and all
other fixtures, belonging to the said Messuages
or tenements, pieces or parcels of ground which
were the property of the said Robert Long, and all
the passage lights, profits or commodious advantages appointed to the tenants of the said messuages
or said pieces of ground, belonging or therewith
held or enjoyed, except reserving to the said
Robert Long, all that small piece of garden ground
and a small tenement built thereon, then in the
possession of Mr. Flanders, and another small
piece of ground with a shed or tenement built
thereon, late in the possession of Mr. Claxton,
but then unlet, and also another small piece of
ground with a tenement or shed built thereon,
then in the possession of Mr. Gray Cutler, and
also another piece of ground with a tenement built
thereon, then in the possession of Mr. Rysbrach,
statuary, all which excepted premises had been
parted off from the said *Great Garden*, and had
been held and enjoyed separately from the same.
And also, except and always reserving to the said
Robert Long and his tenants free liberty to pass
and repass in through and from the public walks
of the said great gardens at all convenient times
to the said excepted premises. *To Hold* the same
(except as before excepted) unto the said Thomas
Lowe, his Executor and Assigns, from the Feast
Day of St. Michael the Archangel, next ensuing,
for and during the full end and term of 14 years

from thence, and fully to be compleat and ended, at and under the yearly rent of 170 pounds of lawful money of Great Britain payable quarterly, in manner thereiu-mentioned.

And on the 31st of Aug. James Dalling, Robert Wright of the Parish of West Ham, in the County of Essex, Coal Merchant, and Francis Walsingham, together with the said Thomas Lowe, became bound to the said Robert Long in the penal sum of five hundred pounds conditioned for the payment of the rent, and performances of the contract.

This property was subsequently in 1768, assigned to George Forbes and Andrew Mitchie, Trustees, for the benefit of the Creditors.

In the Dr. and Cr. Account appear the following items:—

Expenses.	£.	s.	d.
To Mr. Hook, the Music Master	4	4	0
Mr. Lowe's weekly allowance	2	2	0
To Advertisements and Waiters	1	6	10
To Mr. Medhurst, for Chickens	5	8	0
To the Patrol	0	16	0
To Master Brown	4	4	0
To Miss Davies	3	3	0
To Mr. Taylor	2	2	0
To the Gardener	0	9	0
To Candles	3	0	0
To Washing	0	18	10
To One Hundred Lemons	0	10	0
To Water Cakes	0	6	0
To Beer	4	4	0
To Servants Wages	1	8	0
To the Band of Music	27	13	8
To laying out the Books and attending the Music	0	9	0
To the Doorkeepers	2	19	6
To attending the Organ	0	7	6
To Miss Davies	2	2	0

	£.	s.	d.
To Mr. Phillips	2	2	0
To Mr. Taylor	1	8	0
To Mr. Thomas, for the Organ	0	6	0
To 12 Doorkeepers and 2 Patrols	4	3	0
To the Doorkeeper for 6 Sundays	0	6	0
To the Constable for 4 Sundays	0	4	0
To Servants' wages	1	8	6
To one Advertisement	0	5	0
To Writing Music	1	13	6
To one Watchman	0	1	0
To the Music Licence	1	4	9
To Mr. Wakefield	0	12	0

The Expenses of the Establishment from Nov. 12, 1767, to Jan. 31, 1769, were £1534 11s. 9d.

Receipts.	£.	s.	d.
By received in part of the Expenses of Mr. Brown's Benefit	10	10	0
By Ditto Benefit of the Band of Music	9	4	0
By Ditto Mr. Taylor's Benefit	13	2	6
By Ditto Miss Davis's Benefit	6	8	6
By Dr. Arne, for Wine	2	14	6
By one Ticket	1	11	6
The Receipts at the Door do not appear to have exceeded on any one night	15	0	0

But the Receipts at the Bar frequently exceeded £50; and on one occasion, the 8th of Sept. 1768, they amounted to £65. 6s. 4d.

In the Schedule the usual description of furniture is only exhibited, excepting that in the Temple, two Busts of Handel and Shakspeare are mentioned.
*Deed of Trust, dated 3d of Feb. 1769.**

* The above Deed is now in the possession of Sampson Hodgkinson, Esq. who in the most kind and obliging manner, allowed the above Extract to be copied.

PARISH CHARITY SCHOOL.

This Charity was first established in the year 1750, for instructing, clothing, qualifying for useful servants, and apprenticing, the Children of industrious poor Parishioners; and the Countess of Oxford having granted to the Trustees a piece of ground in High-street, at that time called " lower Church Field," for the term of 999 years, from the year 1754, at a peppercorn rent, the Schoolhouse was erected on this site, and the Charity assumed a permanent form. From that time to the present, various donations, legacies, and subscriptions have been received from benevolent individuals; and the objects of the Charity have been modified and altered, from time to time, as its funds extended and the circumstances of the parish changed, until it was enabled to clothe, educate, and maintain Sixty Boys and Sixty Girls.

In 1768, Twenty girls were maintained, and clothed, and forty boys clothed.

    1770, Twenty-six girls maintained, and forty boys clothed.

    1785, Twenty-six girls and forty boys maintained and clothed.

    1789, Twenty-eight girls and forty boys.

    1791, Thirty girls and fifty boys.

    1792, Thirty-two girls and fifty boys.

    1793, Thirty-eight girls and fifty boys.

    1795, Forty-four girls and fifty boys.

    1802, Fifty girls and fifty boys.

    1815, Fifty-four girls and fifty-four boys.

    1818, Sixty girls and sixty boys.

    1820, Sixty girls and fifty boys.

    1822, Sixty girls and sixty boys.

Upwards of Two Thousand and ten Children, *have been Maintained and Educated by this Charity ! ! !*

Upon this plan the Charity was conducted for some years, with various success. The state of the Girls' School was generally such as to satisfy the wishes of the Subscribers, and give them just grounds for believing that great and permanent benefit was secured to the objects of their bounty.

The Boys' School could never be brought into so satisfactory a state; and after every expedient which the deliberate judgment of the Trustees could suggest had been tried without success, and the disposable funds of the Charity had been exhausted in fruitless endeavours to remedy the defects and preserve the discipline of this branch of the Institution, the Subscribers at last resolved, after repeated and anxious discussions of the question, to abolish the Boys' School altogether, from the 5th of January, 1829; and in future to devote the funds of the Charity, exclusively, to the education, clothing, and maintenance of Girls.

The Trustees have already increased the number of Girls in the School to *one hundred and five*. They are also endeavouring to make arrangements which will enable them to receive *twenty more*, as soon as the funds of the Charity appear to justify such a measure; at present it is to be regretted, that the *annual income* of the Charity is found barely to equal its *annual expenditure*; and that the continuance of the Establishment, even upon its present contracted scale, will depend upon the *increased exertions* of its *friends* and *supporters*.

The system of education pursued in the School remains unchanged; the Girls are taught to read and write, and are practised in such of the rules of arithmetic as the Trustees think necessary ; they also learn plain-work, and regularly assist in performing the domestic offices in the house, that they may be trained to the habits and duties of useful servants. Above all, they are carefully instructed in the knowledge of their religion and the practice of its duties.

I 2

When fifteen years of age they are discharged : they then receive a Bible and a Common Prayer Book, a short formulary of private prayer, and a printed exhortation to the proper discharge of their duty.   As a reward for past good conduct, and an encouragement to persevere in the same laudable course, the sum of two guineas is given to such of the girls as can produce a certificate, within three years after leaving the school, of their having remained in the employ of one master or mistress for the space of two years ; or certificates, within five years, of their having been in two employments for periods amounting together to at least three years ; in either case, having, during the time of their respective services, conducted themselves with honesty, sobriety, and diligence.

It is only justice to say, that in their individual capacity, the Trustees of this Charity have been the zealous advocates of the district National Day Schools ; and while it is earnestly hoped, that those Establishments may receive continually increasing support, until they become fully able to supply the wants of those for whose benefit they were opened : still, however, it is of the utmost importance that the *Original School* of the PARISH should not be forgotten ; and that while the opulent and charitable uphold the national day schools of their respective districts, they will also continue to *foster* and *patronise* this Establishment which extends its benefits to the *whole Parish* of St. Mary-le-bone ; and, by the *advantages* it affords to the Girls under its care, advances a *peculiar claim* to the support of every wealthy parishioner.

These advantages consist, not only in the vigilant control which may be exercised over those who live within the walls of a Charity School, and the wholesome discipline to which they are continually subjected ; but in their removal from the contagion of evil example.   Their minds are thus deeply impressed with the principles of religion, before they can be assailed with temptation; and they are inured to habits of industry and sobriety, at a time when the idle cannot approach to seduce, or the profligate to corrupt them. And to these benefits, imparted to the Girls who become inmates of this School, may be justly added, as no small argument in its favour, the substantial relief which is afforded to the industrious mechanic, when struggling hard to maintain his family; if, while he is enabled to procure for his daughters the valuable blessing of a good education, he is also thus exonerated from the expense of their clothing and maintenance. Many, doubtless, are the cases, in which the mere hope of such assistance has encouraged the honest and diligent parent to labour with cheerfulness; and some there may be, whom this important aid, when imparted, has saved from utter despondency, and that last sad retreat of hopeless poverty, the parish workhouse.

The Trustees, therefore (in the Address to the Public printed in their Report of 1832), indulge a hope, that they may be permitted to urge upon the attention of the wealthy and benevolent the *claims* and *necessities* of this Charity.

" They respectfully suggest to their consideration, that it is, *peculiarly* and *exclusively* the PARISH SCHOOL ; that it *receives within* its *walls* ONE HUNDRED AND FIVE GIRLS, daughters of the poor and industrious parishioners, who are instructed in the religious principles of the Established Church, and accustomed to behave with civility, order and morality ; at the same time that they are also trained up in habits of cleanliness and industry, and qualified to fill, with credit to themselves and comfort to their employers, the useful station of domestic servants."

" The number of Girls to be received *may be increased* to any extent, by the bounty of the public : and the Trustees confidently hope, that the more the state of the School is examined, and the conduct of those whom it has sent into the world is investigated, the greater will be the amount of that bounty. They desire that the Charity may be judged by its effects: and they do not doubt that their warmest wishes for its success will be amply gratified, when the advantages which it has bestowed and is still ready to impart to the poor Girls entrusted to its care, are generally understood."

The fact of the Public being invited at all times to inspect the internal domestic arrangement of this Establishment, combined with the judicious Rules and Regulations adopted by the Committee of Management, render this Charity an object of peculiar interest, and worthy of the patronage and support of the wealthy and benevolent of all classes.

Patrons.

His Grace the Duke of Portland.

His Grace the Duke of Newcastle ; the Earls of Macclesfield, and Manvers ; Viscount Duncannon ; the Rt. Rev. the Lord Bishop of London; Lords Kenyon, Bridport, and Radstock; the Hon. B. Bouverie, M. P. Sir James Cockburn, Bart. The Rev. Dr. Spry, Rector of the Parish, and all the District Rectors ; Edward Berkeley Portman, Esq. M. P. ; and Henry Samuel Eyre, Esq.

Treasurer.

The Rev. Bryant Burgess, No. 9, Salisbury Place, New Road.

Physicians.

Dr. Ager.   Dr. Seymour.

Surgeons.

Robert Keate, Esq.   Henry Earle, Esq.

Surgeon-Apothecary. John Propert, Esq.

District Treasurers.

Mr. E. Churton, 140, Oxford Street.
Mr. Joseph Spicer, Duke-Street, Manchester Sq.
Mr. Abrahams, 234, Oxford Street.
Mr. J. Morris, 120, Crawford Street.
W. Marr, Esq. 32, Upper Baker Street.
James Hutchons, Esq. 7, Blandford Square.
Mr. T. Hawkins, 65, Margaret St. Cavendish-Sq.

Bankers.

Sir Claude Scott, Bart. & Co. 1, Cavendish Sq.

Secretary.

Mr. Thomas P. Lowe, School-House, 110, High-
Street, St. Mary-le-Bone.

Collector.

Mr. William Price, 6, Allsop-place, Upper Baker
Street.

Subscriptions and Donations will be received by
the Treasurer, or by the Bankers; also by the
District Treasurers; by the Secretary, at the School
House, 110, High Street, and by the Collector.

*The following important Items appear in the List of
Special Benefactions to this Charity.*

1761 Mrs. Elizabeth Goodere, (legacy)	£.100 0 0	
1762 Hon. Mrs. Mary Stuart, -	200 0 0	
1768 Mrs. Webb, (legacy) . .	100 0 0	
1773 Rt. Hon. Lady Delamer, (legacy) .	200 0 0	
1774 John Allen, Esq. . (do.) .	100 0 0	

1777 Mr. William Lovejoy, many years master
of this Charity School, (do.) the residue of
his estate, which amounted to £120. 18s. 1d.

1788 Mrs. Margaret Anne Adams, (do.)   315 0 0
1802 Mrs. Mary Dover, . (do.)   200 0 0
1814 The Officers and Non-commissioned Officers of the late Royal York St. Mary-le-
Bone Volunteers, by the Rt. Hon. Visct.
Duncannon, their Colonel .   400 0 0

1824 Mr. Thomas Craft, of Wells Street, bequeathed the
sum of 19l. 19s. the Interest to be annually laid
out in Cross Buns, and distributed on Good Friday to the Children of the said School for ever.

Joseph Nollekens, Esq. (Legacy) - 303 13 0
1832 John Pepys, Esq. (in 4 Donations) - 202 10 0

CENTRAL NATIONAL SCHOOL.

A Day School of Industry in which were 300 children, was established in Paradise Street, in the year 1791; and supported by voluntary contributions, charity sermons, and the profits of the children's earnings: the boys were employed in platting straw; the girls both in that and needlework. The School of Industry was one of the first that adopted the system of Dr. Bell. In the beginning of 1808, that distinguished philanthropist Sir Thomas Bernard, Bart. brought forward a project for the general education of the Poor in the Parish of St. Mary-le-bone, and after considerable difficulty in obtaining a situation for the School, he succeeded in purchasing a house and garden in High Street; on which a handsome and commodious school-room was erected under his own immediate inspection. This new Institution was soon afterwards incorporated with the School of Industry, and the whole was placed under the direction of the Governors of the United National Schools. The entrance for the children to the School-Room is in Paddington Street.

In consequence of the establishment of the Eastern and Western National Schools, it was resolved, at the Annual Meeting in 1825, that this School, for the sake of distinction, should thenceforth be denominated " The St. Mary-le-bone Central National School."

It is the object of this Institution to afford useful and religious instruction to the Children of the Resident Poor, whether Parishioners or otherwise; and to qualify them for those situations in life, which they will be called upon to fill. The Children are taught to love and obey God, to honour their Parents, to respect their Superiors, to be faithful to their Masters and Mistresses; to be honest, sober, and cleanly ; to control their tempers ; to be kind in their deportment to their equals, and civil to all. In a word, they are educated in the principles, moral and religious, which the Church of England maintains and inculcates ; and the fruits which these principles, sedulously and constantly impressed upon their minds, have in numerous instances produced, evince the great importance of this Institution, not only to the Poor themselves, but to all classes of society.

It is not doubted, that a Charity, which has so materially contributed to diffuse habits of good order and sound Christian principles among the Poor, will continue to meet with liberal support.

Although at the present moment the finances of this School are far from being in a prosperous state, the Trustees still persevere in their undertaking; not doubting that, under the blessing of Providence, they will be enabled still to open their doors to the helpless children of the poor and ignorant, and to prosecute the important objects of this Institution with vigour and effect.

This School at present contains about 500 Children—337 Boys, and 163 Girls; and, from inquiries which have been recently made, it has appeared, that many of the poor inhabitants have not yet endeavoured to avail themselves of its benefits ; some because they were not aware that such a school was established ; and others because they did not know how easily they might obtain admission for their children.

Patron.
His Grace the Duke of Portland.
President.
His Grace the Archbishop of Canterbury.
Twelve Vice Presidents, including
The Rev. John Hume Spry, D. D. Rector of the Parish.

Treasurer.
Thomas Little, Esq. Maida Hill.

Subscriptions are received by the Treasurer ; by Mr. C. W. Moore, the Master and Secretary, No. 82, High Street; and by Mr. Peter Matthews, the Collector, No. 52, High Street; also at the Banking-house of Sir Claude Scott, Bart. & Co., Margaret Street, Cavendish Square.

CENTRAL DISTRICT PROVIDENT SOCIETY.

This Institution was established by a few benevolent Individuals, for the purpose of encouraging the labouring classes to provide a small fund to meet any unforeseen exigencies that may befal them.   The object of the projectors of this Institution is to establish the principle of saving among the poorer classes, without interfering with that excellent Institution, the St. Mary-le-bone Savings Bank ; the following regulations have therefore been adopted.

The Provident Institution opens for the Season in February, and continues open for business every succeeding Monday until the end of October.

During this period, *any one person in a family,* residing in the District, may deposit a sum not exceeding Eleven pence each week.   On or after the first Monday in November, the whole of the Sum deposited is returned to the Depositor, with the addition of Sixpence for every Five Shillings ; which is given either in Money, Tickets for the purchase of Clothes, Food, or any other Articles, at the choice of the Depositor.

Deposits are received at the Central National School, in High Street, every Monday Evening, between the hours of six and seven.

POLICE OFFICE.

The Police Office was removed by Act of Parliament from Shadwell, and established in High Street in 1821, Lord Sidmouth being Secretary of State at that period : and was opened for transacting business on the 16th of July in that year. The following gentlemen preside as Magistrates at this Office:—John Rawlinson, Esq., Edmund Griffiths, Esq., and William Hoskins, Esq. The establishment of the High Street Police Office has proved an object of great convenience to this populous parish, the increase of population having rendered such an Establishment most desirable ; the celerity and dispatch evinced in transacting the business of the Office, combined with the facility of obtaining legal advice and information, and the general civility and politeness of the Chief Clerk and Officers ; give it a character far superior to Establishments of a similar description. The backway to the Office, is by Grotto Passage, in Paradise Street; the lock-up cells, with some adjacent cottages, having been erected on the site of an Exhibition of Shell-work, called the *Great Grotto*, the property of one *John Castles*, who died in 1757 ; the ingenuity of this artist appears to have been duly appreciated by the Public, his Exhibition having been a celebrated place of fashionable resort.

INFANT SCHOOL OF THE WHOLE PARISH OF ST. MARY-LE-BONE.

This School was projected by the Rev. Dr. Spry, Rector, and established in 1828.

The object of Infant Schools is to provide safety, attention, and suitable Education for the Children of the Poor, during that period of life when they require most care, and generally receive least; it being a fact too well known, that very many Children, from infancy to the age of six or seven years, are entrusted during the working-hours. of the days, to the care of others little older than themselves ;—that others are kept for many hours together confined in the close apartment of some person paid to take charge of them (which restraint, with the injudicious treatment often attending it, injures both their minds and bodies);—while multitudes are left to roam the streets and alleys of the town, liable to painful or fatal accidents, exposed to the temptation of vicious example, and contracting habits of indolence, insubordination, deceit, impurity, and profaneness.   To this perhaps may be traced much of that juvenile delinquency, which continually increases, to the great injury of society, and the deep concern of every Christian mind.

From these evils it is the design of such Schools to preserve the younger Children of the Poor. These establishments, when rightly conducted, combine the advantages of the nursery, the school-room, and play-ground, and are calculated to promote no less the bodily health and activity, than the moral and religious improvement of the Infant-Scholars.   Nor are the benefits of such Institutions confined to the children only whom they receive: their parents are relieved from all anxiety for their infants' safety, while they are necessarily absent from them in pursuit of their several employments; and the elder children of the family, instead of being confined at home (as is now too frequently the case), to tend the younger, are at liberty to avail themselves without interruption, of the excellent course of instruction provided for them in the National Schools.   Those Schools also will become more efficient, where Infant Schools are founded ; for it cannot be doubted, that the striking improvement produced in the temper and behaviour of children subjected to the lenient, yet steady discipline of an Infant School, is in itself a valuable preparation for the Education which it is the object of the National Schools to impart. That these benefits may be secured to some portion of the Infant Poor of the Parish of St. Mary-le-bone, a commodious and retired spot of ground, affording ample space for all the purposes of the plan, has been obtained, contiguous to the garden of the Parish Church. On this ground there is a good and airy play-ground for the children, which has been properly fenced, and fitted with a shed, to shelter them in case of rain. There is also a commodious House for the residence of the School-Mistress ; a School-room has been erected, capable of receiving nearly 300 Children. This has been done in full confidence that the Charity will meet with adequate support from the liberality of the Parishioners; and that support is earnestly and respectfully intreated by the Trustees, as a sum of more than £200. is still required to meet the expenditure.

It is gratifying to know that the Institution is highly valued by the Poor, who cheerfully and regularly contribute their small weekly payments (*one penny*) for the reception of their children ; and the School itself, under the constant and zealous attention of the Mistress, is become what it was intended it should be—not a place of tiresome restraint, but a School for the acquisition of habits of cleanliness and decorum; cheerful subordination, courtesy, kindness, and forbearance; a scene of activity and amusement, and of such a portion of intellectual improvement, and moral and religious discipline, as the tender minds of the Infant Pupils may be capable of receiving.

Among the Rules and Regulations of this School are the following :

That the School be open to all Children of Poor

Inhabitants of St. Mary-le-Bone, under Seven years
of Age, on the recommendation of a Subscriber.

That Parents sending one Child, shall be required to pay One Penny per week for such Child
as long as it shall remain in the School.   Parents
sending more than One Child, shall pay the like
Sum for each Child they send.

That the Officiating Clergy of the Parish, being
Subscribers, be Trustees.

That the Rector of the Parish, and in his absence
one of his Curates appointed by him, be, with two
of the Trustees, elected Monthly Visitors of this
School.

Patronesses.

The Most Noble The Marchioness Cornwallis.
The Rt. Hon. the Dow. Countess Manvers.
The Rt. Hon. Dow. Lady Radstock.
The Right Hon. Ladies Teignmouth ; Eleanor
Dundas ; Bridget Bouverie.
The Hon. Misses Shore, Waldegrave, Watson ;
Ladies Langham, Dalrymple, Johnston, Buller,
Richard King, Astley Cooper, A. Bryce.
Mrs. Spry.   Mrs. Walpole Eyre.

President.

The Lord Bishop of London.

Twelve Vice Presidents, including the Rev. Dr.
Spry, and all the District Rectors.

Treasurers.

Sir Claude Scott, Bart. & Co.

Secretary.

Mr. David Pau, 22, George Street, Portman Sq.

Subscriptions are received by the Treasurers, at
the Vestry of the Parish Church, by the Secretary, Mr. David Pau, and at the School-House
adjoining the Parish Church.

The New Road.

The New Road from Paddington to Islington was cut through this Parish in 1757, commencing from he Edgware Road at the west end of Watery Lane, and passing through the estates of the Rev. Mr. Lloyd, at Lisson Green, Mr. Portman, the Duke of Portland, and the Crown land, crossing the St. Mary-le-bone boundary at the Green Lane opposite the Farthing-Pye-House, continuing through the Duke of Grafton's estate, to Tottenham-Court-Road, and thence through the Duke of Bedford's land to Islington and the City. From an accurate plan of this Road, as surveyed by J. Marsh, 1757, it appears the distance from the west end of Watery Lane along the New Road to Tottenham-Court-Road, is one mile, one quarter, and 277 yards. Opposite the Yorkshire Stingo was a road or lane across Lisson Green to Bell Lane leading to the Harrow Road as exhibited in the above plan.

When the Bill for making this road was before Parliament, the following reasons were offered in support of it:—1. "That a free and easy communication will be opened, between the Counties of Essex and the different parts of the County of Middlesex, and the several roads leading from the western to the eastern parts of the kingdom, without going through the streets, and by a nearer way of about two miles.

2. That the frequent accidents which happen, and the great inconveniencies that arise, by driving cattle from the western road through the streets to Smithfield Market, will be prevented.

3. That the pavements of the streets will be greatly preserved, and the frequent obstructions therein, by the multitude of carriages, which must necessarily pass through the same to go from the western to the eastern parts of the town, will be

in a great measure removed, and the business of the inhabitants of London and Westminster will be transacted in a much easier and more expeditious manner.

4. That in times of public danger, by threatened invasions from foreign enemies, or otherwise, this New Road will form a complete line of circumvallation, and His Majesty's Forces may easily and expeditiously march this way into Essex, and other Counties adjacent, to defend our coasts, without the inconvenience of passing through the Cities of London and Westminster, or interrupting the business thereof."

Notwithstanding all these alleged conveniencies and improvement of communication, the Bill met with strong opposition from the Duke of Bedford, who endeavoured to introduce a clause restricting the erecting of Buildings within an immense distance of the Road; which would have rendered the Bill nugatory : his amendment was rejected, and the Bill was passed. A clause was, however, inserted, prohibiting the erection of buildings, or any erection whatsoever, within 50 feet of the road, and empowering the parochial authorities, upon obtaining an order from a magistrate, to pull down and remove any such erection, and levy the expenses thereof on the offender's goods and chattels, without proceeding in the ordinary way by indictment.

The effect of this restriction, has been the laying out and planting gardens of 50 feet in length in front of all the houses erected on either side of this road, which gives them a most pleasing and picturesque appearance; and has made it necessary to introduce a clause in the Acts of Parliament, for building the Parish and Trinity Churches, to legalize the erection of their respective porticoes, which encroach within the prescribed boundary.

This Road, which is now one of the finest leading

avenues to the Metropolis, is also considered one
of the most convenient; stage Coaches, and Omni-
buses (a vehicle recently brought into use) passing
for the conveyance of passengers, from Paddington
to the City, every five minutes daily, another proof
of the immense increase of population, since, 35
years ago, only one coach ran from Paddington to
London, and the proprietor could scarcely obtain
a subsistence by his speculation.

The New Road is skirted by well-built houses,
some of which were erected soon after the road
was cut. On entering this Parish the Road takes
a slight turn after passing the " Old Farthing Pie
House" on the south; and, crossing Portland Road,
passes through Park Crescent; from this point
the rows of houses on the south side, are named
as follows:—Harley Place, Devonshire Terrace.
Leaving these, we arrive successively. at Church
House, Church Cottage, the Parish Church, and
St. Mary-le-bone Workhouse and Infirmary (described by a late writer, as " possessing as many
windows and covering as much ground as a Russian
Palace"), York Buildings, Salisbury Place,* Cumberland Place, Queen Charlotte Row: at the end
of this Row is situated the extensive bowling-
green and grounds of the Yorkshire Stingo: this
house has been a celebrated House of Entertainment for more than a century; and it appears in
the plan of the New Road of the date of 1757.
Here was formerly held a fair on the 1st of May,
annually, which was tolerated by the Magistracy
for several years, until it became the resort of a
multitude of disorderly and dissolute characters,
and a complete nuisance to the inhabitants of the

* The Rev. Bryant Burgess, Curate of the Parish, resides at
No. 9, in Salisbury Place The grandfather of this gentleman
M. Chassereau, resided many years during the last Century, in a
detached mansion surrounded with a large garden, situated in
High Street, at the North-east corner of Paddington Street.

vicinity, when it was finally suppressed within the
last few years, by order of the magistrates; this
house is now a respectable tavern. Adjoining these
premises is an extensive Brewery, the property of
R. Staines. The road here takes another slight turn
westward, passing an elegant building at the corner
of Harcourt Street, occupied by that excellent
Institution the Queen's Lying-in-Hospital. Paddington Chapel in Homer Place, is the next
prominent building, and the road finally quits the
Parish by Winchester Row, built in the year 1766:
the houses of which have been recently repaired,
the fronts being covered with stucco, and presenting a very neat appearance.

The prominent features of the north side of the
road, are: Trinity Church, Albany Terrace, Park
Square, Ulster Place, Harley House, in the occupation of Charles Day, Esq. Devonshire Place House,
in the occupation of H. M. Dyer, Esq. The Office
of John White, Esq.; Mary-bone Park House, in
the occupation of the Rev. Edward Scott; Nottingham Terrace; Union Place (here is a modern
building with a gothic front occupied by the Exchange Bazaar, and the old established Coach
Manufactory of Mr. Burnand); Allsop Terrace.
In Gloucester Place, New Road, are situated the
following extensive establishments; viz. Jenkins's
Nursery, the Coach Manufactory of Messrs. Tilbury
and Co. and that most respectable and valuable
Institution, the Philological School. In the next
row of houses, named Lisson Grove South, is situated the Western General Dispensary: and the north
side of the road terminates by Middlesex Place,
and Southampton Row. Here is a large cluster
of houses of ancient date, the property of George
Cabbell, Esq.

PHILOLOGICAL SCHOOL,

Gloucester Place, New Road.

Though this School is not confined to the Parish of St. Mary-le-bone, but is open for boys who are otherwise eligible wherever they may reside, yet, as it has been for many years situated within the confines of the Parish, it will not be considered out of place to introduce a short account of it in this work.

Its object is to educate the Sons of Clergymen, Naval and Military Officers, Professional Men, Merchants, Manufacturers, Clerks in Public Offices, the higher order of Tradesmen, and other Persons of an equally respectable class of society, whose families have been in better circumstances and are reduced by accident or misfortune, whereby they are rendered incapable of affording their children a suitable education.

The School is supported by voluntary contributions; and boys duly qualified as above, are admitted on the foundation on the presentation of subscribers; who are entitled to certain rights and privileges in this respect, graduated and regulated according to the amount contributed.

The Boys are educated in English and French, in Writing and Arithmetic, Geometry, Algebra, Geography, the Principles of Drawing, and the Rudiments of Latin; they are at the same time carefully instructed in their religious duties, on the principles maintained by the Established Church.

In addition to this, they are entitled to certain articles of clothing; but are not boarded.

The general administration of the affairs of the School is vested in a Board, composed of the President, Vice-Presidents, and twenty Governors elected at the Annual Meeting of Subscribers.

This Board holds its ordinary sittings for the transaction of business once in every month.

The School was founded in 1792, under the patronage of His Royal Highness the Duke of York, and was for many years carried on in a Building erected for the purpose in King Street, Bryanston Square (now Nutford Place). In the year 1827, the increased number of boys, and the urgency of the further application for admission, pressed upon the Governors the absolute necessity of removing the School to larger premises; and they made choice of the present situation, where the accommodations provided for the School-business, and the advantages offered for air and exercise, render it peculiarly eligible for the purpose to which it is applied.

About the same time, the Governors and friends of the Institution had to lament the death of its first Patron, the Duke of York, under whose countenance and support it had risen and flourished for so many years. The School, however, was not long left without a Royal Patron, His late Majesty, George IV. having graciously condescended to take it under His protection; and on his demise, the present King was pleased to extend to it the same grace and favour. Soon afterwards the Queen honoured the Institution by becoming its Patroness.

At the Annual Meeting of Subscribers, in the year 1831, it was considered that it would greatly tend to promote the welfare of the School, and add stability to it, if a fund were raised for its permanent endowment: and the Meeting, desirous of evincing their gratitude to His Majesty for his munificent contribution in support of the School, came to a resolution that it should be appropriated to lay the foundation of this fund: and it was also provided that, in addition to the King's contribution, all donations of £50 and upwards, and all legacies of any amount, which should be expressly given in augmentation of this fund, should be so applied. The present amount of the contributions has already, it is understood, justified the hopes entertained of the measure on its original formation. Contributors to this fund are entitled to the same privileges as, by the rules of the School, are conferred upon those who subscribe towards its support.

The excellent regulations under which this Institution is conducted, and the sound and useful education which it imparts, have raised it so highly in public estimation, that the number of applications for admission has of late years greatly increased; and it has in consequence become necessary to limit the number of boys.

The Classes of Society to which this Institution affords relief, are such as hide their sorrows from the Public eye; and, while they would shrink from pecuniary assistance, gladly receive an education for their children, which may enable them to fill their proper stations in life; and which has been the means of restoring many a widowed mother and unprotected family to their former comfort and prosperity. With this object, and standing almost alone, this Institution seems to possess peculiar claims on the liberality of the Public; since, under the dispensation of Providence, it may happen that the hand that now affords relief may one day receive the benefit.

List of Officers.

President.
The Right Hon. Lord Teignmouth.

Vice Presidents.
The Right Hon. the Lord Mayor, and eighteen
other Gentlemen.

Treasurer.
John Turner, Esq.
Secretary.   Mr. Edwin Abbott.
Physician.   Thomas Brown, M. D.
Surgeon and Apothecary.   Edgar Barker, Esq.
Surgeon Dentist.   James Snell, Esq.
Solicitor.   W. R. Jupp, Esq. Carpenters' Hall.
Head Master.   Mr. Edwin Abbott.
Writing and Drawing Master.   Mr. Charles
S. Williams.
French Master. Mr. Devolmerange Descroix, B. A.
Assistant Master.   Mr. T. H. Ramsay.
Collector.
Mr. John Whitehead, St. John's Wood Barracks.

The following is an abstract of the Report of the
number and description of the Boys in the School,
made to the Annual Meeting in 1832.

Of the Sons of Naval and Military Officers .	23
Professional Men . . .	8
Clerks in Public Offices . . .	18
Merchants, Manufacturers, and the higher order of Tradesmen . . .	23
Contributory Scholars . .	55
	127

The School is open to the inspection of the
Public; and Reports affording ample information as
to the Plan and Object of the Institution may be
had of the Secretary at the School-House; by whom
also, Subscriptions and Donations are received.

QUEEN CHARLOTTE'S LYING-IN HOSPITAL.

This Charity was instituted in the year 1752, at a house in St. George's Row, near Tyburn Turnpike, from whence it was removed to Bayswater in 1791. It was found to be of material service to the surrounding districts, but in consequence of bad management it had nearly ceased to exist—when the attention of their Royal Highnesses the Dukes of Sussex and Cambridge was awakened to the merits of the Charity; and, at their suggestion a General Meeting was held and many excellent regulations adopted (on the 21st of Oct. 1809). In the year 1810, it was removed to the spacious freehold mansion at the corner of Harcourt Street, New Road (which was originally built by J. Harcourt, Esq. and afterwards occupied by — Tucker, Esq. Secretary to the Admiralty), under the special patronage of Her late Majesty Queen Charlotte, whose name it is distinguished by; and under the direct management of His Royal Highness the Duke of Sussex; who, from the moment he benevolently gave his assistance to its revival, has never ceased to watch over its interests, and to aid and assist its truly benevolent views. The Institution is further honoured by the patronage of Her Majesty Queen Adelaide, and every member of the Royal Family.

The views of the Charity are regularly superintended by a Committee of twenty Governors; and their professed object is eminently promoted by the gratuitous assistance and attendance of a Medical Establishment, comprehending gentlemen of the first-rate professional talent.

This Charity, besides affording an asylum for indigent Females, during the awful period of childbirth, extends its aid also to the habitations of those who prefer remaining with their families, or cannot conveniently be removed:—to such females all the comforts and relief are given, which their immediate wants may demand; although the Hospital cannot, in such cases, afford them the full amount of domestic relief and consolation as proffered under its own roof.

Not only the indigent and helpless, but the wives also of industrious Labourers, Mechanics, and distressed Housekeepers, who, from the pressure of the times, may stand in need of such relief, are made equally partakers of the benefits of this Charity.

The wives too of those indigent brave men, whose lives are devoted to the service of their country, by land or by sea, are more particularly considered as fit objects for its bounty.

Likewise, in the true spirit of Christian charity, which finds not in human frailty any just incitement to utter rejection, this Institution, with a view to facilitate the repentance of a suffering and contrite sinner, and to preclude every motive to suicide, or the murder of a new-born infant, which conscious guilt has been known to excite in the minds of many unlawful mothers—admit penitent patients *once*; but in no instance can they be received a *second* time.

To prevent, however, the possible contagion of evil example, separate wards for the married and unmarried patients are allotted, and all intercourse between them is most carefully precluded.

President for Life.
His Royal Highness The Duke of Sussex, K. G.
Patronesses.
Their Royal Highnesses the Duchesses of Kent, Cambridge and Gloucester.
Vice-Presidents.
Their Graces the Dukes of Grafton, Devonshire, and Northumberland.

The Rt. Hon. the Earls of Shaftesbury, Plymouth,
Dartmouth, Hardwicke, Grosvenor, Ferrers,
Edward Berkeley Portman, Esq. M. P.

Treasurer.
John Wright, Esq.
Consulting Physicians.
Dr. Peter M. Roget, F. R. S.   Dr. James Copland.
Physician Accoucheur.
Dr. Richard Byam Dennison.
Surgeon Accoucheur.   John Sweatman, Esq.
Assistant Surgeon Accoucheur.
Joseph Cholmondeley, Esq.
Solicitor.
Lawrence Walker, Esq. 24, Argyll Street.
Secretary.
Mr. Augustus U. Thiselton, 37, Goodge Street.

Subscriptions are received by the Treasurer; the
Secretary; the Collector; and at the Hospital.

K

THE WESTERN GENERAL DISPENSARY.

This Institution was founded on the 9th of March, 1830, at a public meeting held on that day, and which had been called by a few benevolent gentlemen who felt the necessity of establishing a Medical Institution for the relief of the poorer classes of this district of the Parish of St. Mary-le-bone, and the contiguous Parishes of Paddington and Kilburn. The house now known as the Dispensary-house was engaged, and from its situation holds out the greatest advantages; for though in the Parish of St. Mary-le-bone, it is nearly a mile distant from any other Medical Institution. The St. Mary-le-bone General Dispensary and the Middlesex Hospital, being situated at such a distance from the districts which the Western General Dispensary embraces, rendered it impracticable for the sick poor to resort thither; this Institution has therefore become an object of great importance, to the densely populated district of the north western part of the Parish, consisting principally of the labouring classes. It is only due to the Medical Gentlemen in the neighbourhood to record their unceasing exertions and liberality in affording relief to thousands of cases annually; but it lay alone in the power of the public at large, through the medium of a Charitable Institution, to mitigate to an adequate extent the ravages which disease always makes amongst the poor.

Upon the subject of the great benefit of an Institution of this kind, but little need be said. The claims of an Individual soliciting pecuniary assistance, may be thwarted by imposition and fraud; but the tale of woe, which sickness and disease tells, can never be mistaken; and the contributions of the generous towards relieving distress, which is but too evident, and which there can be no motive for feigning, if it were possible, are of all others the surest to answer the end for which they were intended.

To relieve therefore, as far as human exertions can avail, the miseries to which the poor are exposed in the hour of sickness, the Western General Dispensary was founded; and its objects are thus stated in the prospectus originally issued, namely:

" To give advice and medicines in all cases, both Surgical and Medical, to such poor persons as, from poverty and destitution, have not the means of obtaining relief; subject to such laws and regulations as may from time to time be agreed upon; and, in addition, to supply, under the authority of the Board of Directors, wine, sago, or arrow-root, to those patients whose poverty and ill-health require it."

" To have beds for sufferers from accidents that may occur in the immediate neighbourhood."

A Medical Officer attends at the Dispensary every morning, except Sundays, at twelve o'clock; and will visit, at their own houses, patients whose cases may require such attendance, and who reside within one mile of the Institution.

Another important feature in this Institution, is, that the Medical Officers are Surgeon-Apothecaries, or general practitioners, residing in the immediate neighbourhood; and who from necessity, must be well acquainted with any peculiar local disease which may at any time prevail, or by possibility exist. There is no other Institution of the same description in London.

The utility of this Institution will be obvious, when the Public are informed that in the first twelve months after its establishment, 1618 patients were admitted by Letter; Accidents, 129; of whom 940 were discharged *cured;* Relieved, 268; date of Letter having expired, 96; Discharged for Non-

Attendance, 42; Sent into the Country, 12; Sent to an Hospital, 8; Died, 57; Under treatment, June 30, 1831, 324;. making a total of 1747.

Patron.
H. R. H. The Duke of Sussex, K. G. &c. &c.· &c.

President.
His Grace the Duke of Newcastle.

Treasurer.
The Rev. Bryant Burgess, 9, Salisbury Place, New Road.

Trustees.
Mr. Serjeant Bompas.   James **Parlett**, Esq.
Barry O'Meara, Esq.

Consulting Physicians.
Marshall Hall, M. D.
Anthony Todd Thompson, M. D., F. R. S.

Consulting Surgeons.
B. C. Brodie, Esq. F. R. S.
Edward Stanley, Esq. F. R. S.

Medical Officers in Ordinary
Alexander Anderson, Esq. 17, York Place.
Edgar Barker, Esq. 40, Edgware Road.
J. C. Cox, Esq. 33, Montagu Square.
N. Grant, Esq. 21, Thayer Street.

Dispenser and Secretary.
Mr. T. Y. Cotter, at the Dispensary House.

Subscriptions and Donations are thankfully received by Sir Claude Scott, Bart. & Co. I, Cavendish Square; likewise by the Treasurer, Collector, and at the Dispensary, where Plans of the Charity may he had, and also Letters of Recommendation, on application by Governors.

Portman Square

Was begun about 1764, when the north side of
the square was built ; but it was nearly 20 years
before the whole was completed. This is a very
handsome square, 500 feet by 400, but it is to be
regretted, that the coup-d'œil is wounded by the
total absence of uniformity in the surrounding
buildings, some of them being remarkable for a
profusion of architectural elegance, while others
are distinguished only by a neat simplicity. The
centre of the area is laid out in shrubberies, exhibiting a wilderness of foliage, producing a very
pleasing effect. Here is also a moveable temple or
summer-house, erected by the Turkish Ambassador
about 25 years ago, when he resided at No. 18,
the north-west corner of the square. His Excellency was in the habit of taking the air in this
beautiful spot, surrounded by part of his retinue.
At the north-west angle is the elegant detached
mansion which was built by the celebrated Mrs.
Elizabeth Montagu, who resided here many years,
and whose benevolent feelings led her to regale
all the chimney-sweepers annually, on the 1st of
May, on the lawn in front of this mansion, with
good and wholesome fare: " so that they might
enjoy *one* happy day in the year." This house is
now the residence of Lord Rokeby.

M. Otto, the French Ambassador, resided here
in 1802; his residence was on the south side of the
square. On the occasion of Peace being proclaimed
on the 29th of April, 1802, between His Britannic
Majesty and the French Republic, illuminations
of the most splendid character succeeded the cere-
monial of the day; but the object of universal
attraction was the French Ambassador's House,
which was most brilliantly illuminated with coloured
lamps, disposed in the form of an Ionic temple,

and having in the centre a large transparency, representing England and France, with their various attributes, in the act of uniting their hands, in token of amity, before an altar dedicated to humanity, above which appeared the word PEACE, with olive branches.

The following circumstance, which occurred a few days before the illumination, will shew the true characteristics of national feeling. Immense crowds were daily attracted, by the preparations for the magnificent display which afterwards took place. At length, the word *Concord* was formed in coloured lamps on the entablature of the temple: the reading of John Bull, was, however, *Conquered*, and his inference, that it was intended that *Britain was conquered by France.* Disturbance and riot were about to commence, when M. Otto, after some fruitless attempts at explanation, prudently conceded, and the word *amity* was substituted. But it did not end here, for some sailors found out that the initials G. R. were not surmounted as usual by a crown: this they peremptorily insisted should be done, and a lamp formed diadem was immediately put up.*

This Square contains 40 noble houses, inhabited by the following persons of high rank. The Dukes of Newcastle and Hamilton; Earls Beverley, Manvers, Nelson, Pomfret, Cardigan, Beauchamp; Viscount Newark: Lords Garvagh, Kenyon, Templemore, Teignmouth; Henry Charles and Lady Charlotte Sturt; Hon. Mrs. Leigh; Right Hon. Lieutenant-General Sir John Byng; Henry Skrine, Esq. Henry Elwes, Esq. P. W. Gardiner, Esq. Lady Harriet Chichester; R. R. Pennington, Esq. John Stewart, Esq ; Mrs. Raymond Barker; Miss Johnes; Mrs. H. Nisbet; Countess of Scarborough ; John Giffard, Esq. Charles Morris, Esq. Hon. Miss Kenyon, Mrs. M. H. Beach; James Malony, Esq.

* Lambert's Hist. of London.

Mrs. Denison, Rev. I. H. Sadler; Charles W. G.
Wynne, Esq. Charles Lyne Stephens, Esq. The
Misses Beaumont; Captain Coulson; Colonel Bisse
Chaloner.

In the year 1778, a proposal was made in the
Public Advertiser, to the Inhabitants of Mary-le-
bone, for forming a new road from Portman Square
across the fields to the bottom of Hampstead town,
by the west end of Mr. Allsop's new farm, across
Mr. Willan's field, by the side of the Hill-Field,
commonly called Little Primrose Hill, through a
part of Belsize Park, to the bottom of Hampstead
town: then across the lower side of the Heath, and
to go between the Spaniards and Caen-wood House,
through Bishop's-wood, across the fields into the
Barnet Road, at the bottom of the hill rising up
to Finchley Common, about half a mile below
Highgate Hill: the whole length of this proposed
road was computed to measure barely four miles.
But this proposition was never carried into effect.

MANCHESTER SQUARE.

The north side of this Square was begun in
1776, by the building of Manchester House by
the Duke of Manchester, from whom the Square
derives its name; but it was not completed till the
year 1788. A late writer asserts that it was intended
to have called this Queen Anne's Square, and to
have erected a handsome parochial church in the
centre; but this idea appears to have been erroneous,
a plan having been marked out for the said Square
on or near the site of Portland Place, from which
circumstance Queen Anne Street derives its name.
Upon the sudden death of the Duke of Manchester,
and the minority of his heir, this noble mansion,
which has a very imposing appearance, having a
spacious court-yard inclosed with iron railing, a

handsome portico surmounted by a verandah, &c. became the residence of the Spanish Ambassador; and afterwards the property of the late Marquis of Hertford, who resided here several years. It is now in the occupation of the Dowager Marchioness of Hertford, relict of the late Marquis. During the time the Spanish Ambassador resided here, he erected a small chapel in Spanish Place, which is at the north-east corner of the Square, extending to Charles Street, from designs by Bonomi, which is a very handsome piece of architecture. In 1832 this Chapel was repaired, the exterior being covered with stucco, which not only tends to the preservation of the building, but adds to the classic purity of its style of architecture.

Manchester Square, is small but neat, and the centre, which is laid out in compartments of shrubs and flowers, is surrounded by an iron railing. The principal inhabitants are;—John Liddell, Esq.; J. J. Coney, Esq. Jonas Hall Pope, Esq.;* Colonel Becher; Mrs. Vachell; Mrs. Lowndes Stone; John Leckie, Esq.; Jeremiah Cloves, Esq.; Mrs. Cassamajor; Rev. J. and Lady Cecil Delafield: Richard Norman, Esq.; Dr. M. Hall; George Fuller, Esq.; Sir H. and Lady Lambert; Dr. J. Bright; John M‘Taggart. Esq.; George Lovibond, Esq.; Miss North; Mrs. Dawson; and Mrs. Collins.

At the north-west corner of the Square is Manchester Street, running northward: the houses are plain brick buildings, but occupied by persons of great respectability. The notorious female impostor, Joanna Southcott, resided in this street, and died here in 1814, after having contrived to impose upon six different medical men with the

---

* This gentleman is a Surgeon of extensive practice, and consummate skill; he is also Hon. Medical Secretary to the Local Board of Health, established by Order of the Privy Council; his superior talent and indefatigable activity, are the theme of general admiration.

absurd story of her being about to give birth to
the young " Shiloh." A more particular account
of this woman will be found under the head of
Miscellaneous Biography. Among the residents
in this street, are, the Dowager Lady Synge; Rev.
R. H. Millington; Rev. J. Fanshawe; Captain
Robert Locke; Mrs. Colonel Taylor; W. H.
Harriott, Esq. G. D. Hervey, Esq. James Hakewill,
Esq. &c.

BRYANSTON AND MONTAGU SQUARES.

Since the commencement of the present century
almost all the various streets and avenues in the
north-west part of the parish have been built.
Bryanston and Montagu Squares, which are said
to be the best examples of well constructed town
residences, are built on ground commonly called
Ward's Field; here was formerly a large pond, at
which many fatal accidents occurred every year to
the schoolboys of the neighbourhood; near this
spot was also a cluster of small cottages, called
Apple Village, remarkable from having been the
residence of one of the murderers of Mr. Steele;
the dreadful accident which happened at the execution of these criminals, when nearly 30 persons
were crushed to death, will be fresh in the recollec-
tion of the reader. The above Squares were built
by Mr. David Porter, an eminent builder, who had
formerly been chimney-sweeper to the village, and
resided in Little Welbeck Street, but having acquired a large property, became extensively engaged in the new buildings. On the occasion of
the Jubilee, to celebrate the 50th year of the reign
of George III. this individual gave a substantial
entertainment to his workmen and dependants in
the enclosed area of Montagu Square, which was
then in an unfinished state; when, notwithstanding
the public situation, much conviviality and har-

mony prevailed around the festive board.   Mr.
Porter died in the year 1819, having lived to see
the result of his active labours for many years, in a
most flourishing state.

Bryanston Square, is an oblong ; the dimensions
are 814 feet in length, by 194 in width : it contains
50 handsome uniform houses ; the centre houses
on each side are decorated with columns and pediments, the area is tastefully planted, and enclosed
with an iron railing, forming an agreeable promenade for the occupiers of the surrounding mansions,
who are accommodated with keys.   The following
are among the gentry who reside here :—A. B. and
Lady Mary Drummond ; Joseph Hume, Esq. M. P.
for Middlesex ; Viscountess Dudley ; Dow. Lady
Elcho ; Gen. Sir Joseph Fuller ; Lady Strachan ;
Col. H. S. Eyre, and Walpole Eyre, Esq.; Sir W.
J. Hort, Bt. ; Sir W. Johnstone, Bt. ; Sir W. W.
Pepys, Bt. ; Sir T. B. Lennard, Bt. ; Hon. Newton
Fellowes, and Lady Catherine ; Sir Francis Free-
ling, Bt.; Admiral Douglas; the Hon. Gen.
Meade, &c.

Wyndham Place, extending north from Bryan-
stone Square to St. Mary's Church, contains 16
houses uniform with those in the Square ; and here
reside, Benj. Cohen, Esq. ; the Dow. Countess of
Mountnorris ; M. L. Welch, Esq. ; and the Rev.
Dr. Dibdin, Rector of St. Mary's.

Montagu Square is exactly similar in character
to Bryanston, with the exception that it contains
63 houses, and its dimensions are 820 feet by 156.
Here reside, Baron Wessenberg, *the Austrian
Minister ;* Adm. Maitland; Col. Sutherland; Maj.
J. Y. Bradford; Mrs. Shum ; H. Holland, Esq. ;
C. D. Nevinson, M. D.; Durant St. Andre, *French
Consul General ;* Sir J. Chetwode, Bt. ; Dowager
Ctss of Shrewsbury ; Hon. W. Rodney ; Dr. A.
Gostling, &c.

Dorset Square is a small but handsome Square, with the area enclosed and planted, and is built on the site of Lord's Cricket Ground; in this Square reside, the Rev. Dr. Penfold, Rector of Trinity Church; Lady C. Graham; Count Dupont; the Rev. Dr. Fellowes, &c.

A short distance west of Dorset Square, a new Square is forming, named Blandford Square, the south side of which only is completed.

LORD'S CRICKET GROUND.

This ground was a fine inclosed lawn or plain of large extent, rented by T. Lord, and called after his name. It was formerly a favourite place of resort for amateurs of the athletic game of cricket, many interesting matches for immense sums having been played here, the names of several Noblemen and persons of rank being entered in the list of players. It was also occasionally used as an exercising ground by the St. Mary-le-bone Volunteers, and the stand of colours was presented to the Regiment in this ground, in presence of a vast concourse of the Nobility and Gentry who attended on the occasion.

M. Garnerin made his second ascent in this country, from Lord's Cricket Ground, on the 5th of July 1802, accompanied by Edward Hawke Locker, Esq.; in presence of H. R. H. the Prince of Wales, who attended several ladies of distinction in the ground, and an immense number of the Nobility. His Royal Highness, on this occasion, signed the following letter of recommendation to any gentleman in the neighbourhood where the intrepid aeronauts might descend, that they might not, as on the former excursion, be treated as necromancers coming from the clouds.

July 5, 1802.

" We the undersigned, having been present at the ascension of M. Garnerin, with his balloon, this afternoon

and witnessed the entire satisfaction of the public, beg
leave to recommend him to the notice of any gentleman in
whose neighbourhood he may happen to descend.

Signed. George P. W.   G. Devonshire.
Besborough.   Cathcart.

The balloon rose in the most beautiful and
majestic manner. M. Garnerin had intended to
have descended by the parachute, but the disturbed
state of the elements rendered it impracticable.
From the extreme density of the atmosphere the
balloon was out of sight in three minutes after the
cords were cut, and left one of the most immense
multitudes ever assembled in the metropolis gaz-
ing on the wide expanse. Notwithstanding the
violence of the wind, they rose to the height of a
mile and a half, and descended at 5 minutes after
5 o'clock, without the least injury, at Chingford,
near Epping Forest; having travelled a space of
17 miles in little more than 15 minutes. Such
interest had this famous aeronaut excited, that for
several hours before the ascent all the metropolis
was in an uproar; many accidents occurred, and
many depredations were committed. Mr. Locker
afterwards published an account of his aerial voyage
and says in conclusion:—" Although the mob which
surrounded us on our descent, were as usual, both
troublesome and officiously impertinent, we received great attention and assistance from Mr.
Hughes of the Stamp-Office London, and several
other gentlemen, who beheld our arrival. Attention would, however, have been insured to us, if
necessary, by the paper put into the hands of M.
Garnerin, signed by H. R. H. the Prince of Wales,
and other persons of distinction."* The Cricket
Ground was removed in 1814, to St. John's Wood.

* E. H. Locker, Esq. is still living, and fills an important
situation in Greenwich Hospital. This gentleman recently commenced publishing "The Naval Gallery of Greenwich Hospital,"
which he had the principal share in forming, but was unfortunately
compelled to discontinue it on account of ill health.

Upper and Lower Seymour Street, Edwards Street, Wigmore Street, Mortimer Street, and Charles Street, including the north side of Cavendish Square, and south side of Portman Square, form a spacious avenue from east to west, completely through the Parish, commencing at the Edgware Road, and quitting the boundary at Charles Street. The above streets have been built at various periods : Wigmore Street is the most ancient, having been commenced in 1729. The White Hart at the corner of Welbeck Street, was a detached house of entertainment for many years : it was the practice of travellers to stop at this house for refreshment, and examine their firearms, previously to crossing the fields to Lisson Green. The land, from this house westward, to the banks of the bourn from whence the parish derives its name, formed a deep marshy valley : in this valley a house was erected by one Fenning, which obtained the name of " *Fenning's Folly*," from what was then considered the absurdity of erecting a house in such a situation ; it is shrewdly suspected from the variety of materials used in this building, that they were surreptitiously obtained from the numerous buildings erecting about the neighbourhood at that period. It must, however, have had an excellent foundation, a substantial house, in the occupation of Mr. Williams, Fishmonger to their Majesties, having been erected upon the top of it ; the shop, which is now level with the street, having formed the upper story of " Fenning's Folly." There is also, at the corner of Mary-le-bone Lane, one of the conduits belonging to the City of London ; and in the same building was situated the Armoury and Orderly Room of the St. Mary-le-bone Volunteers. On the north side of Wigmore Street, and at the east corner of Mary-le-bone Lane, lived a respectable Bookseller, named Fiske, in whose house lodged Margaret

Nicholson, the maniac who attempted to stab George III. Aug. 3, 1786. Here is a cluster of small houses occupying a triangular piece of ground between Mary-le-bone Lane and John's Court: this spot was formerly in the occupation of one *Easeley.* The cluster of houses formerly projected across Wigmore Street, and formed an obstruction to the continuation of the line of buildings: the proprietor resisted for some time the offer of the parochial authorities to purchase and remove the obstruction; but finally yielded, on an application to Parliament being threatened; and part of these houses being taken down, this spacious avenue was completed according to the original design. The densely populated mass of buildings north and south of Wigmore Street, from Duke Street, to Mary-le-bone Lane, were not built till after the year 1772: the inhabitants consist of Shopkeepers and the working classes. The remains of the late Lieutenant-General Sir Thomas Picton, who was killed at the Battle of Waterloo, in the moment of victory, were brought over to England, and after lying in state at his house in Edwards Street, were buried at St. George's burial ground. Many shops are interspersed through this fine length of street; there are also many persons of high rank and fashion residing in it, especially in Edwards Street, and Lower and Upper Seymour Streets; among whom are the following distinguished persons:—*Edwards Street,* Dow. Lady Inglis; Hon. B. Bouverie; John Ivatt Briscoe, Esq.; Count de Champemont. *Low. Seymour Street,* Rev. Charles W. Eyre; Lord Mostyn; Rev. P. Le Breton; Dr. Hope. *Upper Seymour Street,* Hon. General Murray; Mrs. Lytton Bulwer; Rev. W. I. Birdwood; Hon. Henry Pierrepoint; Colonel Newbery; Ctss. Macnamara; Gen. Samuel Browne; John Thomas Hope, Esq.; Lady Mary Ann Sturt; Dow. Ctss. of Winterton; Col. Wynyard; Baroness

Montesquieu; Dow. Lady Floyd; Rev. William Toke; Dow. Lady Strachan; George and Lady Anne Wilbraham, &c.

At the east end of this avenue, and directly facing Berners Street, stands

MIDDLESEX HOSPITAL.

This Hospital was instituted in 1745, for the relief of the indigent sick and lame; at which time, and for some years after, it was carried on in two convenient houses adjoining to each other in Windmill-street, Tottenham-court road. The benefactions of the public having greatly increased, the Governors, in 1747, extended their plan to the relief of lying-in married women, when the consequent increase of patients compelled them to think of enlarging their edifice as well as their plan; and by the benevolence of the contributors, they were enabled to erect the present building, which, at that time, stood isolated in the fields.

The anniversary sermon of the Middlesex Hospital, was preached at St. Anne's Church, Westminster, by the Rev. Dr. Nichols, Master of the Temple, May 15, 1755. After Divine Service, the Rt. Hon. the Earl of Northumberland, President, Sir W. Beauchamp Proctor, Bart. and Col. Cornwallis, Vice Presidents, with the Stewards and Governors, walked from the church to the ground appointed for erecting the new building for the Hospital in Marybone Fields; where the President, assisted by the two Vice-Presidents, laid the first stone. They then returned to the great Concert Room in Dean Street, where the collection amounted to 400l. Sir W. Beauchamp Proctor, gave 100l.*

The Resolution of the Governors relating to the admission of pregnant women, was altered in 1792; and it was resolved to provide that class of patients with obstetrical assistance, medicine, &c. at their

* Gent. Mag vol xxv.

own habitations; and the lying-in ward was fitted
up according to a plan suggested by the benevolent
John Howard, for the admission of persons afflicted
with cancer, at the sole expense of *one* benefactor
(Samuel Whitbread, Esq.); who, actuated by the
purest motives of benevolence towards this particular class of distressed individuals, and wishing
only to make a handsome beginning, in the hope
of many contributions from the charitably disposed,
to the further extension of the plan ; settled the
interest of 4000*l.* in the three per cent. Consolidated
Bank Annuities, for ever, by way of endowment ;
and gave 400*l.* for fitting up a ward for the above
purpose.

In consequence of the inadequacy of the Funds
to the increasing expenses, in 1808 this excellent
Institution was in danger of annihilation, the number
of its patients having been for several years necessarily more and more diminished; the whole number
of in-patients admitted during the year 1801, being
675, that for 1808, only 461.   The establishment
was, however, at that time, relieved from its embar-
rassments by an appeal to the Public, and the very
liberal produce of a Benefit at the Opera House.

The munificent donation of £.1000 by Lord
Robert Seymour, enabled the Governors to fur-
nish and open a new Ward at the commencement
of the year 1824; and they appeal with confidence
to the liberality of the Public, and solicit Contributions to the permanent Fund for its maintenance ;
the annual expense of which is upwards of £.400.
Upwards of Two Hundred Beds are continually
occupied in this Establishment, and the more
enlarged usefulness of which it is capable, can only
be obtained by adequate support.

Though the exterior of this building is exceedingly plain, it has a very respectable appearance,
and is replete with every convenience to answer
the charitable purposes for which it was erected.

Patients relieved by the Hospital within the last Ten Years.

	IN-PATIENTS.	OUT-PATIENTS.
1822	1609	5920
1823	1568	3744
1824	1662	5579
1825	1598	3747
1826	1746	3726
1827	1863	4304
1828	1794	4109
1829	1631	3997
1830	1738	4538
1831	1715	4860

In-Patients	16,924	44,524
Out-patients,	44,524	
Total	61,448	

Officers of the Establishment.

Patron.
The King's Most Excellent Majesty.

President.
His Grace the Duke of Northumberland.

Vice-Presidents.
The Dukes of Bedford, Portland, Wellington, and Dorset.
The Marquisses of Stafford, Cholmondeley, and Westminster.
Lord Duncannon, Lord Henley.
Sir William Weller Pepys, Bt. Sir C. Forbes, Bt.
Hon. Bartholomew Bouverie, John Pepys, Esq.
Thomas Lowndes, Esq.

Treasurers.
John Rawlinson, Esq. Thomas Hunt, Esq.

Physicians.

Francis Hawkins, M. D. Thomas Watson, M. D.
John Wilson, M. D. Hugh Ley, M. D.

Surgeons.

Sir Charles Bell. Herbert Mayo, Esq.
J. M. Arnott, Esq.

Chaplain. W. B. Champneys.

House Surgeon. Mr. Edward Lonsdale.

Apothecary at the Hospital. Mr. G. Corfe.

Matron. Mrs. Martin.

Secretary and House Steward.
Mr. Alexander Shedden.

Collector.

Mr. H. O. Knight, 13, Grove End Road, St. John's Wood.

Subscriptions and Donations are received by the Treasurers; at the following Bankers : Messrs. Coutts & Co. *Strand;* Drummond & Co. *Charing Cross;* Hoare & Co. *Fleet Street;* Hammersley, *Pall-Mall;* Ransom & Co. *Pall-Mall East;* Marten & Co. *Old Bond Street;* Herries, Farquhar & Co. *St. James's Street;* Sir Claude Scott & Co. *Cavendish Square;* by the Collector; and by the Secretary, at the Hospital.

It is a singular fact, that, formerly, our pupils went to Paris, to study Surgery, but such has been the improvement of the art in modern times, that Europe now looks up to our Surgeons, as on the summit of the profession.

It will be curious to compare the state of Surgery at the present time, with that of the time of Henry VIII. at which period, as *Gale* tells us,

there were very few worthy to be called Surgeons.
His account of those employed in the army is very
humourous. " I remember," says, he, " when I
was in the wars at Muttril (Montreuil) in the time
of that most famous prince King Henry VIII.
there was a great rabblement, that took on them
to be Surgeons; some were cow-doctors, and some
horse-doctors, with tinkers and cobblers. This
noble sect did such great cures, that they got
themselves a perpetual name; for, like as Thessa-
lus's sect were called Thessalians, so was this
noble rabblement, for their notorious cures, called
dog-leaches; for in two dressings they did commonly make their cures whole and sound for ever;
so that they neither felt heat nor cold, nor no
manner of pain after. But when the Duke of
Norfolk, who was then general, understood how
the people did die, and that of small wounds, he
sent for me, and certain other Surgeons, commanding us to make search, how these men came
to their death; whether it were by the grievousness
of their wounds, or by the lack of knowledge of
the Surgeons; and we, according to our command-
ment, made search through all the camp; and
found many of the same good fellows, which took
upon them the names of Surgeons; not only the
names, but the wages also. We asking of them
whether they were Surgeons or no, they said they
were; we demanded with whom they were brought
up, and they, with shameless faces, would answer,
either with one cunning man, or another, which
was dead. Then we demanded of them what chi-
rurgery stuff they had to cure men withal; and
they would shew us a pot, or a box, which they
had in a budget: wherein was such trumpery as
they did use to grease horses' heels withal, and laid
upon scabbed horses' backs, with rewal and such like.
And others, that were cobblers and tinkers, they
used shoe-maker's wax, with the rust of old pans,

and made therewithal a noble salve, as they did term it. But, in the end, this worthy rabblement was committed to the Marshalsea, and threatened, by the Duke's grace, to be hanged for their worthy deeds, except they would declare the truth what they were and of what occupations; and in the end they did confess as I have declared to you before."—*Aikin's Memoirs of Medicine*, p. 99.

The boundary line of the Parish of St. Mary-le-bone, commences at the east end of Oxford Street, including the whole of the buildings east of Bozier's Court, and continuing in a north-western direction, through the houses into Hanway Yard, crossing the road and passing between Nos. 14 and 15, to the corner of Gresse Street, where it enters Rathbone Place, and includes the remainder of the west side of Rathbone Place, part of Percy Street, and the west side of Upper Rathbone Place; it passes here through the houses, crossing the road at the junction of Charles Street and Goodge Street, and again passes through the houses by the Three Tuns Wine Vaults, four houses on the north side of Charles Street being in the Parish, and includes the whole of Norfolk Street, and the houses at the north and south-west corners of Tottenham Street; and, continuing through the houses, passes through the centre of a house occupied by a Turner, which projects from the south-west corner of the wall inclosing Covent Garden Workhouse; it then passes along the centre of the road in Cleveland Street to the New Road: some alteration was made in the boundary line at this point upon the erection of Trinity Church, an arrangement having been made for that purpose with the adjoining Parish of St. Pancrass, a Clause being introduced in the Act of Parliament 7° 8° Geo. IV. cap. 89, to legalize the transaction. The boundary line, there-

fore, passes from the centre of the New Road opposite Cleveland Street, a short distance westward,
and thence northward, up Osnaburgh Street, including the whole of the site of Trinity Church,
and thence passes through the houses in Albany
Street, entering the Regent's Park at St. Andrew's
Place, crossing the road a few yards south of the
Colosseum.   Hence it passes, in a north western
direction, through the Park and the Zoological
Gardens, continuing across the Primrose Hill Road,
and includes the south-west corner of Primrose
Hill Field, and the whole of Barrow Hill, on which
is situated the reservoir of the West Middlesex
Water works Company: it then crosses the fields
in a zig-zag direction, and the new North Road
about 250 yards above the Eyre Arms Tavern,
and finally proceeds, the boundary stones of St.
Mary-le-bone and St. John's Hampstead, being
placed side by side, till it arrives at a field called
the *Six Acres* or *Hill Field*, a short distance east
of Kilburn Wells.   The boundary line in this field
takes a sweep, forming a complete semicircle, and
finally comes out into the Edgware Road, passing
through a house adjacent to a villa called Kilburn
Priory.   The authorities both of St. John's and St.
Mary-le-bone appear to have been very particular
in defining the boundaries of their respective parishes on this spot, there being no less than six
different stones to mark the line in a space of 100
yards in the above-mentioned field.   The boundary
of St. Mary-le-bone then passes southwards, including the whole of the east side of the Edgware
Road, to Hyde Park Place, at the west end of
Oxford Street: it then passes eastward, including
the whole of the north side of Oxford Street.   There
is a stone placed in the front wall of a house occupied by a tallow-chandler, at the corner of Bozier's
Court, at the east end of Oxford Street, on which
is inscribed *Oxford Street*, 1725, *L. S. M.*

Newman Street and Berners Street were built between the years 1750 and 1770: the former is narrow and curved, and remarkable for the residence of artists, of whom Russell and West in oil and crayon painting, and Bacon senior and junior in sculpture, will be long remembered by their works. The latter will also be remembered for the extensive failure of the Banking house of Fauntleroy & Co. and the delinquency of the managing partner.

Between 1790 and 1793 Clipstone Street, Norton Street, Upper Titchfield Street, &c. were built; but the breaking out of the war in that year, led to a long delay in the completion of the neighbourhood.

The buildings on the east side of Cleveland Street, are of recent erection; the west side of Fitzroy Square having been left a dreary and dangerous chasm, for more than fifteen years. The following dreadful accident happened here on the night of Wednesday, Nov. 27, 1799: the Earl of Scarborough, accompanied by his sister, Lady Louisa Hartley, passing in his Lordship's carriage, the coachman unfortunately drove off the road into the area, which had been dug preparatory to building the houses on that side of the Square. A gentleman named Shield happening to pass near the spot, and hearing violent groans, procured a light, and discovered the accident which had taken place. Proper assistance was immediately procured, and Lord Scarborough and his sister, who had fainted, but most providentially had received no serious injury, were removed to the house of a French surgeon in the neighbourhood, together with the coachman, who had his ribs broken, and the footman, whose leg was shattered in such a dreadful manner, that immediate amputation was found necessary. Lord Scarborough very humanely ordered the best assistance to be procured; and Mr. Heavisides the Surgeon being called in, and concurring with the French Surgeon, the operation was immediately performed. His Lordship and his sister were removed in a hackney-coach to the house of Mr. Hartley in Gower Street. The escape of this nobleman was considered most miraculous, the height of the fall being from 10 to 12 feet. The footman died of the injury he had received, and was buried on the 22d of December.

Great Mary-le-bone Street, New Cavendish Street, and Upper Mary-le-bone Street, form the next longest avenue east and west. In the first of these streets resided a very worthy character known by the familiar cognomen of Dr, Spence, who, in his early days, was the surgeon of the village, he being the only practitioner residing in it. This gentleman, at one time, possessed considerable property, and was highly respected; but becoming a disciple of Emanuel Swedenborg, he lost a considerable sum by publishing his works, and the death of a favourite daughter producing an aberration of intellect, he became reduced, and finally died, at an advanced age, in an obscure lodging in Westmoreland Street, in the receipt of a parochial allowance of 7s. per week. In Upper Mary-le-bone Street, resided another worthy but eccentric character, Mr. Custance, who died in 1799.*

The Edgware Road is skirted with houses, some of ancient date; those of the latter description are occupied by shop-keepers: the Corsican General Paoli resided in a house at the south end of Edgware Road, since occupied by Mr. Mortlock. Hence for three quarters of a mile northward is named Edgware Road, whence the rows of houses are successively named Caroline Place, Portman Place, Lyon Terrace, Windsor Terrace, Northwick Terrace, containing a cluster of detached houses, of a most splendid style of architecture; Clarendon Place, consisting of handsome detached villas, here are also

---

* See notice of Mr. Custance under the head of Biog.

several extensive nursery grounds; Pine Apple Place; and, with the exception of two small fields, which are advertised to be let on building leases, the east side of the Edgware Road is skirted with houses all the way to Kilburn; Abercorn Place, and Kilburn Priory being the last houses, at this extremity of the Parish.

The most important avenues running from west to east, are: Upper Seymour Street, &c. described p. 205; Upper Berkeley Street, including the north side of Portman Square, and Lower Berkeley Street, terminating in Manchester Square. The principal residents, in Upper Berkeley Street, are:—Sir Archibald Murray, Bart.; Colonel Caldwell; Hon. Admiral Sir Courtenay Boyle, Bart.; Captain E. Margoty, R. N.; Capt. T. M'Taggart; Lieutenant-Col. Colston; Col. Elwood; Lady Hammond, &c.

In Lower Berkeley Street, reside Col. Lindsay; Sir W. Dalling, Bart.; John Pepys, Esq.; General Corner; Miss Vaughan, &c.

Upper George Street, and George Street Portman Square, are celebrated for having been the residence of many of the emigrant Nobility of France. M. Otto, the French Ambassador, resided here a short time, while a house was preparing for his residence in Portman Square. The Duke de Berri, and the Archbishop of Sens, also resided in this street; and T. R. G. Rourke, *the Danish Minister*, at present resides here.

In Upper George Street, is situated an extensive building occupied by Messrs. Harwood & Co. as a Decorative Paper Hanging Manufactory. This building was originally erected for a Coach Manufactory, with ample room for carrying on every branch of that trade, but the proprietor becoming bankrupt, the premises were taken by Messrs. Harwood, who removed their business from Chelsea. The above streets form one avenue from the Edgware Road, terminating in Charles Street, leading to Thayer Street, which is a modern elongation of High Street to the southward.

Nutford Place, formerly King Street: in this street was situated the Royal Western Hospital, and, since the failure of that Establishment, the same building has been used as a Cholera Hospital, during the prevalence of that epidemic.

Queen Street: in this street resided Mr. William Taplin, Veterinary Surgeon. This gentleman was author of " The Gentleman's Stable Directory," and various other publications. Mr. Taplin's lively effusions, liberal opinions, and acute judgment, as a writer and veterinary surgeon, will be long remembered by the sporting world. Many of his lesser productions are to be found in the Sporting Magazine; particularly some delightful descriptions of the Royal Chace in Windsor Forest, written in the genuine spirit and language of a true sportsman. About the year 1804, from family affliction, his faculties became impaired; and, from that period, his health had been declining till his death, which took place Jan. 1, 1807.

The celebrated Cato Street passes from Queen Street northward to John Street; it consists of a number of small houses, occupied, chiefly, by the lowest class of Irish, and has frequently been the scene of disgraceful riot and confusion; the military having been repeatedly put into requisition to quell disturbances in this street. Its name has recently been altered to Horace Street. Molyneux and Shouldham Streets named after Adm. Lord Shouldham, also branch northward from Queen Street.

The mass of buildings and streets, from the Edgware Road to Lisson Grove eastward, and to St. John's Wood Road northward, are occupied by the working classes: houses of cheap rent appear to have been the object of the builders; and the principle of speculation has been, to take large tracts of ground by the acre, and to crowd as many

L

streets and alleys into them as possible, in order to create so many feet lineal, to underlet for building; and the fruit of the speculation is the sale of the increased ground rents. In Lisson Grove North, reside Lady Jane Lyon, Charles Rossi, Esq. an eminent Sculptor, &c.

New Church Street West, Church Street and Alpha Road, form one avenue, terminating at the east end in Park Road, Regent's Park. In Church Street is situated

PORTMAN MARKET,

opened as a Haymarket in December, 1830, and for a Vegetable Market and for general purposes in the year following. This market occupies a square piece of ground of about three acres; the shops and buildings are replete with every convenience, and reflect the highest credit on the taste and liberality of the proprietor; the Market Days are Mondays, Wednesdays, and Fridays, and this Market presents far greater convenience than any other Market in London, the produce being all under cover; there is accommodation for more than 100 loads of hay, and for carts and waggons, all sheltered from the weather, with stabling, storehouses, and separate abattoirs for slaughtering Beasts, Sheep and Pigs; and pens for the sale of live stock. Not less than 60,000*l.* must have been sunk in the erection of this Market, which daily improves, and bids fair to become a formidable rival to Covent Garden.

At Aberdeen Place, Maida Hill, the Regent's Canal enters this Parish, passing under the Edgware Road.

REGENT'S CANAL.

The cutting of the Regent's Canal was carried into effect under and by virtue of an Act of Parliament of the 52d Geo. III. cap. 195, intituled " An Act for making and maintaining a navigable Canal in the Parish of Paddington to the River Thames, in the Parish of Limehouse, with a collateral cut in the Parish of St. Leonard, Shoreditch, in the County of Middlesex;" which Act has been explained and amended by several subsequent Statutes.

It commences at Paddington, on the east side of the enlarged part near the first bridge on the Harrow Road, and, proceeding in a north-easterly direction, passes under the Edgware Road, by a tunnel 372 yards long, which continues under the estates of the Governors of Harrow School, and E. B. Portman, Esq. till it enters the property of H. S. Eyre, Esq. where the Canal is partly open, and partly covered; from Mr. Eyre's estate it enters the Regent's Park, and continues its course round the Park to a basin near the Jews' Harp, which is surrounded by warehouses and wharfs. The Canal branches off from the Regent's Park a short distance east of the boundary of this Parish, through the estates of G. Earle, Esq. Lord Southampton, &c. passing through Camden Town, and, crossing the Hampstead and Kentish Town Roads, and Maiden Lane to Islington, supplies a large basin called Horsfall's Basin, in its way to White Conduit Fields. Here it passes through another tunnel 970 yards in length, under the town of Islington and the New River, and emerges into the field adjoining the City Gardens. At this place the water is received into a basin 1600 feet long by 110 feet wide, which, with its wharfs, covers an area of 25 acres. After supplying this basin with water, the canal continues its course over the fields towards the Rosemary Branch; after which, it crosses the Kingsland and Hackney Roads, and passes onward by Stepney Fields, till it falls into the Thames at Limehouse. The length of the Canal is 8 miles 6 furlongs; it has a descent of about 84 feet from its commencement to its termination. There are 12 locks necessary for the purposes of navigation, and it has 40 bridges thrown over it in various places.

The Regent's Canal, which was begun in 1812, was opened Aug. 1, 1820, with an aquatic procession of boats, barges, &c. ornamented with flags and streamers, and filled with ladies and gentlemen, interested in the success of the undertaking.*

St. John's Wood Road is the next important avenue passing eastward from the Edgware Road, terminating at St. John's Wood Chapel: here is situated the New Cricket Ground, and St. John's Wood Tavern, established in 1814: here also is a handsome building occupied by

THE CLERGY ORPHAN SCHOOLS.

The Schools of the incorporated Clergy Orphan Society, at St. John's Wood, have no connection with the Parish, though it has been found convenient to erect them here: but some account of the Institution may well demand a place in this work.

In the year 1749, some benevolent individuals, lamenting the state of destitution in which the families, and especially the younger children, of Clergymen, are frequently left ; and, anxious to rescue them from the evils of poverty, and a neglected education, formed themselves into a Society for the purpose of clothing, maintaining, and educating poor Orphans of Clergymen, until of age to be put apprentice. Their Schools were, at first, established, one at Acton, for the boys, and the

* The plan of bringing a Navigable Canal to London on the same line as the Grand Junction Canal, appears to have been contemplated more than 70 years since. It was then considered of such importance, that the Committee for Canal Navigation for the City of London, in 1773, ordered a Survey to be made of a line from Mary-le-bone to Moorfields, to form a junction with another line proposed to be brought from Waltham Abbey : the Survey was made by Robert Whitworth, and, in the Report which was published on the 5th of October, all the advantages arising from a Canal similar to the Regent's Canal, were ingeniously described and duly appreciated.

other at Lisson Green, for the girls ; and were continued there, on a moderate scale, till 1812, when the present building was erected by subscription ; in which the two schools have been brought together for the purpose of being more effectually superintended by the General Committee of Management, and by the Ladies' Committee ; though they are still, as they were originally, in all respects, distinct and separate. But, though this Institution is situated in the vicinity of London, it is not, either in design or character, a local charity. It has been fixed in the neighbourhood of the metropolis, because no other situation appeared so advantageous for an establishment for poor Orphans of the Clergy of the Church of England. And, that it is not confined or partial, in the selection of those whom it receives under its care and protection, appears from this fact, that, of the orphans now in the Schools, six only belong to London, while one hundred and twenty-four come from other parts of the kingdom.

The Boys are maintained, clothed and educated in the school till they are fourteen ; and the Girls till they are sixteen years of age. Elections of children into the Schools take place twice in the year ; at the Annual General Court, in February, and at a Quarterly General Court, in May. The Institution is under the patronage of their Majesties, is supported by all the Prelates of the Church, by a large number of the Clergy, and by many of the most distinguished individuals among the Laity. The Venerable Archdeacon Cambridge, and Rev. Dr. Shepherd are the Treasurers, and the Rev. John Moore, M. A. is the Secretary.

From St. John's Wood Road northwards the prevailing character of the buildings is that of detached villa residences, situated in large gardens, erected in every variety of architectural elegance, and occupied by persons of the first respectability. A number of artists reside in this neighbourhood, among whom may be mentioned: Thomas Landseer; R. J. Lane; G. Sintzenich; and Edwin Landseer, R. A. Ugo Foscolo, the celebrated Italian Poet, resided in one of these villas.

Portland Town is liable to the same objections as many of the before-mentioned streets, being composed of houses of the meanest description, and inhabited by persons in the humblest class of life: it is said, that there was some unaccountable oversight in the arrangements made for letting out this land on building leases; and that the Duke of Portland was exceedingly angry when he discovered the character of the buildings erected on this property.

The Park Road, Regent's Park, extends from the north end of Pleasant Row in the New Road, along the south western boundary of the Park, to St. John's Wood Chapel; is on the Crown Estate, and was granted, on the application of the Vestrymen of the Parish, " to be used as a Carriage Road for the conveyance of Corpses to the New Burial Ground:" the road is skirted with houses on the east side, and many respectable shops. In this road is a new range of handsome buildings, called Kent Terrace, in memory of a deceased member of the Royal Family.

Cumberland Place.

This Crescent, which was originally intended for a circus, was built about 1774-5, the houses are well built, and uniform; Great Cumberland Street, Cumberland Place, and Cumberland Street, Portman Square, complete the avenue from Cum-

berland Gate Hyde Park, to Bryanston Square;
among the present residents appear the names of
the following distinguished persons;—*Great Cum-
berland Street:* Lord Saltoun; Mrs. Portman; John
Wells, Esq.; Colonel Sherwood; Captain Richard
Manby; John Lodge, Esq.; Major Murray; Robert
Cutlar Fergusson, Esq.; John N. M'Leod, Esq.;
and Lord Bagot. *Great Cumberland Place :* Hans
Busk, Esq.; Sir Clifford Constable; Sir Frederick
Hamilton; Lady C. Underwood; Sir G. Ivison
Tapps; Baron Bulow *(the Prussian Minister) ;*
General Sir R. M'Farlane; Leonard Currie, Esq.;
Sir S. B. Fludyer, Bart.; Lady Trollope; Earl of
Leitrim; Sir Alexander Johnston; and the Hon. and
Right Rev. the Lord Bishop of Norwich.   *Cum-
berland Street, Portman Square:* Rev. Arthur
Pearson; Hon. Captain Curzon, R. N.; Captain
Beaufort, R. N.; Henry Hoare, Esq.; Lady E.
Tufton; William Blount, Esq.; George Buck, Esq.;
Major Robinson; Lieutenant-Colonel Lluellyn;
General D. Douglas Wemyss, &c.

The next important avenue running from south
to north is Portman Street, including the west
side of Portman Square, Gloucester Street, Gloucester Place, Upper Gloucester Street, the east
side of Dorset Square, Dorset Place, and Upper
Gloucester Place, Regent's Park.   In Portman
Street, is situated the Barracks for the Foot Guards;
here also resided for a short time, in the house of
Lady Ann Hamilton, Her late Majesty Queen
Caroline, Consort of George IV. upon her return
from the Continent, in 1821.   In Gloucester Place
resided the American General Arnold, who died
June 14, 1801 : the Veteran Lord Cathcart, resided
here for several years; and the notorious Mrs. Mary
Ann Clarke, also resided here at the period of her
rupture with His late Royal Highness the Duke
of York.   The houses are uniform, and occupied
by persons of distinction, among whom are the

Lieut.-General R. Hopkins; Rev. Robert Walpole, B. D. *Rector of Christchurch;* Vice-Admiral Fellowes; Major-General Orr; Montagu Burgoyne, Esq.; Count de Ludolf, *Sicilian Minister;* the Bishop of Carlisle, &c.

In King Street is situated the Bazaar, for the sale of Horses and Carriages, by Commission and by Auction; for Saddlery, Harness, Furniture and Miscellaneous Articles; lately in the occupation of Mr. Maberly, but now in the possession of Mr. M. C. Allen. The premises contain stabling for nearly 400 Horses, a capacious Riding School, Standing for 500 Carriages, a Ladies' Bazaar, for the Sale of Miscellaneous Articles, the entrance to which is in Baker Street; a Suite of Rooms for the Sale of Furniture; and a splendid Saloon for the reception and display of Works of Art. These extensive premises, which extend over upwards of two acres of ground, were erected for the stables and barracks of the 2d Regiment of Life Guards; but the Government having given them up on the erection of the Regent's Park Barracks, the Bazaar was established, and has been a very successful speculation, having become a fashionable place of resort, for the Nobility and Gentry of the neighbourhood.

Orchard Street, Baker Street, York Place, and Upper Baker Street, including the east side of Portman Square, is a continued line of building, and seems to increase equally in length and splendour, commencing in Oxford Street, and terminating at the Park Road, opposite Clarence Gate. York Place is remarkably beautiful; many of the inhabitants consist of titled persons, and those of the most ancient families; John Farquhar, Esq. of Fonthill Abbey, died in York Place; and that celebrated tragic actress, Mrs. Siddons, breathed her last at her residence in Upper Baker Street. Among the persons of distinction at present residing in *Baker Street*, will

be found: Captain I. W. D. Dundas, R. N.; Gen.
Sir J. Hamilton, Bart.; Sir Bentinck Doyle;
Major-General Mawby; Lady Hawley; Earl of
Huntingdon. In *York Place* reside, Henry Charles
Hoare, Esq.; Hon. Edward and Lady Katherine
Stewart; Sir W. Russell, Bart. M. D.; Major Li-
vingston; Hon. Mrs. Ferguson; Colonel Dacre;
Lady Nightingall; Henry Merrick Hoare, Esq.;
A. J. Mackenzie, Esq.; J. J. Holford, Esq.; Miss
Sainsbury, &c.

Paddington Street was built about 1772, and
continued by Durweston Street, which street has
since been altered to Crawford Street, and form
one long avenue east to west from High Street,
interspersed with many elegant shops. Paddington
Street is celebrated for having been the residence
of Brothers, the pretended Prophet. Devonshire
Street, Weymouth Street, and Queen Anne Street
West, are superior in their buildings, and are
occupied principally by the Nobility and Gentry.

Nottingham Place consists of handsome houses
occupied by persons of the first respectability,
among whom are;—John Turner, Esq.; Mrs. and
Miss Deare; W. Kinnaird Jackson, Esq.; Colonel
Leake; Admiral Sir Edward Hamilton, &c.

STRATFORD PLACE,

which for uniformity and neatness, may be classed
among the principal ornaments of the Parish,
was built about 1774: it consists of two uniform
rows of houses, leading into a small area, or square,
the upper, or north side of which is formed by an
elegant edifice (Aldborough house),* with a stone

---

* Edward Stratford, Earl of Aldborough, Viscount Amiens,
Baron of Baltinglass, Governor of the County of Wicklow, and
F. R. S.   He married, first, Barbara, daughter of the Honourable
Nicholas Herbert, of Great Glenham, Suffolk. Having taken the
lease of the ground, called Conduit Mead, of the city of London,
he planned and built part of Stratford-Place, and Aldborough-

front, which is composed of a rustic basement story, supporting a range of columns of the Ionic order, crowned with an entablature, decorated with ox-sculls, from the horns of which hang neat festoons of flowers and foliage. Above this entablature rises a triangular pediment, from the sides of which a balustrade, ornamented with elegant vases, is continued along the top of the building. From each side of this building, a Doric colonnade, crowned with a balustrade, and ornamented with vases, extends to the east and west sides of the area, the fronts of the houses in which are stuccoed, and the windows of the principal story ornamented with a triangular and a circular pediment, alternately. The sides of the street leading into the area, are exactly similar. All the houses are of brick; but those in the centre, and at the ends, are ornamented with stone, in a style corresponding with the principal building in the area. On each side of the entrance is a small house for a watchman, on the top of which is the figure of a lion carved in stone.

The late Lieut.-General Strode, at whose expense the equestrian statue of William Duke of Cumberland was put up in Cavendish-square, in 1770, also erected, in 1799, in the centre of the circular part of this place, a handsome Corinthian pillar and pedestal, upwards of twenty feet in height,

House, where they resided. At her death, in 1787, he let it on lease, and, marrying, secondly, May 24, 1788, Ann Elizabeth, daughter of Sir John Henniker, of Newton-Hall, near Dunmow, and Stratford-House, West Ham, both in the county of Essex, with a dowry of £50,000. he built a new mansion for himself adjoining Aldborough-House, for their town residence, and finished Stratford-Place according to his original plan. His Lordship died January 2, 1801, of a stroke of the palsy, at his mansion of Belan, in the county of Wicklow, and was buried in a vault in St. Thomas's Church in Dublin, the 7th of the same month. Aldborough-House has been occupied, at various periods, by His Grace the Duke of St. Albans, His Highness, Prince Esterhazy, and other persons of distinction. Their Imperial Highnesses the Arch-Dukes John and Lewis of Austria, also resided at this house during their visit to this country.

commemorative of the naval victories of Great Britain; this pillar supported a statue of His Majesty George III. with trophies, &c. and the following inscriptions:—

On the Front Square.

" Sacred to British Glory and the Heroes
of its Empire;
who, aided by the Almighty,
have carried their victorious arms
throughout every region
of the earth;
liberating mankind
from the Atheistical principles,
unjust usurpations,
and tyrannical subjugation
of rapacious France,
restoring due subordination, felicity, and
civilization throughout
Europe."

On the right-hand Square.

" In this memorable year,
on the 4th of May, 1799,
Seringapatam was taken by storm,
and the perfidious Tippoo Saib
slain in his capital,
by the English forces under General Harris;
the territory of Mysore,
and Port of Mangalore,
annexed to the Eastern dominions
of Great Britain;
and quiet and security restored
to that quarter of the
Globe."

On the left-hand Square.

" In memory of
the atchievements of Admirals
Lords Hawke, Rodney, Howe, Hood,
Bridport, St. Vincent, Nelson, Duncan,
Sir John Borlase Warren,
Sir Sidney Smith, and Mitchell,
who, in different actions with the
Spanish, French, and Dutch,
took the Admirals of each nation:

captured, sunk, and destroyed,
above one thousand of their ships,
annihilating their Fleets and commerce,
and ascertained and maintained,
under the Divine Providence,
the Empire of Great Britain over the
Globe."

On the Back Square.

" Stet columna,
in secula stet,
magis floreant res Britannicæ ;
sic sperat precat
Edw. Aug. Stratford,
Comes de Aldborough, de Ormond Super,
Vicecomes Amiens,
Baro de Baltinglass, &c. &c. &c.
Qui,
regnante Georgio Tertio,
sub auspiciis Dei Omnipotentis,
annoque Salutis, 1799,
posuit."

The foundation of this pillar having given way,
the whole was taken down about the year 1805.

Stratford Place comprises twenty-one houses;
the present residents are, Sir Giffin Wilson ; Dow-
ager Lady Ellenborough ; G. W. Tapps, Esq.; Sir
Robert Smirke ; Edward Drummond, Esq. ; Lieut.-
Colonel Marton ; George Hayter, Esq. ; Hon. Col.
J. W. Stratford; Right Hon. Sir J. and Lady Anne
Beckett; Sir Thomas Phillips, Bart. ; Lewis De-
sanges ; Lieut.-General Sir W. H. Pringle ; Mrs.
Joseph Cotton ; Earl of Wemyss and March ;
Thomas Emmerson, Esq. ; Thomas John Burgoyne,
Esq.

The Estate of John Thomas Hope, Esq.

This estate, which was formerly called Conduit
Field, came into the possession of the present
proprietor, by his marriage with the daughter
and heiress of Sir Thomas Edwardes, Bart. and
comprises 20 acres of land, on which are erected
part of Oxford Street, Somerset Street, Edwards

Street, Duke Street, and that densely populated mass of buildings known by the names of Gee's Court, Barrett's Court, &c. It had been originally intended to have formed one long avenue from Henrietta Street to Somerset Street, and to have erected a line of handsome and uniform houses, but the building of Stratford Place by the Earl of Aldborough, preventing this design being carried into effect, did considerable injury to this property ; the Builders of that period refusing to speculate in erecting large houses on this spot ; hence arise the above narrow courts and mean buildings. It appears that the City of London, in defining the boundary of their land, in the early part of the last century, made an encroachment upon this property, which the unaccountable apathy of the then proprietor suffered to take place without resistance, and a small portion of this land was therefore lost to the family. The Earl of Aldborough, likewise forgetting to respect the rights of property, in his anxiety to render Stratford Place the most magnificent pile of buildings of that period, made a still further encroachment on this estate, by erecting the buildings on the west side of Stratford Place, over the brook which formed the boundary line between the two estates ; but for which a compensation has recently been made.

The present respected proprietor, actuated by the most liberal and praiseworthy motives, has offered to resign to the Vestry, certain buildings, which project in Oxford Street, to be taken down, for the purpose of advancing the improvement of the neighbourhood, and promoting the convenience of the public, by widening the foot pavement. The Vestry have not yet, however, thought proper to avail themselves of this liberal and spirited offer, but the tenants of these buildings hold possession, with an understanding to quit whenever the Vestry may require them.

WELBECK STREET.

Is a handsome well-built street, named after the Duke of Portland's seat at Welbeck. It will long be famous in the annals of London, for having been the residence of Lord George Gordon, who figured so conspicuously in the Riots of 1780. A very different character also resided in this street, dying in 1769, viz. Edmund Hoyle, Esq. to whom the gaming portion of the community are under the deepest obligations for his treatises on the Game of Whist, &c. Here, also, resided, for a short time before his death, that celebrated and eccentric character John Elwes, Esq. He removed to his seat at Marcham in Berkshire, in the year 1789, where he expired on the 26th of November, after an illness of eight days. This street, which was one of the earliest built after Cavendish Square, appears to have been the most fashionable street of that time. The following are the principal residents of the present day;—General Sir Charles Doyle; Jesse Cole, Esq. *Solicitor;* Captain Whish, R. N.; John Harrison, Esq. *Architect;* Sir David Barry, M. D.; Rev. James Smirnove; Captain Griffiths; Sir Peter Pole, Bart.; Mrs. Colonel Scott; Major-General Clitherow; Count Mortara; Lady Nisbet; Lieutenant-Colonel Chaplin; Dow. Lady Knatchbull; Hon. Mrs. Stopford; Colonel Nugent; and John Hill, Esq. *Solicitor.* Here is also situated the

St. Mary-le-bone General Dispensary.

Instituted 1785, for administering advice and Medicines for the relief of the Sick and Lame Poor and Pregnant Women of the Parishes of St. George, Hanover Square; St. Mary-le-Bone; St. Anne, Soho; St. Martin; St. Pancras; St. Giles; St. George, Bloomsbury : St. James ; Paddington, and places adjacent; at the Dispensary, or at their own Habitations.

The object of this Institution is to administer Advice and Medicine to the Sick Poor of all Classes.

To Females its benefits must appear the most forcible; the industrious Wife being attended with the utmost care at the time of her greatest distress.

The treatment of the Diseases of Children is specially attended to; and Vaccination is performed without any letter of recommendation.

The better to afford efficacy to Medicine, as the Poor are often in want of suitable food, they are supplied, at the discretion of the Medical Officers, with wine, rice, sago, barley, tapioca, &c. in all cases that particularly require such assistance.

The great number of Patients that have been, and continue to be daily relieved by this Charity, and the great encouragement it has long experienced by the voluntary Subscriptions of the Nobility, Gentry, and others, afford the most convincing proof of its utility; which it is hoped may be extended by additional benefactions.

Patron.

His Most Gracious Majesty.

President.

His Grace the Duke of Portland.

Treasurers.

Joseph Hobbs, Esq.   Edward Young, Esq.

Physicians.

James Bartlet, M. D.   George Sigmond, M. D.

Physician-Accoucheur.

Henry Davies, M. D.

Surgeons.

Titus Berry, Esq.   F. B. Samwell, Esq.

Apothecary.

Mr. G. Grice, at the Dispensary.

Secretary.

Mr. Thomas P. Lowe, 110, High Street.

Wimpole Street, is a beautiful uniform street, terminating in Devonshire Place, which is 72 feet wide; and skirted with splendid mansions. In Devonshire Place resided the Rev. W. Holwell Carr, B. D. who died Jan. 24, 1830. This gentleman was a distinguished patron of the Fine Arts, and bequeathed his valuable collection of Pictures to the National Gallery. The principal residents in Devonshire Place, are:—Col. Hanmer; Lieut. Col. J. Baillie; Hon. M. Fortescue; Dr. H. Young; Sir Thomas Baring, Bart.; Rev. Stowel Chudleigh; Lieut. Gen. Sir W. Anson; Lady Stanley; Major-Gen. Sir T. Reynell, and Lady Elizabeth; Wastel Brisco, Esq. &c.

In Wimpole Street, formerly resided Her Grace the late Duchess of Wellington, during the Peninsular War; the late Sir Thomas Bernard also resided here. The principal present residents are:—Sir C. Scudamore, M.D.; Lady B. Bouverie; Col. Sir T. H. Doyle; Lord Bridport; Lord Edward Somerset; Lady Durrant; Capt. W. Patterson, R.N.; Rear Admiral Sir J. T. Rodd; J. Rawlinson, Esq.; Col. Higginson: Admiral Sir T. Byam Martin; Right Hon. Sir C. Robinson; Lady Rowley; Right Hon. Sir H. Russell, Bart.; Hon. Lady Murray; Sir W. Brisco, Bart.; Rev. G. A. Thursby; Lieut.-Gen. Hodgson, &c.

In Upper Wimpole Street, reside Lady Fras. Fitzwilliam; Godfrey Meynell, Esq.; I. W. Freshfield, Esq.; Capt. Johnstone; Sir W. Young, Bart.; G. Arbuthnot, Esq.; Rev. Richard Bouchier, Esq.

Harley Street. In this street, resided the late Rt. Hon. Frances, Dowager Viscountess Nelson, Duchess of Brontè, relict of the Hero of the Nile and Trafalgar. Her ladyship was the widow of Josiah Nisbet, M. D. when his present Majesty performed the ceremony of giving her away in marriage to Lord Nelson, at the Island of Nevis, in the year 1787. Her maiden name was Woodward, and she

was niece to William Herbert, Esq. President of
the Island : her Ladyship died, May 4, 1831. The
principal residents in this street, are: Lady Mary
Petre; Dr. H. Southey; Hon. Capt. Waldegrave;
Sir W. Beechey, R. A.; Sir G. A. Lewin; Rev.
H. Latham; Capt. Bullock; Gen. Bradshaw; Rt.
Hon. Sir L. Shadwell; Hon. Mrs. Fitzroy; Lord
Redesdale; Sir C. Des Vœux, Bt.; the Duke of
Dorset; Gen. Sir J. Champagne; Gen. Sir G.
Walker; Dow. Lady Rodney; Viscount Strang-
ford; Lady Hunter; Lady Farquhar; Adm. Don-
nelly; Sir Robt. Buxton, Bt.; Adm. Sir Henry
Digby; Visctss. Andover; Rt. Hon. J. Sullivan,
&c.

Upper Harley Street. Died at his house in this
street, June 21, 1800, in consequence of a melancholy accident, which he met with on the preceding
night, William Bosanquet, Esq. He had been
making some alterations in his house, and, among
others, had removed the balcony from his back
drawing room window: unfortunately forgetting
this circumstance he walked out, and immediately
fell into the area, and, in his fall, broke the vertebræ
of his back, and was otherwise severely bruised
and injured. He was sensible of his inevitable
dissolution, and bore his sufferings with a fortitude
almost unparalleled; dictating, in the extremity of
torture, some additions to his will. He left a most
amiable lady, and ten children, to deplore his loss.
Mr. Bosanquet was son of the respected Bank
Director of that name; and brother of Jacob Bosanquet, Esq. of Broxbourn, formerly Chairman of
the East-India Company; and he was a partner in
the Banking-house of Foster and Lubbock. Another lamentable occurrence also took place in this
street, on the 27th of April, 1831 : at two o'clock in
the morning, the house of Lord Walsingham was
discovered to be on fire. His Lordship was unfortunately burnt to death in his bed chamber; and

Lady Walsingham, in her fright, precipitated herself out of the window of her room, on to some leads at the back of the house, and shortly after expired, from the injuries she had received. The present residents in this street, are :—The Hon. W. F. Elphinstone; Lady Walsh; Hon. Col. Hen. Windsor; Marquis De la Belynaye; Rev. R. S. Dixon; Baron de Cetto, *Bavarian Minister;* Lt. Col. Vans-Agnew; Pascoe St. Leger Grenfell, Esq.; Lady Pole; Adm. Sir Robert Stopford; Col. W. B. Davis; S. Bosanquet, Esq.; Sir Wm. Horne, *Attorney-General, and M. P. for the Borough of Mary-le-bone;* Sir W. Earle Welby, Bt.; Sir H. W. Martin, Bt., &c.

In Chandos Street, resided Prince Esterhazy, the *Austrian Ambassador*, and Baron de Neumann. The magnificent structure called Chandos House was built by the Duke of Chandos; and James, third and last Duke of Chandos, resided at this mansion; the following agonizing catastrophe occurred here, on the occasion of the christening of His Grace's infant daughter, in September, 1778, when their Majesties stood sponsors in person; and when, melancholy to relate, the child was seized with convulsions and died in the nurse's arms, during the ceremony; the glare of light being the presumed cause of its death. After the above dreadful occurrence, the family never held up their heads: the Duke died in 1789, and the Duchess retired from the world, but not from the house, in which she took a melancholy pleasure to reside until removed by death.

In Mansfield-Street reside : H. T. Hope, Esq.; Marquis of Sligo; Lord Petre; Earl of Limerick; W. Camac, Esq.; Rt. Hon. T. Spring Rice, Esq. and Lady Theodosia; Chev. de Cordoba, *Spanish Charge d'Affaires;* Lord Stourton; Sir S. Scott, Bt.; Enoch Durant, Esq. &c.

At the back of Chandos House in Duchess Street

is situated the mansion of the late Thomas Hope, Esq.; which has long been an object of interest to lovers of the Fine Arts, on account of the valuable collection of sculpture, antique vases and pictures, and the splendid and original style of interior decoration with which it was fitted up from the designs of its late proprietor. The house was originally built by M. Adams, and was the property of Gen. Clarke, the husband of the Dowager Countess of Warwick, who was sister to Sir W. Hamilton. The exterior presents plain brick walls only, without dressings or ornament of any kind; the building is rendered fire proof; the floors being raised on groined arches, and the ceilings of all the principal rooms are arched, supporting over them floors of Roman cement. The approach or entrance is through a gateway leading to a square court-yard. At the south end of this court is the dwelling-house, the basement story of which is appropriated to domestic offices, and the first floor is occupied by a series of reception rooms; and a Picture gallery. This floor, extending round three sides of the court, constitutes the principal suite of apartments, comprising, in its rich and varied contents, a most interesting and highly valued series of works of art. The following description of the decoration of the apartments of this house, is taken from *Westmacott's British Galleries*, 8vo. 1824.

Egyptian or Black Room.—The ornaments that adorn the walls of this little Canopus, are taken from Egyptian scrolls of papyrus, and those of the ceiling from various mummy cases; and the prevailing colours, both of the furniture and ornaments, are that pale yellow and bluish green which holds so conspicuous a rank among the Egyptian pigments, skilfully relieved by the occasional introduction of masses of black and gold.

Blue or Indian Room.—The decorations of this apartment are in the most costly style of Oriental splendour ; the curtains, ottomans, &c. are all of rich damask silk.

Star-Room.—The whole surrounding decoration of this apartment is in unison with the classic subject by Flaxman, which forms the centre object of attraction. Aurora visiting Cephalus on Mount Ida ; the design has been rendered in some degree analagous to these personages, and to the face of nature, at the moment when the first of the two, the goddess of the morn, is supposed to announce the break of day. Round the bottom of the room still reign the emblems of night. In the rail of a black marble table are introduced medallions of the God of Sleep and the Goddess of Night. The bird consecrated to the latter deity is seen perched on the pillars of a black marble chimney-piece, whose broad frieze is studded with the emblems of night. Figures of the youthful hours, adorned with wreaths of foliage, form the chief decorations of the furniture, which is mostly gilt, to give relief to the azure, black and orange compartment of the draperies.

The Closet.—The Closet or Boudoir, is fitted up for the reception of a few Egyptian, Hindoo, and Chinese Idols and curiosities. The sides of this Lararium are formed of pillars, and the tops of laths of bamboo ; from which is suspended a cotton drapery, in the manner of a tent. The mantelpiece is designed in imitation of an Egyptian portico, which being placed against a background of looking glass, appears insulated. On the steps of this architectural ornament are placed Idols, and in the niches bas-reliefs.

Picture Gallery.—In this apartment, the centre of the ceiling is supported by small columns, which divide the light, and are imitated from those seen at Athens, in the upper division of the octagon building, vulgarly called the Temple of the Winds.

These columns rest on massy beams, similar to

those in marble, which lie across the peristyle of the Temple of Theseus ; the larger columns, which support the entablature, are profiles of those of the Propylæa. The organ assumes the appearance of a sanctuary. The Ionic columns, entablature and pediment, are copied from the exquisitely beautiful specimen in the Temple of Erechtheus, in the Acropolis of Athens: over the centre of the pediment, is the car of Apollo; the tripods, sacred to the god of music, surmount the angles; the drapery which descends over the pipes in the form of an ancient pepluus or veil, is embroidered with laurel wreaths, and other emblems appropriate to the son of Latona. The massive tables, with recesses for books and portfolios, and the antique pedestals and implements, which adorn the sides of the chamber, have all the classic uniformity of the general decoration.

The splendid and unique Collection of Greek Vases.—These treasures of antiquity are arranged in four separate apartments leading to the Picture Gallery, and may be safely pronounced the most interesting and unique collection in the world. The furniture is decorated with the scenic mask of the Thyrsus, twined round with ivy leaf; the panther's muzzle and claw ; and chimeras in bronze, from models of ideal animals found among the ruins of Pompeia. The vases consist of nearly two hundred specimens, among which, are two beautiful modern copies of the Barbarini or Portland vase.

The New Gallery.—This splendid apartment has been recently added to the extensive galleries of Mr. Hope, and affords additional proof of the distinguished talent and fine taste of this liberal patron of the arts. It is of an oblong form, 48 feet in length, by 22 in breadth, and was erected by Mr. W. Atkinson, from designs and under the direction of Mr. T. Hope, for the reception of one hundred pictures in the Flemish school of painting, and in the superlative class of art.

The apartment may, with great justice, be termed a Jewel Closet; not less from the treasures of art contained therein, than from its splendour of decoration, appropriate elegance, and tasteful arrangement. The centre of the ceiling, which is divided into sunk pannels with gold patres in the centre, rises from a gallery of circular-headed lights, which are continued on the four sides of a quadrangle, with very slight divisions. The under part of the ceiling springs from a cove, and is enriched with gold mouldings, and five sunk pannels at each end of the room; the doors are of polished mahogany, inlaid with classical designs in brass, richly engraved. Opposite the door, is a light blue Ottoman spreading round the end of the room, on the sides of which, are disposed Grecian couch-chairs carved, of the most beautiful designs, and tripod-tables of elegant structure, crowned with rich specimens of variegated marble slabs, under some of which are fine antique bronze casts of the Dying Gladiator, the Wrestlers, and curious antique vases. Down the centre of the room, from end to end, leaving a sufficient passage, is a beautiful screen, executed in mahogany, the lower compartments of which extend on each side, and are adapted for the reception of splendid books of fine art, with which it is well stored. Six elegant chased gold brackets, supporting Grecian lamps, spring from each side, and, ranged along the top, are several beautiful bronze figures, and choice vases, mostly antiques of great value; on each side of the screen, ten of the choicest paintings are arranged, and hung on centres, so that the connoisseur may turn them to obtain a suitable light. As a collection, the pictures contained therein are perfectly unique, every work of the least doubtful character, or second-rate class, being carefully excluded.

This splendid mansion is liberally opened to the Public, under similar restrictions to those adopted

by the Marquis of Stafford, Earl Grosvenor, &c.
Visitors are admitted on the Mondays during the
season of the Nobility being in town, between the
hours of 11 and 3.

REGENT CIRCUS,

and the continuation of Regent Street, from Oxford
Street, built from the Plan of Mr. Nash, which
was adopted in 1814, is composed of houses with
handsome fronts, calculated for broad showy shop
windows, where goods and manufactured articles
are displayed to the greatest advantage, with wide
private doors for entrance to the upper apartments;
such is the prevailing character of the houses extending from Oxford Street to Margaret Street;
and from thence to Mortimer Street, there is much
novelty and picturesque effect displayed in the
otherwise clumsy piers and sepulchral arches of
the entrance story to the houses, their deep recesses afford a solid base for the superstructure
of the elevation; the handsome arched façade to
the row of stables on the west side, is an ingenious
contrivance to conceal an obvious defect, and highly
creditable to the artist; the front of Mr. Marks's
Coach Manufactory on the east side of the street,
would have been admired for a gentleman's mansion
a few years ago, but is now lost among the architectural beauties in its immediate vicinity. Passing
All Souls' Church, the street here takes a handsome sweep round the elegant mansion and grounds
of Sir James Langham, to Langham Place, which
is an elongation of Portland Place, built on part
of the site of Foley House. Langham Place consists of 15 noble mansions occupied by persons of
rank, among whom are: the Lord Bishop of Bath
and Wells; Sir Anthony Carlisle; Right Hon.
Lady Ongley; Mr. Baron Vaughan; and the Right
Hon. Lady St. John; Sir John D. Astley, Bart;
and Sir Gilbert Heathcote,

PORTLAND PLACE,

which is considered the handsomest street in
London, consists of 73 houses of the very first-rate
description: it is 126 feet wide, and was built
about 1772. The houses, for the most part, have
Ionic fronts, with balustrades concealing the attics;
at certain regular intervals they have pediments :
the houses having this addition are facing each
other all the way on both sides of the street; the
intermediate houses without pediments are Tuscan
or Doric. This noble street owes its origin to
Mr. Robert Adams, and to a restrictive clause in
the agreement between the Duke of Portland and
the ancestor of the present Lord Foley. " When
the latter determined to build Foley House in the
fields near Cavendish Square, he stipulated, that
no other building should be erected upon the same
estate to the north ; this stipulation, it is probable,
had no other object than to prevent any accidental
nuisance to Foley House; but when the riches
which flowed into the country after the peace of
1763, had excited a rage for building, and houses
rose like exhalations in the Parish of St. Mary-le-
bone, both parties discovered its importance : the
ancestor of Lord Foley then saw the cheerfulness
of his house preserved by the force of this
stipulation, and the Duke of Portland felt that
his projected improvements were checked by the
same means. Mr. Adams contrived, in some
measure, to reconcile their jarring interests, by
making a street, equal in width to the whole extent
of Foley House; thus conforming to the letter of
the covenant, without materially affecting the prospect, or obstructing the ardour of speculation."
Foley House was an elegant mansion and possessed
an enviable situation, with an extensive garden,
&c. the last occupier of Foley House was Lord
Rendlesham. Portland Place was originally bounded
on the south, by the fields, but in the progress of

modern improvement: it has been extended by the addition of four houses on each side, named Upper Portland Place, to Park Crescent. The following distinguished persons at present reside in Portland Place: Sir S. Graham, Bart.; Count Batthyany; Robert Farquhar, Esq.; Viscount Boyne; Hon. G. F. Hamilton; Earl of Sheffield; Earl of Stirling; Martin Stapylton, Esq.; Admiral Lord Colville; Sir Robert Sheffield, Bart.; Hon. Edward Monckton; Earl of Mansfield; Sir Richard Borough, Bart.; Lord Skelmersdale; Rev. Sir W. H. Cooper, Bart.; Sir Richard B. Philipps, Bart.; Charles and Lady Mary Ross; Sir William Curtis, Bart.; Sir Richard Paul Joddrell, Bart. &c. In Upper Portland Place reside the Dow. Duchess of Richmond; Lord Arthur Lennox; Lord Walsingham; Hon. Major-General King, and Col. William Blackburne, &c.

PARK CRESCENT.

The fronts of the Houses in Park Crescent have a very neat colonnade of double Ionic pillars with a balustrade and balcony. The area of this Crescent is laid out in planted pleasure grounds, and surrounded with a beautiful ornamental iron railing. In this garden immediately facing Portland Place is placed a statue of His Royal Highness the late Duke of Kent, executed in bronze by *Gahagan*, and elevated on a granite pedestal. The figure is 7 feet 2 inches in height, and the weight of metal is two tons. The Royal Duke is represented in a standing posture, dressed in a Field Marshal's uniform, with a drapery of his robes and the collar of the Order of the Garter. The attitude is simple and unaffected, and the whole figure is an excellent likeness of the Royal Personage it represents. In Park Crescent reside the Marchioness Cornwallis; Count de Surveilliers; Countess St. Germains; Hon. Mr. Justice Alderson; Admiral Sir Richard King; Hon. Lady Edmonstone, &c.

M

242   MARY-LE-BONE PARK.

In Portland Road, died Sir Francis Bourgeois, who bequeathed his valuable collection of Pictures to Dulwich College. It appears that this gentleman intended to have left this beautiful Collection as the commencement of the foundation of a National Gallery, and offered the Duke of Portland, provided he would give a piece of ground on some part of his estate, to erect a Gallery, and to leave £10,000. for the purpose of assisting in the erection, and endowing a keeper; but, through some unaccountable neglect, no answer was returned to the application until it was too late; Sir Francis having determined to bequeath them to Dulwich College, where a new wing was erected for their reception. Thus was lost an establishment, which would have proved an object of general attraction to the amateur, the student, and the connoisseur.

MARY-LE-BONE PARK.*

It has been mentioned, that, when the Manor of Marybone was granted to Edward Forset, King James reserved Marybone Park in his own hands. It continued in the Crown till the year 1646, when King Charles, by letters patent, dated at Oxford (May 6), granted it to Sir George Strode and John Wanderford, Esq. as security for a debt of 2318*l.* 11*s.* 9*d.* due to them for supplying arms and ammunition during the troubles. After the

---

* In Queen Elizabeth's Progresses, it is recorded, that, on the 3d of February, 1600, the Ambassadors from the Emperor of Russia, and their retinue, rode through the City of London to *Marybone Park*, and there hunted at their pleasure, and shortly after returned homeward.

" Sir Charles Blount, afterwards Earl of Devonshire, a very comely young man, having distinguished himself at a tilt, Her Majesty (Q. Elizabeth), sent him a chess Queen of gold enamelled, which he tied upon his arm with a crimson ribband. Essex perceiving it, said with affected scorn, ' Now I perceive, every fool must have a favour!' On this, Sir Charles challenged, fought him in Marybone Park, disarmed him, and wounded him in the thigh."—*Royal and Noble Authors,* vol. i. p. 131.

King's death, when the Crown lands in general were sold by the usurpers, this park, without any regard to the claim of the grantees above-mentioned, was sold to John Spencer of London, Gentleman, on behalf of Colonel Thomas Harrison's Regiment of Dragoons, on whom Marybone Park was settled for their pay ; Sir John Ipsley was at this time ranger, by authority of the Protector. The purchase-money was 13,215*l.* 6*s.* 8*d.*, including 130*l.* for the deer (124 in number, of several sorts), and 1774*l.* 8*s.* for the timber, exclusive of 2976 trees marked for the Navy. On the Restoration of Charles the Second, Sir George Strode and Mr. Wandeford were reinstated in their possession of the Park, which they held till their debt was discharged, except the great lodge and 60 acres of land, which had been granted for a term of years to Sir William Clarke, Secretary to the Lord General the Duke of Albemarle. A compensation was made also to John Carey, Esq. for the loss of the Rangership, which he had held before the usurpation. The site of the Park (for it was disparked before the Restoration, and never afterwards stocked) was leased in 1668 to Henry, Earl of Arlington ;—in 1696 to Charles Bertie and others, in trust for the Duke of Leeds ;—in 1724 to Samuel Grey, Esq. whose interest in the lease was purchased by Thomas Gibson, John Jacob, and Robert Jacomb, Esqs. who renewed in 1730, 1735, and 1742. In 1754, a lease was granted to Lucy Jacomb, widow, and Peter Hinde, Esq. In 1765, William Jacomb, Esq. had a fresh lease for an undivided share, being 15 parts in 24. The term of this share was prolonged in 1772, and again in 1780 for eight years, to commence from January 24, 1803. In the year 1789, Mr. Jacomb sold his interest in the estate to the Duke of Portland, in whom the said share was vested until the expiration of the lease in Jan. 1811. In 1765, and 1772,

Jacob Hinde, Esq. had new leases of the remaining undivided share, being nine parts in 24. This was never renewed, and expired in 1803.*

Summary of a Plan of the Estate called Mary-le-Bone Park Farm, in the Parishes of St. Mary-le-Bone and St. Pancras, in the County of Middlesex, belonging to the Crown ; taken by Order of the Right Honourable the Lords Commissioners of His Majesty's Treasury, and under the direction of John Fordyce, Esq. His Majesty's Surveyor-General, by G. Richardson, 1794.

Names of Tenants, Fields, &c.
Farm in possession of Mr. Thomas Willan and his Under Tenants.

		A.	R.	P.
1. Farm-house, Barn, Stables, Cow-houses, Yards, Garden, &c.	-	2	0	36
2. Small Tenements, Sheds, Yards, and Gardens, let to divers Tenants,	-	1	0	8
3. Ditto,	-	0	2	25
4. The Six Closes,	-	72	1	37
5. Butchers' Field,	-	27	1	28
6. The Long Mead,	-	24	3	36
7. Long Forty Acres,		34	0	11
8. Short Forty Acres,	-	14	2	17
9. Harris's Field,	-	34	1	32
10. Hill Field,	-	18	2	14
11. Gravel Pit Field,	-	20	2	32
12. Part of Home Seven Acres,	-	6	3	32
13. Remainder of Ditto,	-	2	0	25
14. Bell Field,	-	9	2	32
15. Pightle, let to Thomas Hammond,	-	1	1	17
16. Copal Varnish Manufactory and Garden, let to Mr. Alexander Wall,	-	0	1	3
17. Cottages, Sheds, Yards and Gardens, let to divers Tenants,	- -	2	0	8
18. The Five Acres,	-	4	0	18
19. Paddock let to Thomas Hammond,	-	1	1	18
20. White House Field,	-	9	0	6
Total.		288	0	35

* Lysons' Environs.

Farm in possession of Mr. Richard Kendall, and his Under Tenants.

		A.	R.	P.
21. Part of Saltpetre Field,	-	12	3	23
22. Ditto let to John White, Esq.	-	1	1	12
23. *a.* Ditto. Ditto,	-	0	3	16
23. *b.* Late part of the Five Acres, Ditto -		1	1	24
24. Garden let to George Stewart, Esq.	-	0	2	12
25. House, Garden, and Shed, Do.	-	0	1	20
26. Dupper Field,	-	9	1	18
27. Garden let to Sir Richard Hill, Bart. -		0	1	7
28. Farm-house, Cow-houses, Yards, and Cow-lair,	-	1	2	19
29. Cow-houses, Sheds, &c.	-	0	1	11
30. Tenements, Yards, Gardens, &c.	-	2	3	24
31. White House Field,	-	8	0	32
32. Bell Field,	-	15	1	35
33. White Hall Field,	-	20	3	36
34. Rugg Moor and Lodge Field, in one, -		57	0	12
	Total.	133	2	21

Farm in the occupation of Mr. Richard Mortimer and his Under Tenants.

		A.	R.	P.
35. The Nether Paddock,	-	16	1	16
36. Pound Field,	-	22	1	30
37. The Thirty Acres,	-	34	0	12
38. The Twenty Nine Acres,	-	34	1	21
39. Home Field, Farm-House, Cow-House, &c.	-	10	1	9
40. Six Cottages and Gardens, with small Sheds, let to Mr. Richard Holdbrook,		0	1	2
	Total.	117	3	10

Abstract.

	A.	R.	P.		A.	R.	P.
41. Mr. White's Garden,	0	2	26				
42. Small triangular piece on the south side of the road, -	0	0	16		0	3	2

	A.	R.	P
Brought forward	0	3	2

43. Part of the Turnpike-
road belonging to
this Estate,   - -   0 1 31

Other part of Ditto, -   2 0 38   2 2 29

(Both rented by the   3 1 31
Trustees of the road.)
Farm rented by Mr.
  Willan,   -   -   288 0 35

Ditto by Mr. Kendall,   -   -   133 2 21

Ditto by Mr. Mortimer,   -   -   117 3 10

                Total. 543 0 17

This Estate is bounded on the south by that of the Duke of Portland; on the West by those of E. B. Portman, Esq. and Col. Eyre; on the north, by the Barrow-hill farm, and a small portion of College land; and the estate of Lord Southampton, extending along the whole of the east side.

The Truschessian Gallery,

was exhibited in 1804, in a temporary building erected in a field on the site of Park Square: the interior of this building was fitted up with great taste and elegance, and attracted the attention of all lovers of the Fine Arts, throughout the Kingdom. The pictures were subsequently sold by auction, and many of them are now to be found in the various splendid Collections of the Nobility.

This Collection was the property of Joseph Count Truschess of Zeyl Wurzach, Grand Dean of the Cathedral of Strasbourg, and Canon of the Metropolitan Chapter of Cologne; who was originally possessed of very considerable property on the left bank of the Rhine, which he lost by means of the French Revolution, and which induced him thus to dispose of his splendid gallery of pictures, which he had been more than thirty years collecting at an immense expense, and with more than common judgment. And from the testimony of the Vienna Academicians it was considered one of the most complete galleries of Painting in Europe, consisting of such a number of pictures by the most capital artists of every country. A subscription was entered into to defray the expense of bringing them to this country, and a general feeling was entertained that they would be purchased by Government, and formed into a National Gallery; but after they had been exhibited some time, a portion of the pictures were discovered to be copies of the Ancient Masters, and the whole exhibition was consequently brought to the hammer.

In 1793, the late Mr. White, architect to the Duke of Portland, exhibited to Mr. Fordyce, the Surveyor-General, a plan for the Improvement of Mary-le-bone Park, which attracted his attention, and which he noticed in his Report to the Lords of the Treasury; who directed him to take the necessary steps accordingly, and to offer a reward not exceeding 1000l. to the successful author of a plan for the improvement of the whole estate. A copy of the Treasury Minute, dated July 2, 1793, was communicated to Mr. White, with six engraved plans of the estate, which induced him to dedicate much attention to the improvement thereof; and he made several plans, which are noticed in the First Report of the Commissioners of Woods, Forests, and Land Revenues.

After the death of Mr. Fordyce, the Office of Surveyor-General of the Land Revenue, was amalgamated with the Commission for the management of His Majesty's Woods and Forests; and Messrs. Leverton and Chawner, architects and surveyors of buildings of the Land Revenue; and Mr. Nash, Architect and Surveyor of the Woods and Forests; were required to deliver in plans for the arrange-

ment of the Mary-le-bone Park Estate; the result
of their labours, was the delivery of several plans
by Messrs. Leverton and Chawner, and of several
others by Mr. Nash.

Mr. Fordyce, in April 1809, had laid before the
Commissioners of the Treasury, a memorandum
respecting the extension of the town over Mary-
le-bone Park, leading the attention of architects
to the proper consideration of the sewer, supplies
of water, markets, police, churches, and a public
ride or drive. He had, antecedent to this period,
in May, 1796, particularly brought into notice the
forming a direct and commodious communication
to Mary-le-bone from Westminster, by Tichborne
Street, &c. and recommended its execution.

The Commissioners directed Mr. Nash to consider the subject of this communication, and he
produced a plan, which was submitted to Parliament, and an Act obtained for carrying it into
execution.

His Royal Highness the Prince Regent having
manifested his anxiety for the embellishment and
comfort of the metropolis, by encouraging the
improvement of this estate, it was named the *Regent's Park*, and will be a lasting monument of his
taste and liberality.

REGENT'S PARK.

PARK SQUARE.—On this spot it was originally
intended to have completed the crescent opposite
into a circus, which would have been the largest
circle of buildings in Europe. The foundations
of the western quadrant of it were even laid, and
the arches for the coal cellars turned. For some
reasons, however, this plan was abandoned, and
the entire chord of the semi-circle left open to the
park, instead of being closed in by the intended
half circus. This alteration is a manifest improvement of the entire design, and is productive of

great benefit to the houses in the crescent and in Portland Place. Park Square is erected in its stead, and consists of two rows of houses, elongated upon the extremities of the crescent, and separated from the New Road, from the Park, and from each other, by a spacious quadrangular area, laid out with planted pleasure grounds and enclosed by handsome ornamental iron railings, communicating by a tunnel under the New Road into the semi-circular garden of Park Crescent.

ULSTER TERRACE.—This Terrace adjoins the west corner of the Square, and derives its name from the Earldom of Ulster, one of the titles of the late Duke of York; it consists of eight houses three stories high, having their basement stories adorned with Ionic columns; the attics have a neat balustrade. Handsome Doric columns adorn the outer divisions of the terrace.

YORK TERRACE.—Named in honour of his late Royal Highness the Duke of York, extends to both sides of the entrance to the park, and consists of 61 handsome mansions, built from the designs of Mr. Nash; whose principal entrances are in the rear, where large porches protect the vestibules, an arrangement of great convenience to company alighting from their carriages in wet weather. Passing westward, this splendid row of princely mansions, has the appearance of one single building, rather than a row of private dwellings; all the doors and windows are uniform, opening on a lawn, ex-tending along the whole front of the terrace. This appearance is kept up by the arrangement of the trees and shrubs, there being no divisions, but laid out in the style of grounds belonging to a palace. The elevation of this principal front is in the Græco-Italian style of architecture, and consists of a ground story, with semi-circular headed windows, and rusticated piers : a continued pedestal above the windows, divided between the columns into balustrades, forms balconies in front of the windows of the drawing-room story. Lofty well-proportioned windows, giving light to the splendid drawing-rooms, are perforated immediately on the cornice of the pedestal, and in conformity with the simplicity of the Order, are left without decoration. A similar range of windows, of the same width, but less in height, are constructed for the third story. These two stories form the principal architectural feature of the terrace, and are decorated with a colonnade of the Ilyssus-Ionic Order. Above the third story is a blocking course, over which are the attics; the windows correspond with those of the basement story.

York Gate.—In entering the Park by this Gate, the pedestrian will be gratified by proceeding to view the Lake from the bridge which is immediately opposite to it. This sheet of water is a beautiful addition to the landscape, being adorned with rare and beautiful water-fowl, aquatic plants, and other appropriate embellishment. In returning from this Bridge, the beautiful façade of Mary-le-bone Church is seen to great advantage, the two rows of splendid mansions, forming an architectural avenue to the park, and a picturesque border to the view of that sacred edifice.

Cornwall Terrace.—This Terrace inclines to the north, and is one of the first erected in the Park, and named after His late Majesty's ducal title when Regent. The architecture is Corinthian, from the designs of Mr. Decimus Burton. The houses are not on so large a scale as those in York Terrace, but are remarkable for regular beauty. The elevation consists of a rusticated ground story, which forms the basement. This rusticated story

projects beyond the face of the upper, which consists of Corinthian Columns, with fluted shafts,
well-proportioned capitals, and an equally appropriate entablature. The windows, dressings, em-
bellishments, &c. of this elegant terrace, consisting
of 21 houses, are in excellent taste, and have a
singularly beautiful effect.

CLARENCE GATE.—Forming the entrance to the
Park from North Baker Street, is at the end of
Cornwall Terrace ; and on this spot a statue of
Earl Grey is proposed to be erected, in commemo-
ration of the passing of the Reform Bill, a subscrip-
tion having been opened for that purpose, and His
Majesty having graciously signified his consent.

CLARENCE TERRACE.—This terrace is the smallest
in the Park, comprising only 12 houses, and derives
its name from his present Majesty, when Duke of
Clarence, and Lord High Admiral of England; it
was built from the designs of Mr. Decimus Burton,
and consists of a centre and two projecting wings,
of the Corinthian Order, connected by two colonnades of the Ilyssus-Ionic Order. The elevation
is divided into three stories, viz. a rusticated basement story, supporting a drawing-room and chamber
story, also surmounted by an elegant entablature
and open balustrade; fluted Corinthian pilasters,
with proportionate capitals, adorn the wings of this
pleasing specimen of architectural elegance. One
of the most pleasing views in the Park is seen from
the windows of this Terrace, the beautiful expanse
of lake, and the two beautiful villas, the Holme,
and South Villa, surrounded by a luxuriant exuberance of shrubs, trees, and flowers, form prominent
features in the landscape. The next range of
building northward, is

SUSSEX PLACE. Built from the designs of Mr.

Nash, and named after His Royal Highness the
Duke of Sussex. Sussex Place, comprising twenty-
four houses, is arranged in the form of a half
moon, the garden in front being tastefully laid out :
the principal entrances are by a coach drive in the
rear.   The elevation has a novel appearance, and
presents a singular contrast to the more chaste
beauties of the other terraces, and places, by which
the Park is surrounded; it is presumed that this
novel style of architecture, was purposely introduced for the sake of picturesque variety.   It comprises a centre, and extensive wings, the summit
crowned with cupolas and minarets.   The principal
story has a balcony, from which arise columns of
the Corinthian Order, supporting a pedestal to the
chamber story, above which is an open balustrade.
Nearly opposite the end of Sussex Place, is an entrance by a gate to the Promenade of the enclosure,
which, however, is at present only available to the
inhabitants of the adjoining terraces, or annual
subscribers of two guineas, who are allowed keys.
But it is confidently anticipated that, in the next
year, this promenade will be thrown open to the
public generally, under similar restrictions to those
of Kensington Gardens, and the enclosure in St.
James's Park.

HANOVER TERRACE.   Named after His Majesty's dominions on the continent, succeeds Sussex
Place; and is the last range of building on this side
the Park, and is also from the designs of Mr. Nash.
This terrace is built in the Italian, or Palladian
style of architecture, with a beautiful shrubbery in
front, separated from the terrace by a fine level
carriage drive; the stories of the mansions are lofty,
and elegantly finished : and the domestic arrangements of the apartments, conveniently and tastefully laid out.   The front elevation comprises a
centre and two wings, buildings of the Doric Order,

the acroteria of which are surmounted by statues,
and other sepulchral ornaments, in terra cotta. The
centre building is crowned by a pediment, the tympanum of which is embellished with statues and
figures in high relief, representing Medicine, Sculpture, Architecture, Poetry, and other Arts and
Sciences. The windows throughout are embellished with neat and appropriate decorations, and
the attic story is surrounded by an open parapet.
The islet on the lake which faces the northernmost
wing of this terrace, sweetly diversifies the scene,
and adds to the beauty of the prospect from the
houses. At the extremity of Hanover Terrace,
there is a road leading out of the Park, by Hanover
Gate, into St. John's Wood road. The Lodge at
this gate is a neat and handsome quadrangular
building, ornamented with statues and scrolls. Situate between Hanover Terrace, and Gate, is

ALBANY COTTAGE,

the picturesque residence of Thomas Raikes, Esq·
an exquisite specimen of the English Cottage
ornée, the plantations surrounding the house being
laid out with singularly happy effect. The next
object to attract the attention is

HANOVER LODGE,

the tasteful dwelling of the gallant Earl of Dun-
donald. This pleasing mansion has greater pretensions to architectural character than the preceding.
It is situated on an eminence to the left, and forms
a handsome square villa residence, having only one
story above the basement. The house is entered
under a noble portico, opening into a spacious hall,
the cieling of which is supported by marble columns,
and its floor decorated with a beautiful tessellated
pavement. A commodious dining room, 19 feet
6 inches in length, by 16 feet in width, adjoins the

hall on one side, and on another is a splendid suite of drawing rooms, extending above sixty feet in length, by 18 feet in breadth. The upper story, which is attained by means of a stone staircase, comprises nine bed chambers, a bathing-room with every accommodation for that luxury, and convenient dressing-rooms. The lodges and out-offices are upon a very extensive scale. A dense plantation screens the villa from the view on the north and west sides, at the back of which the Regent's Canal enters the Park, and after skirting it to the north, terminates in a basin on the east side. Between the Canal and St. John's Wood road, to the left of the drive, is another elegant villa called

Grove House,

the residence of George Bellas Greenough, Esq. built from the designs of Mr. Decimus Burton. This house possesses two fronts. The garden front is divided into three portions, a centre and two wings. The wings have recesses, supported by three-quarter columns of the Doric Order. Between these columns are well-proportioned niches, each of which contains a statue. The centre is composed of a noble portico of four columns, of the Ionic Order, raised on a terrace. Three windows fill the apertures between these columns, and a long panel over them, gives an apparent height to the apartment thus ornamented. No other window or door appears on this front, which has a remarkable and pleasing effect. The portico, which is composed of one of the purest Grecian Orders, is surmounted by a pediment and acroteria; and the cornice by a blocking course. The entrance front has also a centre and two wings. The centre is inferior to the garden front, having no pediment, and being finished with a simple blocking course over the level Ionic cornice. The entrance door is protected by a semi-circular portico of the Doric Order.

The Marquis of Hertford's Villa.

On the right hand side of the drive, and nearly facing Hanover Lodge, stands the beautiful Italian villa, which is the suburban retreat of the Marquis of Hertford; and was designed by Mr. Decimus Burton. Its buildings and offices are on a larger scale than any other in the Park, and are accordant in style with the wealth of the noble owner. Simplicity and chastity of style, characterize the exterior, and its interior is in the same style of beauty. The entrance-hall, in the principal front, is adorned with a portico of six columns, of that singular Athenian Order, which embellishes the vestibule of the Temple of the Winds at Athens. The roof is Venetian, with broad projecting eaves, supported by cantalivres, and concealed gutters to prevent the dropping of the rain water from the eaves. On each side of the portico, on the ground floor, are three handsome windows, and a series of dormers range along the upper story. Contiguous to the west end of the mansion is a large tent-like canopy with a spiral finish of copper, of considerable height. This canopy forms the roof of a spacious room fitted up in the most splendid style, and used for the entertainment of visitors to the Noble Marquis's public breakfasts. The offices are abundantly spacious, being spread out, like the villas of the ancients, upon the ground floor, and are designed in the same style of architecture as the mansion. In a recess near the entrance, are the two gigantic wooden figures, with their bells, which formerly stood on the south side of St. Dunstan's church, Fleet-street, where they had stood from the year 1671. They were purchased by the Marquis for £200.

The drive now takes an easterly direction, and, at the termination of the shrubbery, surrounding the Marquis's villa, a beautiful opening to the south presents a rich dioramic view. From this spot may be seen the terraces on the east side of the Park, St. Catharine's Hospital, and the Master's House ; pursuing the line of the drive, the Collosseum, Diorama, and the various modern churches, successively meet the eye. The spire of All Souls' church, is here distinctly visible.

MACCLESFIELD BRIDGE

is the next object worthy of attention. The construction of this bridge, designed by Mr. Morgan, is very picturesque, appropriate, and architectural. Its piers are composed of a series of cast iron columns of the Grecian Order ; from the summits of which spring the lofty arches, three in number, which support a flat road way, and, expanding over the towing path, the canal itself, and the shrubberies on its southern bank. The canal winds under this bridge in a deep dell; the grounds of the Park descend to a precipitous bank, which protects them from the incursions of the bargemen and other persons whose occupations lead them to frequent the canal and the towing path. An iron plate on each side of the balustrade exhibits the Macclesfield Arms. The bridge, on the whole, has a light and beautiful appearance. The gate, at the northern end of the bridge, which, with others, is closed at ten o'clock every night, to all but those who are going to the houses within the Park, is in three divisions, a carriage way, and two posterns for foot passengers, divided by stone piers, and a plain lodge on the western side for the attendant porter. In a direct line with this bridge is a branch of the New North Road which leads to Barnet, winding round the foot of Hampstead Hills, which are 150 feet higher than any part of this road. The road to the right, leads to Barrow and Primrose Hills, on the former of which an extensive reservoir has been formed by the West Middlesex Water Works Company.

PRIMROSE HILL.

This spot of ground, which for so many years formed the termination to the rural walks of the inhabitants of London, was formerly famous for Primroses, whence it derives its name. The place is notorious in history for the murder of Sir Edmondbury Godfrey, or rather, perhaps, for his body having been found there in Oct. 1678, after he had been murdered elsewhere. The Coroner's Jury, after an adjourned Inquest, returned the following verdict: "That he was murdered by certain persons unknown to the Jurors, and that his death proceeded from suffocation and strangling; and that his sword had been thrust through his body some time after his death, and *when he was quite cold;* because not the least sign of blood was seen upon his shirt, or his clothes, or the place where he was found." The odium of this murder was thrown entirely upon the Papists.

As Charles II. did not find it compatible with his gallantries that his spouse Catherine should be resident at Whitehall, she resided during some part of his reign, at Somerset House. This made it the haunt of the Catholics; and, possibly, during the phrenetic rage of the nation at that period against the professors of her religion, occasioned it to have been made the pretended scene of the murder of this gentleman. Three persons, viz. Robert Green, Cushion-Man to the Queen's Chapel; Laurence Hill, Servant to Dr. Godden, Treasurer of the Chapel; and Henry Berry, Porter to Somerset House, were tried for this Murder at the King's Bench Bar, before the Lord Chief Justice Scroggs, on the 10th of Feb. 1679; the infamous witnesses Oates, Prance, and Bedloe, declared " that he was waylaid, and inveigled into the Palace, under the pretence of keeping the peace between two servants who were fighting in the yard; that he was there strangled, his neck broke, and his own sword run through his body; that he was kept four days before they ventured to remove him; at length, his corpse was first carried in a sedan-chair to Soho, and then on a horse to Primrose Hill." The Jury found them all guilty of the murder, and the Lord Chief Justice, said, " They had found the same verdict that he would have found if he had been one of them."

The abandoned characters of the witnesses, however, together with the absurd and irreconcileable testimony they gave on the trial, has made unprejudiced times to doubt the whole. But the innocence of these poor men could not avail, the torrent of prejudice prevailing against them; and Green and Hill were executed on the 21st of February, declaring their innocence to the last; as did likewise Berry, who was executed on the 28th of May, having been reprieved till that time.

Sir Edmondbury's corpse being embalmed, was kept till October 31, when it was carried from Bridewell Hospital, of which he was one of the Governors, to the Church of St. Martin in the Fields, where he was buried. The pall was supported by eight Knights, all Justices of the Peace; all the Aldermen of the City of London attended the Funeral. Seventy-two Ministers marched two and two before the body, and great multitudes followed after in the same order. A Sermon was preached on the occasion, by Dr. William Lloyd, Vicar of St. Martin's, from 2 Sam. c. iii. v. 24.

Primrose Hill and its neighbourhood has also been the scene of several sanguinary duels, one of which took place on April 6, 1803, between Lieut. Col. Montgomery, and Captain Macnamara, in consequence of a quarrel between them in Hyde Park, when a Meeting was appointed for 7 o'clock the same evening, near Primrose Hill; the consequence of which proved fatal. Captain M.'s ball entered the right side of Colonel M.'s chest, and passed through the heart; he instantly fell without uttering a word, but rolled over two or three times, as if in great agony, and groaned; being carried into Chalk Farm, he expired in about five minutes. Colonel Montgomery's ball went through Captain Macnamara, entering on the right side, just above the hip, and passing through the left side, carrying part of the coat and waistcoat in with it, and taking part of his leather breeches and the hip button away with it on the other side. A Coroner's Inquest returned a verdict of Manslaughter against Captain Macnamara, who was tried at the Old Bailey on the 22d of April, when he received an excellent character from Lords Hood, Nelson, Hotham and Minto, and a great number of highly respectable gentlemen, and the jury pronounced a verdict of Not Guilty.

The splendid architectural view from the summit of Primrose Hill, is of a most imposing character, the beautiful landscape and water, the splendid palatial terraces, which surround the Park, the gothic spires of St. Catharine's Chapel, and the capacious dome of the Colosseum, to use the language of a late celebrated writer, " delight our eyes, and appeal forcibly to our understandings; compelling us to exclaim, that London ought not to be inferior to Rome in any of these marks of her greatness. Greater far is our metropolis than that boasted city, both in the virtue and the opulence of its inhabitants; in virtue more transcendent, from a sublimer religion, and in opulence more pre-eminent, because its riches are derived from industry and commerce, and not from the plunder of the world."

The road to the left of Macclesfield Gate, leads to St. John's Wood Chapel and Cemetery; the north side being bounded by a row of pleasant houses, called Portland Terrace, which, from the

salubrity of their situation, are exceedingly eligible
for the residence of Invalids.

On the west side of St. John's Wood Chapel is
Wellington Road, leading to the New North Road
to Barnet, made by Act of Parliament in 1826 ;
this road proves of great convenience to the inhabitants of the western part of the metropolis ; travellers by this road, avoid both Hampstead and
Highgate hills, and only one toll is exacted on the
whole line of road, extending a distance of nine
miles and a half.

At the commencement of the New North Road,
is situated the *Eyre Arms Tavern, and Assembly
Rooms ;* this splendid edifice was erected by Mr.
White, and is capable of accommodating more than
1500 persons, the grounds attached to the house
are upon a very extensive scale, and laid out with
great taste and ability.

A short distance from the Eyre Arms, and on the
east side of the road, are situated the Artillery
Barracks, and capacious Riding School ; being at
present the last pile of buildings at this northern
extremity of the parish : the land, however, on
both sides of the road, which is on the Eyre estate,
is now advertised to be let on building leases, for
the erection of detached villa residences.

To return to the Park. A short distance from Macclesfield Bridge are situated the Gardens of that
useful and praise-worthy Institution, the Zoological
Society. This Society was founded in 1826, by
Sir Thomas Stamford Raffles, Sir Humphry Davy,
Lord Auckland, and other noblemen and gentlemen, patrons of science. A grant of land having
been obtained from the Government, the gardens
were formed and opened to the Public in 1828.
The rustic entrance to the gardens is on the right
hand side of the road. The original grant of land
being found inadequate to contain the various
specimens of zoology with which the Society had

been presented, an additional piece of ground was granted for the purpose, on the north side of the road, which communicates with the establishment on the south side, by means of a tunnel under the road. These gardens have acquired great celebrity, and are the favourite resort of the Nobility and the fashionable world ; and present an ample field for the study of Natural History and Botany.

The boundary line of St. Mary-le-bone Parish passes through the Zoological Gardens, crossing the road opposite the head keeper's apartments ; the whole of the east side of the park being in the parish of St. Pancras. The prominent features of this side of the park are

Gloucester Gate, of the Doric order, flanked by two well-proportioned stone lodges.

Gloucester Lodge, a handsome villa of the Ionic Order, in the occupation of the Rt. Hon. Sir B. Martinez Taylor, C. B.

Gloucester Terrace, consisting of eight houses three stories high, ornamented with Ionic columns.

The collegiate Church of St. Catharine, Hospital, and Master's House. This small ecclesiastical establishment, whose proper title is, " The peculiar and exempt Jurisdiction of the Collegiate Church or Free Chapel of St. Catharine, the Virgin and Martyr ;" was founded by the bold and ambitious Matilda, Queen consort of King Stephen, in the year 1148, and dedicated to St. Catharine. It was dissolved in 1272, and the present hospital founded in the following year by Q. Eleanor, and dedicated to the same saint; and continued unaltered till its removal in 1826 to its present site, on the formation of St. Catharine's Docks.

The building is a pure specimen of gothic architecture, and forms a quadrangle, the church being situated on the east side. The pulpit, stalls, organ, &c. were brought from the old church. The pulpit was the gift of Sir Julius Cæsar, in the reign of

James I. and has six sides, on which are carved
four views of the ancient hospital, with the outer
and inner gate, and round the whole is this inscription:—" *Ezra the scribe—stood upon a—pulpit of
wood—which he had—made for the preachen.*"—
Neheh, viii. 4.

On each side of the quadrangle are three houses
in the style of domestic architecture of the six-
teenth century.

*The Master's House** is situated on the opposite
side of the road, and presents the same style of
architecture, but displays more embellishment.
The following pleasing description of this house,
is taken from that valuable and ingenious work,
Elmes's Metropolitan Improvements, 1830. "Now
for the Master's mansion. Truly were it finished,
and some of the tawny tints of time deposited upon
its surface, we might really take it for the habita-
tion of the Prior to some mitred abbey. Its separated angle chimney flues, their ornamented tops,
the fastigated gables, and narrow cell-like windows
in the attics, the mullioned windows of the upper
story, the bow and bay windows and porches to the
doors of the principal story, give the whole a con-
ventual or collegiate appearance. The handsome
well laid out pleasure grounds, the store of kitchen
gardens, and the stable offices, reminding one of
the tithe barn, keep up the illusion ; and nothing
but a Father Paul or two at the windows, rubifying
the scene like the coloured bottles in a chemist's
window, and a living skeleton or two in the shape
of lay brothers, labouring in the gardens, are wanting to complete the picture."

Passing *Cumberland Terrace,* which consists of
thirty-three richly decorated houses, we arrive successively at *Chester Place, Chester Terrace, Cambridge Terrace,* and

The Colosseum. This building is a polygon of

* The present Master is General Sir Herbert Taylor, G.C. B.

sixteen faces, each 25 feet in length, making the circuit of the building 400 feet. It was commenced in 1824, and completed in 1827, under the superintendence of Mr. Decimus Burton. The portico of this building is one of the finest and best proportioned in the metropolis, and gives a majestic feature to this part of the park, that cannot be surpassed. This building was originally erected to exhibit *Mr. Horner's* panoramic view of London, as seen from St. Paul's; but several curious exhibitions of art have since been added, among which may be mentioned, a Swiss cottage, conservatories, a Marine Cave and Grotto, Waterfalls, &c. The original price of admission was 5s. each person; but the proprietors have recently divided the exhibition into two parts, and liberally reduced the price to 1s. for admission to the Panorama; and 1s. for admission to the Swiss Cottage, &c.

Leaving the Colosseum, we re-enter the parish of St. Mary-le-bone at *St. Andrew's Place*, and arrive at the east side of *Park Square*, which completes the tour of the outer circle of the Regent's Park. About the centre of the east side of the Square, is

The Diorama, an exhibition of paintings, which are changed from time to time; introduced into London from Paris, by Messrs. Bouton and Daguerre, in 1823. The body of the picture is painted on what is technically termed a flat, and the perpendicular subject is aided by wings, by painting on the floor, by raised bodies, and by other optical and pictorial effects, till the delusion is perfect and almost incredible. Two pictures are always exhibited; one representing architectural, and the other landscape scenery.

The inner circle of the park is adorned with the following villas: *South Villa*, a handsome structure of the Doric order, the residence of James Holford, Esq. *The Holme*, consisting of two stories, exclusive of the domestic offices, which are contained in a basement. The garden front is very handsome, and a well-proportioned cupola covers the roof. On the opposite side of the road, is a very picturesque *Thatched Cottage*, in the occupation of Mr. Jenkins, whose nursery comprises the whole of the land within the enclosure. *St. John's Wood Lodge,* is a handsome mansion built in the Grecian style of architecture, for C. A. Tulk, Esq. from the designs of Mr. Raffield. The centre is ornamented by two piers which support a pediment with acroteria, and include between them two Corinthian pilasters, and between these is a large and lofty Palladian window ; below this window is a spacious porch of two piers, each supporting a lion: the centre is marked by two columns, and an entablature of the Doric order. The wings project a little from the centre, and are likewise embellished by two large piers with neat panels, and Grecian honeysuckles in the caps. This house is now the occasional residence of the Marquis of Wellesley.

THE VOLUNTEERS.

Whilst the French Revolution was in progress, the inhabitants of St. Mary-le-bone formed themselves into a military Association for the defence of the country, under the command of Colonel Phipps, who was appointed by his Majesty's commission, Lieut. Col. Commandant of the St. Mary-le-bone Volunteers. This Association consisted of a corps of Infantry, and amounted to upwards of 800 effective members. The uniform consisted of a blue jacket, turned up with red, blue pantaloons, &c. from which they were facetiously termed " *Blue*

Bottles." The arms were provided by Government, and deposited at the workhouse; the parade ground being situated in George Street. This Corps was formed in 1797, and disbanded in 1801.

THE ROYAL YORK ST. MARY-LE-BONE VOLUNTEERS.

In 1802, after the short interval of peace, the old threat of invasion being repeated, a second Volunteer Corps of Infantry was speedily established under the above title, in compliment to His Royal Highness the late Duke of York, who at that time resided in the parish. This Corps soon arrived to great perfection in order and discipline, under the command of Colonel, the Right Honourable Viscount Duncannon, and T. Phillips, Esq. their Adjutant; and comprised upwards of 1000 effective members. The uniform was different to that of the original corps, being a handsome scarlet jacket, trimmed with gold lace, blue pantaloons, &c. The arms were provided by Government, and the Armoury and Orderly Room were first established at No. 4, Nottingham Street, and afterwards removed to a building at the corner of Mary-le-bone Lane and Wigmore Street; and the expenses of the Corps were defrayed by a subscription among its members. A subscription was, however, solicited in 1804, from those inhabitants who were exempt, or not eligible to serve in the Corps; when it was stated in the circulars distributed on the occasion, that nearly 20,000*l.* had been expended in establishing the Association, which was decidedly one of the most respectable, being composed principally of master tradesmen, and officered by gentlemen. This Corps was broken up in 1814, and the remains of their fund amounting to £.700, was presented to the Parish Charity School, and Middlesex Hospital; viz. £.400 to the School, and £.300 to the Hospital.

In the prosecution of the study of military tactics, various were the dangers and fatigues encountered both by "flood and field," by this gallant corps, and none but those who have "followed to the field some warlike lord," can attempt to describe the numerous battles, skirmishes, and gallant achievements accomplished by this loyal band of patriots. The following poetical effusion is one of the many which appeared at the time.

Expedition of the
Royal York St. Mary-le-bone Volunteers, or
THE BATTLE OF HOUNSLOW.
Tune.—Drops of Brandy.

T'other day we were sent out of town,
　And sure it was one of our gay days;
Oh! how we astonish'd each clown,
　And charm'd many beautiful ladies:
We muster'd so neat and so clean,
　They made us all pay down four stivers,
For which we'd a car 'mongst sixteen,
　Four horses, and one pair of drivers.
　　　　　　　　　　Sing ri fol lol, &c.

All were mounted, fat, lean, short, and tall:
　Mr. Cubitt as brisk as an eel, Sir,
Captains, Majors, and Colonel, and all,
　Which made us look vastly genteel, Sir;
Drummers, Fifers, and Blacks were so cramm'd,
　They wish'd that the cars were made larger;
Says Mr. Phillips, sit still and be d——d,
　As he gallop'd along on his charger.
　　　　　　　　　　Sing, &c.

Sure the French they are landed, cry'd some,
　As we rattled along like thunder;
To Hounslow at last we did come
　Safe and sound, which I thought was a wonder;
Then over the heath we did scramble,
　The light Bobs were at home to a peg, Sir,
For they fir'd every hedge, bush, and bramble,
　But their Captain got shot in the leg, Sir.
　　　　　　　　　　Sing, &c.

We search'd all the country in vain,
　For no enemy there could be found, Sir;
So we ended a glorious campaign,
　Then our dinners we took on the ground, Sir,
In our sacks Sir, we all found good cheer,
　And our canteens are sure very handy,
For they carry a good quart of beer,
　With a place for a few drops of brandy.
　　　　　　　　　　　　　Sing, &c.

Then some danc'd when they struck up the band,
　But we rode home quite sober and steady,
And should the foe dare for to land,
　They'll find that we always are ready,
For our lads have got true British hearts,
　And I'm sure they will do the neat thing, Sir,
Those may ride to the gallows in carts,
　That won't fight for their country and King, Sir.
　　　　　　　　　　　　　Sing, &c.

COURT HOUSE.

The Old Court House and Watch House were erected
in 1729, and rebuilt in 1804, but in consequence of the
great increase of population, it being found too small and
insufficient for conveniently carrying on the business
of the Parish, the Vestrymen, by virtue of the powers
vested in them by the Act of Parliament, 3d Geo. IV. cap.
84, erected the New Court House, adjoining the Old
Watch House in Mary-le-bone Lane, on ground on which
was formerly situated a Pound, but latterly occupied by
livery stables: this ground was purchased by the Parish,
of His Grace the Duke of Portland. The building is designed with great taste, surmounted by a pediment, in the
tympanum of which is placed a Clock; and the apartments
are replete with every convenience for the purposes for
which they were designed.

The Court House was opened for business in 1825. It
contains on the *Basement Story*:—Sealing office for weights
and measures; and Kitchen for House Porter and Beadles.
Ground Floor.—Offices, Porter's Hall, and Committee
Room. *First Floor.*—A spacious circular Board Room,
elegantly fitted up, and offices attached; also a Waiting
Room for Appellants. *Second Floor.*—Sleeping rooms
for Porter's Family and domestics, and Lumber rooms for
old Office Books and Papers.

The Establishment of the Court House consists of the following persons;
James Hugo Greenwell, Esq. Vestry Clerk.
C. Flood, Esq. Assistant Vestry Clerk and Accountant.
R. Scace, Surveyor.
B. Warden, Paving Clerk.
J. Drew, Assistant Clerk.
J. Moore, Ditto.
House Porter. Housekeeper. Five Beadles.

VESTRY.

This Parish is governed under the Act of the 35th Geo. III. (which Act repealed the former Acts of the 8th, 10th, 13th and 15th years of the Reign of Geo. III.) by a Vestry consisting of 120 Vestrymen including the Rector and Churchwardens, who are empowered by the Act, to take examinations upon Oath, in any matter or Business concerning the Parish.   To appoint all Officers, with Salaries and Allowances as they may see reasonable. All the Parish property to be vested in the Vestrymen. The Vestrymen are also directed by the Act, as soon as they shall have ascertained the money sufficient for the current year, to make once a year, or oftener if necessary, five distinct and equal pound Rates; viz. one for the maintenance of the Poor, one for repairing the Highways; one for Watching, one for Paving; and one for repairing, cleansing and lighting; all such Rates and Accounts to commence on the first of January in each and every year.
The Vestrymen are also directed to appoint annually, in the month of February, thirty substantial and discreet Persons, to be Directors and Guardians of the Poor, who, with the Ministers and Churchwardens, are to carry into execution the powers given by the Acts relating to the Poor.   The Directors and Guardians are also directed to form themselves into six distinct Committees, each Committee to consist of five Members, and fix an annual rule or rotation for their attendance.   One Committee to meet every week, and no business transacted to be valid unless five members are present.   The Directors and Guardians are also directed to hold Four General Quarterly Meetings in every year, viz. on the 25th of March, the 24th of June, th 29th of September, and the 24th of December; and no business transacted at the said Quarterly Meetings to be valid, unless Nine Directors and Guardians attend, and unless the same shall be confirmed at the next Quarterly General Meeting.   It is also provided that each Director

and Guardian shall make Oath that he will without favour
or affection truly and impartially, according to the best of
his skill and knowledge, execute and perform all the trusts,
powers and authorities vested in him as a Director and
Guardian, according to the said Act. It is also enacted,
that all Furniture, Apparel, Tools, Utensils, Materials, &c.
provided for the use of the Poor of the said Parish shall
be vested in the Directors and Guardians of the Poor.

It is also directed that no Vestryman shall hold any
Office or Place of Profit, or have any share or interest
in any Contract or Work to be made or done in pursuance
of this Act, during the time he acts as Vestryman; and it
is provided that, at all their meetings, the Vestrymen
shall pay their own expences.

By the 7th section of the said Act, it is directed, that it
shall be lawful, in the month of March in every year for
the said Vestrymen, to elect and appoint, by ballot, at
any Vestry, duly convened, one or more fit and substantial
parishioner or parishioners to be a Vestryman or Vestrymen
of the said Parish, in the stead of any Vestryman who may
die, or cease to dwell in the said Parish, or refuse to act;
and such person or persons so elected or appointed, shall
be vested with the same power and authority as his pre-
decessor.

By Act of Parliament, 3d Geo. IV. cap. 84, intituled an
" Act for altering, amending and enlarging the Powers of
three several Acts made in the 35th, 46th, and 53d years
of the Reign of Geo. III." sec. 43, Provides, that from and
after the passing of this Act, no person shall be eligible
to be chosen or elected a Vestryman of this Parish, except
he shall for one year at the least, previously to the time of
electing new Vestrymen have been a Housekeeper, rated
in the Parish Books, at a Rent of not less than fifty pounds
per annum.

By an Act passed 20th Oct. 1831, 1st and 2d William
IV. cap. 59, intituled " An Act for the better Regulation
of Vestries, and for the Appointment of Auditors of Accounts, in certain Parishes of England and Wales;" it
was provided that the said Act might be adopted by any
Parish where the inhabitants do not meet in open Vestry;
under certain Regulations contained therein: the following
of which were the principal.

1. That any number of Rate Payers, amounting at least
to one-fifth of the Rate Payers of the Parish, being desirous
that the Parish should come under the operation of this
Act, may, between the 1st of Dec. and the 1st of March
deliver a Requisition, by them signed, and describing
their places of Residence, to the Churchwardens, requiring

them to ascertain, according to the provisions of the Act, whether the majority of the Rate Payers do wish and require that this Act and the Provisions thereof, should be adopted therein.

2. And it was further enacted, that the Churchwardens, shall, on the 1st Sunday in the month of March after the receipt of such requisition, cause a public notice to be affixed on the door of every Church or Chapel in the Parish, specifying some day, not earlier than ten, nor later than twenty-one days after such Sunday, and at what place or places within the said Parish, the Rate Payers are required to signify their Votes for or against the adoption of this Act; which Votes shall be received on three successive days, commencing at eight o'clock in the forenoon, and ending at four o'clock in the afternoon of each day.

A large number of the Inhabitants of the Parish of St. Mary-le-bone, being desirous that the Parish should be brought under the operation of this Act (which indeed they had been instrumental in getting passed into a Law), complied with the provisions of the Act, and, after votes being received for three days at the Court House, there appeared a large majority in favour of the adoption of the Act; and it was accordingly adopted.

The adoption of this Act, repealed or rendered nugatory, so much only of the former Acts of the 35th Geo. III. cap. 73, and 3d Geo. IV. cap. 84, as related to the Election of Vestrymen and Auditors of Accounts :—" Provided always that nothing shall be construed or taken to repeal or invalidate any Local Act for the Government of any Parish by Vestries, or for the Management of the Poor by any Board of Directors and Guardians, or for the due provision for Divine Worship within the Parish, and the Maintenance of the Clergy officiating therein ; otherwise than is by this expressly enacted, regarding the Election of Vestrymen and Auditors of Accounts.

It was therefore enacted, that the Election of Vestrymen and Auditors of Accounts, shall take place in the month of May in every year. That the Vestry consist of not more than 120. And it was also further enacted, that at the first election after the adoption of this Act, one third of the then existing Vestry shall retire from office, and an equal number be elected by the Rate Payers, duly qualified according to the provisions of the Act ; and that on the next election one half of the remainder of the old Vestry shall retire from office, the same number being re-elected by the Rate Payers, and on the third annual election, the last remaining portion of the Old Vestry shall retire, an equal number of Vestrymen being in like manner re-elected so as to fill up the Vestry to the exact number as prescribed by the Act.

And it was further enacted, that, at every subsequent Annual Election, those Vestrymen who have been three years in office shall retire, and the Rate Payers shall elect other Vestrymen, to the number of those who retire, filling up likewise any vacancies which may have occurred from death or other causes; provided always, that any or all of the Vestrymen so going out by rotation, may be immediately eligible for re-election.

It is also provided, that, in the Parishes adopting this Act within the Metropolitan Police District, if the resident Householders therein should amount to more than 3000, then and in that case each Vestryman elected under this Act shall be a resident Householder rated at the relief of the Poor, upon a rental of not less than £40. per annum. Vestries appointed under this Act to exercise the authority of all former Vestries. No business transacted at a Meeting of the Vestry to be valid unless Nine Vestrymen are present. Vestrymen, in the absence of the persons authorized by law or custom to take the Chair, to elect a Chairman for the occasion, before proceeding to other business. Five Rate Payers to be elected annually, to serve the office of Auditors of Accounts, who shall not be Vestrymen, nor shall be interested directly or indirectly in any contract, office or employ, for the Parish for which he is to serve.

According to the Provisions of the above Act, the Election for Vestrymen, took place in May, 1832, when 40 gentlemen retired from office, and 40 other gentlemen were elected by a majority of the Rate Payers.

According to *Maitland*, in 1734, the Vestry was general, and the Parish Officers consisted of two Churchwardens; two Overseers of the Poor; two Constables; two Headboroughs; two Surveyors of the Highways; no Scavengers, but the person who carried away the ashes, received by a voluntary contribution, about 50*l.* per annum; one Beadle, and six watchmen.

WORKHOUSE AND INFIRMARY.

A spacious and commodious Workhouse, situate in Northumberland Street, was erected in 1775. The plans for the erection of this building were made by John White, Esq. Architect to the Duke of Portland, *gratuitously ;* he having become a convert to the prevailing opinions of the time, of the advantages of large establishments of this nature ; Mr. White died in 1813, and, after having dedicated much attention to the interests of the Poor of this extensive Parish, was satisfied, that the opinions he entertained in early life on this subject were erroneous, and that the congregating large bodies of people, particularly children, was detrimental to the true interests of Society.

So much has been written on the Poor Laws, and on the Establishment of Workhouses, that it will scarcely be necessary to say, that viewing these Establishments open for the reception of the aged and infirm, the lame, the blind, or the indigent, reduced by unavoidable calamity, to fly to this last sad retreat of hopeless poverty and distress : as alike honourable to the benevolent character of the British Nation, and gratifying to contemplate; yet the certainty of parochial relief frequently tends to destroy the motives to economy and diligence among the labouring classes, and makes the poor man careless of his conduct, and indifferent whether he work or play : agreeably to the old song with which our Poor Laws were insulted, soon after their first institution :

> " Hang sorrow ! and cast away care !
> " The Parish is bound to find us."

St. Mary-le-bone Workhouse, however, bears a superior character for cleanly and orderly management, every attention being paid to the necessary comforts of the paupers.*

The Infirmary was built at a later period : the old Infirmary having been situated at the north-east corner of the cemetery on the south side of Paddington Street, in a

---

* Died in Mary-le-bone Workhouse, Dec. 27, 1793, in his 78th year, Lieutenant John M'Culloch, a native of the North of Ireland. This gentleman had rendered great services to the British Government during the American War. In 1755, he was appointed Commissary Assistant of Stores, to the garrison of Oswego ; but the garrison being taken prisoners by the French in 1756, he was carried to Quebec. He took an opportunity while there to make a Survey of the rocks and fortifications above the town, which he reported to General Shirley, with a view of reducing Quebec to the British arms. He returned to England in 1757, on an exchange of prisoners, and was introduced to General Wolfe, as a proper person to assist in the reduction of Quebec. The General took his memoranda in writing, the morning before he left London ; and it is well known that General Wolfe made the attempt, first, on a different plan, at Montmorency, and was repulsed ; but making a second attempt agreeably to the plan of Mr. M'Culloch, he proved completely successful. In 1760, Mr. M'Culloch was appointed a Lieutenant of Marines, and served on board the Richmond, Capt. Elphinston, and was solely the cause of taking the Félicité French Man of War. He subsequently fell into difficulties, and was finally compelled to seek refuge in the POOR-HOUSE of Mary-le-bone.

house which had formerly been the country villa of some private gentleman ; it was taken down in 1795-6.

Different Branches of the Workhouse Management.

Superintendent's Department.—Embraces the general management of the paupers in the house, paying and visiting out-door poor, executing orders for removal, apprehensions, &c. attending the Boards of Directors and Guardians, and keeping the accounts connected with and arising out of this business.—Consists of clerk and assistant clerk, 4 inspectors, and 3 messengers.

Steward's Department.—Comprises the management of the interior of the house, as to ordering, receiving, and delivering out provisions and stores.

Matron's Department.—The domestic economy of the house, as to household linen, clothing, kitchen, nursery, and girls' school.

Medical Department.—The care of the patients in the infirmary, and also out of the house, averaging about 485.—Surgeon-apothecary, 2 assistants, 2 dispensers, and 1 laboratory man.

Manufacturing Department.—For sacks and sacking mats, cordage, &c. &c.

Boys' School.—(Generally about 275 boys.)

Girl's School.—(Generally about 200 Girls).

Accountant's Department.—For keeping the books of the establishment, as to the supply of provisions, stores, and raw materials for the manufactory ; sale of manufactured articles, &c.

Clerk of the Works.—For the superintendence of new buildings, repairs, alterations, cleansing, &c.

The duty of the *Chaplain* is to read prayers in some one or more of the wards every day, and throughout the wards of the infirmary once at least every week ;—occasionally to expound portions of Scripture ;—to administer the Sacrament to individual sick persons, to perform two full services in the chapel of the house on Sundays, including two sermons, baptisms, and churchings. Also to supervise and examine the children in the schools of the workhouse.

Overseers of the Poor's Account, anno 1734.

John Deschamps, &c. received		- £.529	4	11	
Paid on Account of the Church	176	7	5		
Paid on Account of the Poor	301	19	5½		
			478	6	10½
Balance due to the Parish.		£50	18	0½	

*From an official Return made to Parliament in 1762,
by John Austin, Vestry Clerk.*

The first Rate for the poor made in May 1761, at 6*d.* in
the pound.   Total of the rent-charge 18,920*l.*

The second Rate for the Poor made in November 1761.
The rents having increased, the total of the rent-charge
amounted to 20,194*l.* at 6*d.* in the pound.

The composition with the Trustees of the Turnpike
Road from St. Giles's Pound to Kilburn bridge, in lieu of
Statute work, and towards repairing the pavement of
Oxford Street, is 75*l.*

The present contract with the Lamp-lighter, for lighting
about 112 lamps, is 1*l.* 12*s.* per *annum* each.

*From Papers Ordered to be laid before the House
of Lords, in 1805.*

Assessment for the Poor Rate in 1776,	£.4534	6	7
Medium Average of 1783-4-5, -	£.8556	5	3
Total sum of money raised in 1803, at 2*s.*			
3*d.* in the pound - - -	40,557	1	2
Expended in Suits at Law, Removal of			
Paupers, &c. in that year	331	2	6

Number of persons relieved in and out of the workhouse,
1523.   Number not Parishioners relieved, 40.

*Statement of the Average Number of Paupers in the year
ending 30th June, 1832, with the heads under which
they were receiving relief.*

In the workhouse, including the Infirmary,	1344 persons
Permanent out-door Poor -	592
Casual out-door Poor - -	5655
Illegitimate children - -	708
Lunatics - - -	81
Out-door Dispensary patients - -	207
Total	8587

Mr. Stephen Watts, principal Clerk at the Workhouse,
has filled that situation 34 years, and been in the Parish
employ 57 years.

The Rev. Stephen Weston, late of Edward Street, Portman Square, bequeathed by his Will to the Minister
and Churchwardens of the Parish of St. Mary-le-bone,
In Trust for the Poor of that Parish not receiving Alms :
Five Pounds Long Annuities.

Will dated October 10, 1829. Proved at Doctor's Commons, April 2, 1830. Vested in the names of the Rev. John Hume Spry, *Rector.* Hon. Bartholomew Bouverie, John Hall, Esq. *then Churchwardens.**

Table shewing the Number of Houses on a graduated Scale of Rental.

Rental.					Number of Houses.
Not exceeding 10*l.* per annum.				-	964
Above 10*l.* and not exceeding 20*l.*				-	2077
Do.	20	ditto	50	-	5010
Do.	50	ditto	100	-	2614
Do.	100	ditto	200	-	1262
Do.	200	-	-	-	516
					12443

* His Excellency the late Count Simon Woronzow, bequeathed the sum of £.500 to the Poor of this Parish, which was liberally paid without deducting the legacy duty, by his daughter the Countess of Pembroke and Montgomery. It is to be regretted that no public memorial exists of this munificent bequest, the terms of the will *(au maison des pauvres)* having precluded any disposition of the legacy, calculated to produce that effect. Had the benevolent intentions of His Excellency been differently expressed in the Will, the money might have been placed in the Public Funds, and the Interest annually devoted to the relief of a number of the industrious Poor, for ever; in the present instance it became absorbed in the Poor's Rate, and appears only in the Minutes of the Directors and Guardians of the Poor.

BOROUGH OF MARY-LE-BONE.

By the provisions of an Act of Parliament, intituled an " Act to Amend the Representation of the People in England and Wales,"* passed the 7th of June, 1832, the Borough of Mary-le-bone was created. It being enacted in the 3d section of the Act, that Mary-le-bone (in common with other places named in the Schedule marked C, annexed to the said Act), shall for the purposes of this Act be a Borough, and shall as such Borough include the place or places respectively, which shall be comprehended within the Boundaries of such Borough, as such Boundaries shall be settled and described by an Act to be passed for that purpose in this present Parliament; which Act when passed, shall be deemed and taken to be part of this Act as fully and effectually, as if the same was incorporated herewith ; and that each of the said Boroughs named in the said Schedule C, shall from and after the end of this present Parliament, return two Members to serve in Parliament."

By the Act above alluded to, intituled " An Act to settle and describe the Divisions of Counties, and the Limits of Cities and Boroughs, in England and Wales, in so far as respects the Election of Members to serve in Parliament," passed the 11th of July, 1832 ; the Boundary of the Borough of Mary-le-bone is settled to extend to, and include, the whole of the three Parishes of St. Mary-le-bone, St. Pancras, and Paddington.

---

* In the debate on the above Bill, in the House of Commons, Mr. Macaulay, the Honourable Member for Calne, thus elegantly described this favoured spot:—" He (Mr. Macaulay) would take this imaginary foreigner to that great city north of Oxford-street, a city equal in population to most Capitals, and in intelligence and wealth not inferior to any on the Globe. He would take him to that almost interminable range of Streets and Squares ; he would point out to him the brilliancy of the shops ; he would exhibit to him those Palaces that encircled the Regent's Park ; he would inform him that the rental exceeded that of all Scotland at the time of the Union, and then he would inform him, that all these were *unrepresented* in the Great Council of the Nation."

By the Parliamentary Census of 1831, it is ascertained that this Borough contains a population of 240,294 persons, viz.

Paddington,	14,540	Inhabitants.
St. Pancras,	103,548	ditto.
St. Mary-le-bone,	122,206	ditto.

THE ELECTION.

On Parliament being dissolved by Proclamation in the Gazette of December 4, 1832, immediate preparation was made for the Election, by the erection of hustings, polling booths, at various places, and the establishment of Committee Rooms by the different Candidates, several meetings having been previously held, and an active canvass made by the friends of each Candidate.

The Right Honourable the Lord Mayor, Sir Peter Laurie was appointed the Returning Officer.

The principal polling booth and hustings whence the Candidates addressed the Electors, were erected in a most commanding part of Park Crescent, facing Portland Place; and polling booths were erected at seven other places, for the convenience of the Electors of the different districts. There were originally six Candidates for the Suffrages of the Electors of this Borough, but Mr. Savage resigned, previously to the day of nomination.

On Saturday the 8th of December (being the Day of Nomination), shortly after 12 o'clock, Sir Peter Laurie, attended by the different Candidates, and a number of gentlemen, appeared on the hustings. There were about 2500 persons assembled, beyond which number there was but a trifling increase during the day.

After the reading of the Precept, the Bribery Act, and the swearing of the Returning Officer, Sir Peter Laurie came forward, and proposed, that the Candidates should draw lots to decide the order of nomination; he also expressed a wish that all the Candidates should be nominated, before either of them addressed the Electors; and suggested, that, to enable the business to be finished by daylight, each Candidate should confine his address to a quarter of an hour. He then announced the days of polling, and the hours at which the polling would commence, viz.—To commence on Monday the 10th at 9 o'clock in the morning, and close at 4 in the afternoon; and on Tuesday the 11th, to commence at 8, and close at 4; the state of the poll to be announced, and the Candidates returned to be declared, on Wednesday the 12th, at 10 o'clock in the morning,

The names of the Candidates were then written on pieces of paper, and Sir Peter Laurie drew them forth in the following order: 1. Sir Samuel Whalley; 2. Mr. Thomas Murphy; 3. Col. Leslie Grove Jones; 4. Sir William Horne; 5. Edward Berkeley Portman, Esq.

Sir Samuel Whalley was then proposed by John Mills, Esq. and Mr. Potter, seconded the Nomination.

Mr. Thomas Murphy was proposed by J. R. Elmore, Esq., and seconded by Major Revell.

Colonel Leslie Grove Jones was proposed by W. Skrine, Esq. and seconded by W. Shaw, Esq.

Sir William Horne was proposed by Major Carnac, and seconded by Dr. Southey.

Edward Berkeley Portman, Esq. was proposed by Sir Samuel Hawker, and seconded by Raikes Currie, Esq.

The Candidates having severally addressed the Electors; Sir Peter Laurie proceeded to put the names by show of hands in the order of nomination; the result was declared to be in favour of Sir Samuel Whalley, and Mr. Murphy. It was, however, computed that not one-half of the persons assembled in front of the hustings, were Electors. Each of the other Candidates having demanded a poll, a vote of thanks to the returning officer, was proposed by Mr. Savage, seconded by Mr. Haydon, and carried by acclamation. Sir Peter Laurie, having acknowledged the compliment, dismissed the assemblage, which dispersed in a few minutes, in the most orderly manner.

The polling commenced on Monday the 10th, and was carried on with great activity both days.

On Wednesday the 12th, the Returning Officer, Candidates, &c. re-assembled at the hustings; when the State of the Poll was declared as follows:

E. B. Portman, Esq. -	4,317
Sir W. Horne, - -	3,320
Sir S. Whalley, -	2,165
T. Murphy, Esq. - -	913
Col. Jones, - -	316

In all, 11,031

The number of householders qualified to vote in this Borough, are 21,630.

Sir Peter Laurie having declared Edward Berkeley Portman, Esq. and Sir William Horne, to be the Members duly elected and returned for the Borough of Maryle-bone, to serve in the Imperial Parliament of the United Kingdom. Both these gentlemen, and the unsuccessful Candidates, addressed the assembled Electors, and the business of the Election closed, by a unanimous vote of thanks to Sir Peter Laurie, whose impartial conduct in the execution of the arduous task he had to perform, met with the approbation of all parties ; and presents an example worthy of imitation by Returning Officers throughout the Kingdom.

It is likewise, a subject of proud congratulation, that the exercise of the elective franchise for the first time, by the inhabitants of this populous Borough, has been conducted with such harmony and good humour; that, while it might have been expected, that great excitement would have existed, from the novelty of the proceedings, yet, not a single breach of the peace occurred during the whole of the Election;—reflecting the highest credit on the good taste, discernment and moderation, of the enlightened inhabitants of this important Borough.

Edward Berkeley Portman, Esq. succeeded his father* as Representative for the County of Dorset, and during the four Parliaments he has sat in the House, has made many great sacrifices both of money and personal convenience in defence of liberal principles ; and uniformly supported the Whig interest. Mr. Portman voted for the repeal of the Test and Corporation Acts ; a repeal of the Law of Settlement, and for Reform : and stands pledged to support, a cheap supply of corn by a fixed duty ; free

* See p 43, ante.

trade; cheap and speedy justice; national education; the commutation of tithes; thĕ reduction of all monopolies, sinecures, and church pluralities; the total abolition of slaverÿ; of the taxes on knowledge; the substitution of a property-tax for taxes pressing on the poor; and lastly, to vote conditionally for triennial Parliaments.

Sir William Horne, is a Chancery Barrister, was appointed Attorney General to the Queen on the accession of his present Majesty; Solicitor-General in 1830, upon the formation of Lord Grey's administration; and Attorney-General in 1832, on the promotion of Sir Thomas Denman to the Chief Justice-ship of England, vacant by the death of Lord Tenterden. Sir William sat in Parliament many years ago for Helston, and in the two last Parliaments for Bletchingley, and Newton, Isle of Wight. This is Sir William's fourth Parliament. He stands pledged to a vigilant and unremitted attention to the correction of all abuses.

BIOGRAPHICAL NOTICES.

Humphrey Wanley, F. R. S. son of the Rev. Nathaniel Wanley, Vicar of Trinity Church, Coventry, who wrote " Microcosmos ; or, The Wonders of the Little World," was born March 21, 1671-2. He was an eminent antiquary, and Librarian to Robert and Edward, Earls of Oxford. Several of his Letters are in the British Museum. He is thus facetiously noticed in *Dr. Dibdin's Bibliomania, p.* 458, " Mr. Wanley was, I believe, as honest a man, and as learned a librarian, as ever sat down to morning chocolate in velvet slippers. There is a portrait of him in oil in the British Museum, and a similar one in the Bodleian Library—from which latter, it is evident on the slightest observation, that the inestimable, I ought to say immortal, founder of the *Cow Pox system* (my ever respected and sincere friend, Dr. Jenner) had not then made known the blessings resulting from the vaccine operation : —for poor Wanley's face is absolutely *peppered* with *variolous* indentations! Yet he seems to have been a hale and hearty man, in spite of these merciless inroads upon his visage ; for his cheeks are full, his hair is cropt and curly, and his shoulders have a breadth, which shew that the unrolling of the *Harleian MSS.* did not produce any enervating effluvia or miasmata. Our poet, Gray, in his epistle to Pope, *ep.* 18, thus hits off his countenance :

> " O Wanley, whence com'st thou with *shorten'd hair,*
> And visage, from thy shelves, *with dust besprent ?* "

" The following desultory information is translated from the preface to Hearne's *Annales Prioratûs de Dunstaple*—wherein, by the bye, there is a good deal of pleasant information relating to Wanley.

" We are here told, that Wanley was born at Coventry ; and in his younger days, employed his leisure hours in turning over ancient MSS. and imitating the several hands in which they were written. Lloyd, Bishop of Litchfield and Coventry, in one of his episcopal visitations, was the first who noticed and patronised him. He demanded that Wanley should be brought to him ; he examined him " suis ipsius, non alterius, oculis :" and ascertained whether, what so many respectable persons had said of his talents, was true or false. " A few words with you, young man," said the Bishop. Wanley approached with timidity— " What are your pursuits, and where are the ancient MSS.

which you have in your possession?" Wanley answered
readily—exhibited his MSS.; and entered into a minute
discussion respecting the ancient method of painting.
His hobby-horse seems to have been the discovery of the
ancient method of colouring or painting, yet towards
British History and Antiquities he constantly cast a fond
and faithful eye. How admirably well calculated he was
for filling the situation of librarian to Lord Oxford, is
abundantly evinced by his Catalogue of the Harleian MSS.
which was most ably executed, and it is to be sincerely
lamented that he did not live to complete it." He died,
July 6, 1726, in his 55th year.

John Abbadie, D. D. An eminent divine, born in
the Canton de Berne, and educated in France. He left
that kingdom on account of the persecutions, and went to
Berlin, where he resided many years as Minister of the
French church. When the Prince of Orange came to
England, Dr. Abbadie accompanied his patron Marshal
Schomberg, and was some years Minister of the French
Church in the Savoy. He was afterwards made Dean of
Killaloe. His writings are numerous. On the Truth of
the Reformed Religion. A Commentary on the Revela-
tions. The Art of Self Knowledge. Several Sermons.
An Account of the Assassination Plot. A Defence of the
Revelation; and some Panegyrical Orations. They were
all written in French, but most of them have been translated.
Dr. Abbadie was esteemed one of the most eloquent men
of his time. He is erroneously called *John* in the Register.
His name was James. He died, Sept. 1727.

James Gibbs, Esq. The celebrated architect; he was
born in 1683, being the son of Peter Gibbs, a merchant in
Aberdeen, at the University of which place he received
his education, and took the degree of M. A. The Earl of
Mar was his first patron in life, and assisted him with
money to prosecute his studies in Italy. He settled in
England in 1710, and in the course of a few years became
the architect most in vogue. His principal works are the
Radcliffe Library, and the New Quadrangle at All Souls'
College in Oxford, the new building at King's College,
Cambridge, and the Senate House at Cambridge; the
Duke of Newcastle's Monument in Westminster Abbey,
the New Church in the Strand, and St. Martin's in the
Fields. In 1728, he published a large volume folio of
his own designs. He gave an instance of grateful re-
membrance to his patron the Earl of Mar, by leaving a
considerable legacy to his son. All his books, prints, &c.

he bequeathed to the Radcliffe Library in Oxford. He died Aug. 1754, aged 71.

William Guthrie. Guthrie was a native of Scotland, where, if we may believe Churchill and some other writers, he followed the profession of a schoolmaster. About the year 1730 he came to London, and having connected himself with the booksellers, was in constant literary employ. He succeeded Dr. Johnson in supplying the Gentleman's Magazine with the Debates in Parliament. He wrote a History of England, a History of Scotland; compiled some parts of the Universal History, and for several years carried on the Critical Review, with little or no assistance. In conjunction with Ralph, he published a Political Journal in defence of the broad bottom administration, and was engaged in many other Political works. He wrote a novel also; translated Quintilian and some parts of Cicero, and assisted in various literary undertakings. There is good reason for supposing that the geographical grammar, which passes under his name, was compiled by another hand. Mr. Guthrie was buried in the Cemetery on the south side of Paddington Street, where, against the east wall is his monument. He died, March, 1770.

Anthony Relhan. Dr. Relhan, who was a Fellow of the College of Physicians in Ireland, resided for some time at Brighthelmstone, of which place he published a short history in 1761, with observations on the mineral springs and sea-bathing. He was author also of a Treatise on the effects of Music in medicine, and several medical Tracts. His son, who was a Fellow of King's College, has published an account of the plants growing near Cambridge. He died, Oct. 1796.

James Ferguson. This man exhibited a remarkable instance of native genius, surmounting the obstacles of poverty and obscurity, and distinguishing itself in no mean degree in the walks of science. Ferguson was born in the County of Banff, about the year 1710. The bent of his mind towards mechanic pursuits first discovered itself by the accidental circumstance of his father's making use of a lever in his presence, and applying it as a prop to his decayed cottage, when he was only eight years of age. His own account of the manner in which he prosecuted his favourite studies, during hours snatched from the most laborious employments (for he was many years a farmer's servant), is very curious and interesting. After struggling with various difficulties, his merit procured him patrons, and he was enabled to pursue his studies with more advantage. Having attained a great proficiency in natural philosophy and astronomy, he came to London in 1743; and having constructed an apparatus for experiments, read lectures in those sciences. Before he left Scotland he had learned to draw portraits, and for a few years after he came to town, practised as a limner in China ink. His price in 1746, was 9s. at home, or 10s. 6d. any where within the distance of a mile. At the same time he read lectures on the globes and the orrery, at his lodgings in Great Pulteney Street, at a shilling each lecture. In 1748, he tells us that he left off limning, which he never liked as an employment; it was certainly an art in which he did not excel. He continued his lectures till near the time of his death, which happened at his house in Bolt Court, in the month of November, 1776. He left behind him a very amiable character. His principal writings were, a Dissertation on the Harvest Moon; a Description of an Orrery; Astronomical and Mechanical Lectures; Tables and Tracts relating to various Arts and Sciences; and a Treatise on Electricity. His last publication was intituled, Select Mechanical Exercises. He wrote his own life, to accompany this work, which was not published till after his decease. Mr. Ferguson was a Fellow of the Royal Society. It should not be omitted, as reflecting honour both on the Royal Donor and himself, that His Majesty allowed him £50. per annum, out of the privy purse, subject to no deductions.

Archibald Bower. Bower was a native of Scotland, being born at or near Dundee, in the year 1686. He was educated at the college of Douay, whence he removed to Rome, and was admitted into the order of Jesus. He resided afterwards at several of the Italian Universities, where he read lectures in the sciences, and at length became counsellor to the Inquisition at Macerata. In the year 1726, he quitted the territories of the Pope, flying, according to his own account, by hairbreadth escapes from the resentment of the Inquisition. He bent his course to London, where, after a residence of some years, he publicly conformed to the Church of England. Meantime he supported himself by private pupils, and by writing for the booksellers. He contributed to a work called the Historia Literaria (in the nature of a review), and when that was discontinued in 1734, he engaged in the Universal History, upon which he was employed several years. In 1748, he published the first volume of his principal work, the History of the Popes, which was not completed till a short time before his death. After the publication of the third volume, the work fell into discredit, and its author into disgrace, by the discovery of his clandestine correspondence with the Jesuits, into whose society he had been a second time admitted. A controversy relating to these transactions commenced in the year 1756, which ended to the disadvantage of Mr. Bower, who was convicted of many wilful falsehoods and misrepresentations. This controversy was principally carried on by a learned divine, who then held a distinguished rank in the church. Bower's defence was spirited, but ineffectual. The material charges alleged against him were never satisfactorily answered, yet he continued to assert his innocence till his death. He died, Sept. 1766.

Mark-Anthony-Joseph Baretti. This well known character was son of an architect at Turin, where he was born about the year 1716. After struggling with great difficulties in the early part of his life, he came to England in 1750, and settled in London as a teacher of Italian. He gave a proof of his extraordinary facility in acquiring languages, by publishing in English, within three months after his arrival, a defence of the Italian poetry against Voltaire. About this period he was introduced to Dr. Johnson, with whom he maintained an intimacy till nearly the end of his life. In 1760, he revisited his native country, and whilst resident at Venice, published a periodical paper, which added much to his reputation. At his return he was engaged in a controversy with Sharp, who had published, Letters from Italy, in which a very unfavourable account was given of that country and its inhabitants. Soon after his return from a visit to Spain in 1769, he had the misfortune to kill a man in an accidental affray in the streets. He was tried at the Old Bailey, when after a full investigation of the case, during which the most honourable testimony was borne to his character, the jury gave a verdict of Manslaughter. In 1770, he published an account of his travels, which met with a very favourable reception from the public. At the first institution of the Royal Academy, Baretti was made their Secretary for Foreign Correspondence. About the same time he had a pension of £80. per annum from the crown. He died on the 5th of May, 1789, and was interred in the cemetery on the north side of Paddington Street; Dr. Vincent, Sir William Chambers, and some gentlemen of the academy attending his funeral. His letters, among which were several from Dr. Johnson, were burnt by his representatives.* His principal works were, an Italian Grammar ; a Dictionary of that language, which is in very general use ; his Travels ; A View of the customs and manners of Italy ; a Discourse of Shakspeare and Voltaire, and an edition of Machiavell's Works, Some of his later writings were of a personal nature, and are replete with acrimony.

John Dominick Serres. An eminent artist, who excelled in painting sea-pieces. He was marine painter to His Majesty. He died, Jan. 1793.

Francis Wheatley, Esq. R. A. Mr. Wheatley, was an artist of eminence, and a Royal Academician : in the former part of his life he chiefly painted portraits in small whole lengths; he resided for some time in Ireland, where he was much patronized, and gained considerable reputation by his picture of the Irish House of Commons, taken at the time of Mr. Grattan's making his motion for the repeal of Poyning's Act. Latterly, Mr. Wheatley devoted his attention to the painting of rural scenery, and exhibited several pictures of that description, which were much admired. Mr. Wheatley, at the age of 54, fell a sacrifice to the gout, with which he had been many years afflicted. There is a tombstone to his memory in the south Cemetery. He died, June, 1801.

George Stubbs, Esq. This celebrated painter and anatomist, was in his 82d year, having been born at Liverpool in the year 1724. He was long distinguished for his eminence as a painter of animals, and the exhibitions of the Incorporated Society of Artists, and afterwards at the Royal Academy, of which he was an Associate, were many years enriched by his works; of these, " the Lion and Horse," " the Lion and Stag," and the " Brood Mares," were amongst the most celebrated. Having devoted much labour and attention to the practice and study of comparative anatomy, in 1766 he brought out his magnificent and much-esteemed work, on the anatomy of the Horse ; being the result of observations made by himself, during a long course of dissecting : the drawings and engravings were all made with the utmost accuracy by his own hand. Mr. Stubbs, at the time of his death, had completed both the anatomical preparations and the drawings for a work on the structure of the human body compared with that of a tiger and a fowl. Of this work, which was to be com-

* See Life of Baretti, in the European Magazine for 1789, whence the above account is principally taken.

prised in six parts, containing thirty plates, three parts only were published. Mr. Stubbs died at his house in Somerset Street, Portman Square, in July, 1806, where he had resided many years; he was remarkable for his abstemious way of life, and a very robust constitution, which enabled him, even after he was fourscore, to take an extraordinary degree of exercise for his advanced time of life, and to pursue his professional occupations almost to the last.

Admiral Sir Richard King, Bart. Sir Richard King, a brave and meritorious officer, who chiefly distinguished himself on the East India station, where he had the rank of Commodore, and was engaged in all the actions with Mr. De Suffrein's squadron, during the war that terminated in 1783. Having gone through all the inferior promotions, he was made Admiral of the White in 1799. In the year 1792, he was created a baronet, in which title he was succeeded by his eldest and only surviving son, Sir Richard King, Bart., Captain of the Achilles man of war, who married the only daughter of Admiral Sir John Duckworth, K. B. He died, Nov. 1806.

Stephen Riou. This gentleman, who was a Captain of Horse, and had served in Flanders in the year 1741, distinguished himself as a man of taste, by the publication of a splendid work, in imperial folio, on the Grecian orders of Architecture, explained by delineations of the Antiquities of Athens, made during his travels into Greece. He published also an Essay on the Construction of Bridges.* He died, March, 1780.

Allan Ramsay, Esq. Mr. Ramsay was principal portrait painter to His Majesty. He was one of the writers in the controversy on Elizabeth Canning's Case, and was author of a pamphlet called the Investigator, and various Political Tracts.† His father wrote a well-known drama called the Gentle Shepherd, and several other Poems. He died, Aug. 1784.

Sir George Collier, Knt. Sir George Collier, who was made a Post Captain in 1762, was employed chiefly on the Coast of America during the American War. In 1775, he brought out at Drury Lane Theatre, a Dramatic Romance, taken from the French, called " Selima and Azor." He died, April, 1795.

---

* Gentleman's Magazine.   † Ibid. and Biog. Dram.

Stephen Storace. An eminent musical composer, to whom the public are indebted for the music of several well-known comic operas; of which, the Haunted Tower and Siege of Belgrade, are spoken of by Professors as having the most distinguished merit. His last work was the music of the "Doctor and Apothecary," for Drury Lane Theatre. He died, March, 1796

William Cramer. This celebrated musician, who was a native of Manheim, resided many years in this country, where he was long at the head of his profession, and led the band at the Opera House, and at most of the great public concerts; he was particularly eminent as a leader of Handel's music. Mr. Cramer left two sons both eminent in the same profession: the elder is one of the principal leaders of the present day; his brother is well-known as a piano forte player, and a teacher of that instrument. Miss Jane Cramer, a daughter by his second wife, is distinguished by her extraordinary talents for elocution, which shewed themselves at an early age. He died at his house in Charles Street, Oct. 1799.

The Rev. Charles Wesley. Mr. Wesley was a younger brother of the celebrated John Wesley, one of the founders of a very numerous body of men, generally known by the name of Methodists. Their father, Samuel Wesley, was author of "The Life of Christ," a Poem: a "Commentary on the Book of Job," and other works. Charles Wesley was born in 1708, at Epworth; he was educated at Westminster school, and Christchurch, of which college he was a student. He accompanied his brother during most of his travels, and encountered with him many dangers and difficulties. After his marriage, he divided his time between Bristol and London. His writings, not so numerous as those of his brother, consist chiefly of hymns and sacred poems. His son Charles, before he was three years of age, exhibited uncommon musical talents; his youngest son Samuel, at an age not much more advanced, discovered the same talents and inclination for music, and composed an Oratorio and several other pieces, whilst a child. A minute account of their progress in the science, from the information of their father, is given in the Hon. Daines Barrington's Miscellanies, p. 289-310. They both embraced a profession for which nature had so evidently designed them. Some years ago select concerts were given at their father's house in Chesterfield Street, Marybone, at which the joint performances of the brothers, particularly their double lessons on the organ, were received with much admiration and applause. Mr. Wesley was buried in the Church-yard of Mary-le-bone, by his own desire, his pall being supported by eight clergymen of the Church of England.—*See his Life by Dr. Whitehead, to which is prefixed a portrait.*

Mr. Samuel Wesley, an elder brother of the above-mentioned Charles, had a design of publishing an edition of Hudibras with notes. He applied to the Earl of Oxford for the use of the books in his library, and his Lordship wrote him the following obliging answer from Dover Street, August 7, 1734. " I am very glad you was reduced to read over Hudibras three times with care : I find you are perfectly of my mind, that it much wants notes, and that it will be a great work ; certainly it will be, to do it as it should be. I do not know one so capable of doing it as yourself. I speak this very sincerely. Lilly's life I have, and any books that I have you shall see, and have the perusal of them ; and any other part that I can assist. I own I am very fond of the work, and it would be of excellent use and entertainment.

The news you read in the papers of a match with my daughter and the Duke of Portland was completed at Mary-le-bone chapel," &c.*

What progress he made in the work, or what became of his notes, does not appear.

Alexander Dalrymple. The late Alexander Dalrymple, F. R. S., F. A. S., &c. was the seventh son of Sir James Dalrymple, Bart., of New Hailes, near Edinburgh, by Lady Christian, daughter of the Earl of Haddington. In 1752, he was appointed a writer in the East India Company's service, on the Madras Establishment ; and having from his earliest years had a great thirst for geographical knowledge, he was induced to forego considerable advantages, which he might have derived from remaining at Madras ; and in 1759 proceeded on a voyage of discovery to the eastward, which had been proposed by himself, and acceded to by the Governor, Sir George Pigot. In this voyage he visited Sooloo, and concluded a treaty with the Sultan ; in 1762, he returned to Madras, and the same year embarked on another voyage to Sooloo, in the course of which he visited the Island of Balambangan, and obtained a grant of it for the East India Company. In 1765,

---

* Extract of a letter from Lord Oxford, taken from original letters by the Reverend John Wesley and his friends, illustrative of his early history, published by Joseph Priestley, LL. D. printed at Birmingham, 1791.

o

he returned to England. In 1769, when the Royal Society proposed to send out persons to the South Seas to observe the transit of Venus, Mr. Dalrymple was fixed upon for the superintendence of the voyage, and the prosecution of discoveries in that quarter; but Lord Hawke, then at the head of the Admiralty, refusing to give the command to any but a naval officer, he declined the undertaking.

In 1775, Mr. Dalrymple was appointed one of the Council at Madras; iu 1779, hydrographer to the East India Company, and in 1795, hydrographer to the Admiralty. On the 20th of May, 1808, having refused to resign the last-mentioned office, on the ground of superannuation, and to accept of a pension, he was dismissed from his situation; and it is said, that in the opinion of his medical attendants, his death was occasioned by vexation arising from that event. A motion was shortly afterwards made on this subject in the House of Commons, when the Secretary to the Admiralty, after bearing the most ample testimony to the talents and services of Mr. Dalrymple, fully justified the conduct of that board, which had adopted a necessary measure with much reluctance. Mr. Dalrymple died on the 19th of June, 1808, at his house in High Street, Mary-le-bone, and was buried in the small cemetery adjoining the church. There is no monument to his memory.

Thomas Holcroft. This well-known writer was of humble origin, having been originally, as it is said, a shoemaker in the north. Possessing great natural endowments, and much industry, he acquired such a knowledge of the modern languages as enabled him to translate from them with great facility. He was for some years a performer in the provincial theatres, and soon after his coming to London, in 1778, he obtained an inferior engagement at Drury Lane Theatre, but never distinguished himself as an actor; he produced several pieces for the stage; but none that were very successful, excepting " The Road to Ruin," which had a great run, and still continues to be popular. Mr. Holcroft was author of " Anna St. Ives," and other novels; a Tour in France and Normandy; some Poems, and numerous translations of Memoirs, Novels, &c. from the French and German. He died at his house in Clipstone Street on the 23d of March, 1809, and was buried in the larger cemetery at Mary-le-bone. There is no memorial for him.

John Vandrebank. A portrait painter much in fashion during the reigns of George I. and II. is said by Vertue to be an Englishman (though by his name, at least of foreign extraction), and to have attained his skill without any assistance from study abroad. Had he not been careless and extravagant, says that author, he might have made a greater figure than almost any painter this nation had produced; so bold and free was his pencil, and so masterly his drawing.* He died of a consumption when he was not above forty-five years of age, at his house in Holles Street, Cavendish Square, December 23, 1739. He had a brother of the same profession.

John Michael Rysbrach. This celebrated statuary was born at Antwerp in 1693. His father was a Landscape Painter, and had been in England, but quitted it with Largilliere and went to Paris, where he married, and returning to Brussels and Antwerp, died at the latter in 1726, at the age of fourscore. Michael his son arrived here in 1720, then about the age of twenty-six, and began by modelling small figures in clay, to show his skill. The Earl of Nottingham sat to him for his bust, in which the artist succeeded so well, that he began to be employed on large works, particularly monuments. For some time he was engaged by Gibbs, who was sensible of the young man's merit, but turned it to his own account, contracting for the figures' with the persons who bespoke the tombs, and gaining the chief benefit from the execution. The statuary, though no vain man, soon felt his own merit, and shook off his dependence on the architect, as he became more known and more admired. Business crouded upon him, and for many years all great works were committed to him; and his deep knowledge of his art, and singular industry, gave general satisfaction. His models were thoroughly studied, and ably executed; and as a sculptor capable of furnishing statues was now found, our taste in monuments improved, which till Rysbrach's time had depended more on masonry and marbles, than statuary. Besides numbers more, Rysbrach executed the monuments of Sir Isaac Newton, and of the Duke of Marlborough at Blenheim, and the equestrian statue in bronze of King William at Bristol in 1733, for which he received £1800. He also made a great many busts, and most of them very like, as of Mr. Pope, Gibbs, Sir Robert Walpole, the Duke and Duchess of Argyle, the Duchess of

* In 1735, he made drawings for Lord Carteret's edition of Don Quixote which were engraved by Vandergutcht. Hogarth's designs were paid for, but rejected, and were likewise afterwards engraved.—*Nichols.*

Marlborough, Lord Bolingbroke, Wootton, Ben Johnson, Butler, Milton, Cromwell, and himself; the statues of King George I. and of King George II. at the Royal Exchange; the heads in the Hermitage at Richmond, and those of the English worthies, in the Elysian fields at Stowe.

This enjoyment of deserved fame was at length interrupted by the appearance of Mr. Scheemaker's Shakspeare in Westminster Abbey, which besides its merit, had the additional recommendation of Mr. Kent's fashionable name. Piqued at Mr. Scheemaker's success, Rysbrach produced his three statues of Palladio, Inigo Jones, and Fiamingo, and, at last, his chef-d'œuvre, his Hercules; an exquisite summary of his skill, knowledge, and judgment. This athletic statue, for which he borrowed the head of the Farnesian god, was compiled from various parts and limbs of seven or eight of the strongest and best made men in London; chiefly the bruisers and boxers of the then flourishing amphitheatre for boxing; the sculptor selecting the parts which were the most truly formed in each. The arms were Broughton's, the breast, a celebrated coachman's, a bruiser; and the legs were those of Ellis the painter, a great frequenter of that gymnasium. As the games of that Olympic Academy frequently terminated to its heroes at the gallows, it was soon afterwards suppressed by Act of Parliament; so that in reality Rysbrach's Hercules is the monument of those gladiators. It was purchased by Sir R. C. Hoare, and is the principal ornament of the noble temple at Stourhead, that beautiful assemblage of art, taste, and landscape.

Mr. Rysbrach, who had by no means raised a fortune equal to his deserts, before his death made a public sale of his remaining works and models, to which he added a large collection of his own historic drawings, conceived and executed in the true taste of the great Italian masters. Another sale followed his death, which happened Jan. 8, 1770. He resided in High Street.

John Wootton. A scholar of Wyck, was an excellent master of that branch of his profession to which he principally devoted himself, viz. painting horses and dogs, which he both drew and coloured with consummate skill, fire and truth. He was first distinguished by frequenting Newmarket, and drawing race-horses. The prints from his hunting-pieces are well known. He afterwards applied himself to landscape, approached towards Gaspar Poussin, and sometimes imitated happily the glow of Claud Lorrain. He died in January 1765, at his house in

Cavendish-Square, which he built, and had painted with much taste and judgment.

J. Sigismond Tanner, Esq. Engraver to the Mint for forty years, was appointed chief graver in 1740. He had retired from business, and died at his house in Edward Street, Cavendish Square, March 16, 1773.

Benjamin West, Pres. R. A. This distinguished artist was born at Springfield, in Chester County, Pennsylvania, Oct. 10, 1738. He was the youngest of ten children of John West, who removed to Pennsylvania, in 1714, where he married Sarah, the daughter of Mr. Thomas Pearson, who had accompanied Penn thither in 1681. His genius exhibited itself at the early age of six years, when he made a pen and ink sketch of his sister's infant, while it was sleeping in its cradle. Though entirely destitute of the requisite materials, yet he triumphed over every obstacle that fortune had placed in the way of the indulgence of his favourite pursuit. Having obtained some red and yellow colours from the Indians, and some Indigo from his mother, he supplied himself with a pencil, by plucking the hairs from a cat's back. After struggling with innumerable difficulties, he was at last permitted by his friends to yield himself to the impulse of his genius. At the age of fifteen he painted portraits at Lancaster, and was established as a portrait painter in Philadelphia at the age of 18, he also painted some historical compositions. By the liberality of his friends and patrons, he was enabled to visit Rome in the 22d year of his age, for the purpose of studying the works of Raphael and Michael Angelo. He was here patronized by Lord Grantham, whose portrait he painted, which was submitted to many artists and connoisseurs, and had the honour to be taken for one of the *best coloured* pieces of *Mengs.* He now visited Bologna, Mantua, Parma, Venice, and Verona, and made himself acquainted with the style of the best masters of the Italian School. In 1763, he came to England, arrived in London on the 20th of June, and shortly after took lodgings in Bedford Street, Covent Garden, where he set up his easel. The first pictures he exhibited, were Angelica and Medora ; Cimon and Iphigenia; and a portrait of General Monckton. These productions were well received, and he obtained the patronage of many dignitaries of the church, and especially of Dr. Drummond, Archbishop of York. Mr. West was married in September, 1765, at the church of St. Martin in the Fields, to Miss Shewell, daughter of a respectable merchant at Philadelphia, to

whom he had formed an attachment, before he visited
Rome, and who came over accompanied by a relation, that
the ceremony might be performed, without impeding the
progress of his studies. The Archbishop of York now
introduced Mr. West to the King, who commanded him
to paint the subject of the ' Departure of Regulus;' the
production of this picture gained him the personal confidence of his Majesty, which was rendered eminently serviceable in the establishment of the Royal Academy,
founded in 1768. He now devoted himself entirely to
historical compositions, which are exceedingly numerous,
his later productions were ' Christ Rejected,' and ' Death
on the Pale Horse :' the latter was painted when the artist
was nearly 80 years of age. Mr. West succeeded Sir
Joshua Reynolds, as President of the Royal Academy in
1792, and held it till his death, with the exception of the
year 1806, when Mr. Wyatt filled that office. He died at
his house in Newman Street, on the 11th of March, 1820.

Joseph Nollekens, Esq. R. A. This celebrated sculptor
was born on the 11th of August, 1737, in Dean Street,
Soho. In his thirteenth year he was placed in the studio
of Scheemakers ; and went to Rome in 1760. He was
admitted an Associate of the Royal Academy in 1771, and
Royal Academician in the following year. Mr. Nollekens
enjoyed the patronage of His Majesty George III. and by
habits of strict parsimony, amassed an immense fortune.
He died at his house in Mortimer Street, April 23, 1823,
leaving property amounting to nearly £.300,000, which,
with the exception of about £.6000 divided in legacies,
was bequeathed to Francis Palmer, Esq. and the well-
known antiquary, Francis Douce, Esq. ; the latter gentleman being residuary legatee. John Thomas Smith, Esq.
of the British Museum, one of the executors to his will,
who had a legacy of £.100, has published " The Life of
Nollekens, comprising Memoirs of Contemporary Artists,"
this work is written with great feeling and taste, and is
replete with strokes of humour, traits of character, and
anecdotes of genius and manners of life.

John Bacon, Esq. R. A. An eminent sculptor, was
born in London on the 24th of November, 1740. His
father was a clothworker in Southwark. In 1755, and
at the age of 14, he was bound apprentice to Mr. Crispe,
of Bow Churchyard, where he was employed in painting
on porcelain. Mr. Crispe had a manufactory of China at
Lambeth, where Mr. B. occasionally assisted. In attending this manufactory, he had an opportunity of observing

the models of different sculptors, which were sent to a pottery on the same premises, to be burnt. The sight of these models, inspired him with an inclination for the art of sculpture, to the study of which he applied himself with the most unremitted diligence; his progress was as rapid as his turn for it was sudden and unpremeditated; and between the years 1763 and 1766, the first premiums awarded by the Society for the Encouragement of Arts, in those classes for which he contended, were no less than nine times adjudged to him. About the year 1763, he commenced working on marble. In 1768, he attended the Royal Academy, which was instituted in that year; and the following year, the first gold medal for sculpture, given by that body, was decreed to Mr. Bacon. He became an Associate in 1770, and a Royal Academician in 1778. His reputation was, however, publicly established by the exhibition of his statue of Mars, which recommended him to the notice of that liberal patron of the Arts, the Archbishop of York, who presented him to His Majesty, who was graciously pleased to sit to him for a bust, which the Archbishop designed to place in the hall of Christ Church College, Oxford. His execution of this work procured him the Royal patronage, and Mr. Bacon afterwards executed three other busts of His Majesty, one of which has been placed in the meeting room of the Society of Antiquaries. He was soon afterwards employed by the Dean and Chapter of Christchurch in forming several busts for them, particularly of the late General Guise, the Bishop of Durham, and the Primate of Ireland.

It would far exceed the limits of this notice, to give a list of his numerous works; among the principal, may be mentioned, Lord Chatham's monument in Guildhall; the bronze group in the Square at Somerset House; Sir G. Pococke's and Bishop Thomas's Monuments in Westminster Abbey; Mr. Howard's and Dr. Johnson's, in St. Paul's, and the Pediment at the East India House. Mr. Bacon had under his hand at the time of his death, several important commissions, among which were, a group for India, containing a colossal statue of the Marquis Cornwallis; an equestrian bronze of William III. for St. James's Square, with some others of minor importance.

This distinguished artist and excellent man was suddenly attacked with an inflammation in his stomach, on the evening of Sunday, Aug. 4, 1799, which carried him off in two days. During this short illness he expressed a firm reliance on that sure foundation on which he had long and consistently built. He departed this life on Wednesday morning, August 7, in the 59th year of his age; leaving two sons and three daughters by his first wife, and three sons, by his last, the surviving widow. He was buried under the north gallery of Whitfield's Chapel, Tottenham Court Road, and according to his direction, a plain tablet was placed over his grave, for which he had written the following inscription :

" What I was as an Artist, seemed to me of some importance while I lived. BUT what I really was, as a Believer in Christ Jesus, is the only thing of importance to me NOW."

Sir Francis Bourgeois, R. A. This gentleman was descended from a Swiss family, but was born at London in 1756. His original destination was to the army, but having been taught to draw when a child, he became so much attached to the art, that he resolved to pursue it professionally. He was accordingly placed as a pupil with Mr. Loutherbourg, whose style he adopted, and acquired considerable reputation by his landscapes and sea-pieces. After travelling for improvement, he settled in London, and rose to distinction. He was appointed painter to the King of Poland, who honoured him with the Order of Merit; and his knighthood was confirmed by His Majesty George III. by whom he was nominated his landscape painter. He acquired a large collection of pictures by the will of Mr. Desenfans; these, with the bulk of his property, he bequeathed to Dulwich College. He died at his house in Portland Road, January 8, 1811.

John Jackson, R. A. This eminent portrait painter, was born at Lastingham, a small village in the North Riding of Yorkshire, May 31, 1778. His father was the village tailor, and he himself commenced his career in that humble occupation. He had from his childhood, a predilection for drawing, and in 1797, at the age of 19, he ventured to offer himself as a portrait painter at York ; during one of his excursions to Whitby, he obtained the honour of an introduction to Lord Mulgrave, who patronized, and recommended him to the notice of the Earl of Carlisle. At Castle Howard he copied the Three Mary's, by Annibal Caracci, with considerable success. He was also patronized by the late Sir George Beaumont, Bart. came to London in 1804, and in the following year became a student at the Royal Academy. In 1807, he was established as a portrait painter, and every succeeding year furnished specimens of his abilities for the Exhibition at Somerset-House. He was elected an Associate of the Royal Academy in 1816, and a Royal Academician, in 1818. In the former year he accompanied General the

Hon. Edmund Phipps in a tour through Holland and Flanders; and in 1819, he accompanied Mr. Chantrey in a tour of Italy; at Rome, he was elected a member of the Academy of St. Luke, and met with great attention from Canova, who sat to him for his portrait. One of his last exhibition pictures was a portrait of his intimate friend Chantrey, painted for Sir Robert Peel. He had an uncommon readiness and skill of hand, his colouring was deep, clear, and splendid, and in this he resembled Reynolds more than any artist since his day. He died at his house at St. John's Wood, June 1, 1831.

The Rev. William Holwell Carr, B. D. F. R. S. Vicar of Menhenniot, Cornwall. This gentleman's paternal name was Holwell. He was of Exeter College, Oxford, M. A. 1754, B. D. 1790, and was presented to the Vicarage of Menhenniot, one of the most valuable benefices in Cornwall, by the Dean and Chapter of Exeter. Mr. Carr was for many years a distinguished patron, as well as an exquisite connoisseur of the Fine Arts, and was a Director of the British Institution. His private collection of pictures consisted principally of productions of the Italian School; one of which, " Christ disputing with the Doctors," was bought of Lord Northwick, in 1824, it is said, for £.2600. Mr. Carr bequeathed his valuable collection to the Nation, stipulating however, that a gallery should be provided, where they might be properly seen and justly appreciated. He died at his house in Devonshire Place, Dec. 24, 1830, aged 72.

David Pike Watts, Esq. This gentleman received the first rudiments of his education from Alexander Cruden, the Author of the " Concordance to the Bible." He became connected with Benjamin Kenton, Esq. an eminent wine merchant in very early life: Mr. Kenton had an only daughter, and a mutual affection arose between this lady and Mr. Watts, but Mr. Kenton refused his consent to their union, which had such an effect upon the young lady, that she fell into a gradual decline, and sunk into a premature grave: and the conduct of Mr. Watts on this trying occasion, so endeared him to his patron, that upon retiring from business, he left him the management of the whole of his extensive concern.

Mr. Watts married Miss Morrison of Durham, by whom he had two sons and one daughter. Both the sons were brought up to the army. David, the elder, died in the 20th year of his age, in Jamaica, of the yellow fever; and Michael, who was Ensign in the Coldstream Guards, fell

at Barossa, also in his 20th year. His daughter was united
to Jesse Watts Russell, Esq. of Ham Hall near Ashbourne,
Derbyshire, and proved, with her family, the solace of his
declining years.

Mr. Kenton died May 25, 1800; leaving the chief part
of his fortune to Mr. Watts, who shortly afterwards retired from business, and devoted his active mind to the
extension of his fortune in the promotion of the public
welfare; in which he may be literally said, to have gone
about doing good. Thus he became the liberal friend of
literature and learned men—he respected their talents, and
lamented and secretly relieved the severe privations of
many, whose studies had not always secured them from
temporal distress; and whose station or professional
habits were such as to depress their merit.

The same disposition led him to patronize Christ's
Hospital, the Institution of Sunday Schools, and all the
methods adopted for the religious instruction of youth:
he gave a hearty encouragement to the Institution of the
Central National School in Baldwin's Gardens, and also
to those Parochial and Ward Schools more immediately
attached to his places of business and residence.

His private charities were boundless. The conciliatory
manner in which he bestowed his relief, filled many a
heart with joy, and many an eye with tears of gratitude,
and his name will be blessed by the remembrance of his
deeds, in the hearts of numerous individuals, and of as
many public institutions, of which he never suffered himself to be an inactive benefactor. It may be truly said
that this gentleman lived beloved and died lamented, at
his house in Portland Place, on the 29th of July, 1816, in
the 62d year of his age

Sir Thomas Bernard, Bart. This gentleman was son
of Sir Francis Bernard, Bart. Governor of New Jersey,
who was created a Baronet in 1780; and was born at
Lincoln, April 27, 1750. During his father's life-time
he was appointed to the official situation of Commissary
of Musters; he also studied the law, and was called to the
Bar in 1780, by the Hon. Society of the Middle Temple;
he however selected the more retired business of Convey-
ancing, in which he rapidly rose to a high degree of
reputation and practice.

In 1782, he married Margaret, daughter and co-heiress
of Patrick Adair, Esq. by which marriage, and by assiduous
attention to his profession for fifteen years, he acquired a
sufficient competency, withdrew himself from the Law,
and devoted his future life to an occupation more congenial
to his feelings.

The endeavour to ameliorate the condition of the poor, was his first object, and from his unceasing exertions to attain that object, he became the most distinguished philanthropist of the age.

Mr. Bernard had taken an active part on the Committee of the Foundling Hospital for some years before he retired from business, and he was elected Treasurer to the Hospital in 1795, which opened a new field for his benevolent exertions. In conjunction with Count Rumford, he introduced a system of economy, in cooking and fuel, on the Count's principle, which effected a saving of twenty-five chaldrons of coals in the first year, also saving the labour of one of the two cooks, rendering that of the remaining one more easy, and dressing the food better than before.

The success of this experiment led to the formation of a scheme in 1796, for introducing the same system of economy into the Mary-le-bone Workhouse. For this object a subscription of £100. each from Mr. Bernard, the Bishop of Durham, Mr. Eliot, Mr. Wilberforce, and some others, was raised in order to commence operations; but the proposal was not acceded to by the Vestry.

He was the author of the plan for the formation of the " *Society for Bettering the Condition of the Poor*," and was one of the founders of the " *School for the Indigent Blind*," in the year 1800. He also fitted up at an expense of £1000. a large Chapel in West Street, Seven Dials, the whole body of the Chapel being free for the Poor. This Chapel was opened on the 25th of May, the sermon being preached by Dr. Porteous, Bishop of London.

He was a Member of the Committee of the London Fever Institution, and of the Jennerian Society; and was one of the founders of the Royal Institution, in 1799, and in 1805, furnished the outline of the plan for forming " *The British Institution for Promoting the Fine Arts in the United Kingdom*," which was established on the 4th of June in that year; and on the 29th of June Mr. Bernard, agreed, on behalf of the Committee, for the purchase of the Shakspeare Gallery in Pall Mall; which Gallery was opened for the Exhibition and Sale of the productions of British Artists, in the following spring.

In the year 1804, on account of ill health, Mr. Bernard purchased a house in Wimpole Street, and resigned his office of Treasurer to the Foundling Hospital.

He formed the Alfred Club in Albemarle Street, which was opened on the 1st of January, 1809. In January, 1810, he succeeded to the Baronetage on the death of Sir John Bernard in the West Indies. In 1811, he raised a subscription of 3000 guineas for the purchase of Mr.

West's Picture of " Christ Healing the Sick," which the Artist had intended to present to his native city Philadelphia. This picture was exhibited in the Gallery of the British Institution, and has since been presented by the Directors, to the National Gallery.

In 1812, Lady Bernard was attacked by a severe illness, and Sir Thomas accompanied her Ladyship to Brighton, where he raised a subscription of £2500. to complete a chapel, which had been commenced, but neglected for want of funds. In this year, he began his work on the " Comforts of Old Age," which was about half finished on the day of her Ladyship's death, which happened after a happy union of 31 years, on Whitsunday morning June 6, 1813, she having suddenly expired while preparing to go to Church. The " Comforts of Old Age," has passed through four editions.

In 1813, Sir Thomas arranged, " The Political Life of Lord Barrington," which was published in 1814, as coming from the Bishop of Durham, but his Lordship in the Preface, very handsomely gave the credit of the work to the person who had so kindly undertaken the labour.

On the 15th of June, 1815, Sir Thomas Bernard, celebrated his second marriage with Miss Hulse, the youngest sister of Sir Edward Hulse of Breamore House, Hants, Bart.; and continued to his death in the uninterrupted enjoyment of all the advantages to be derived from congenial habits, and from a pure and benevolent heart.

In 1816, and 1817, Sir Thomas exerted himself to obtain a repeal of the Salt Duties, and in December, 1817, published " The Case of the Salt Duties with Proofs and Illustrations." In the next Session of Parliament a Committee was appointed to enquire into the Salt Laws. The increased exertion he now used in procuring evidence for the Committee brought on a severe illness, and he was induced to leave London at the earliest possible time; and from medical advice, proceeded to Leamington Spa, where he arrived in the middle of June: from this moment he gradually grew weaker, until the morning of the 1st of July, 1818, when his valuable life terminated without a struggle.

In private life he was serene, cheerful, and hospitable. His memory retained much useful information and lively anecdote collected in his various and extensive reading, which rendered his society at once instructive and entertaining. His table was the resort of many of the most distinguished characters of the day, in Literature, Science, and the Fine Arts.

Leaving no issue, he was succeeded in the Baronetage

by his only surviving brother, the late Sir Scrope Bernard
Moreland, of Nether Winchendon, Bucks, and Pall Mall,
London.

Mrs. Elizabeth Montague. This learned and ingenious
Lady, was the daughter of Matthew Robinson, Esq. of
West Layton, in Yorkshire; of Coveney, Cambridgeshire;
and of Mount Morris, in Kent; by Elizabeth, daughter
and heiress of Robert Drake, Esq. She was born at
York, Oct. 2, 1720, but lived, for some of her early years,
with her parents, at Cambridge, where she derived great
assistance in her education from Dr. Conyers Middleton,
whom her grandmother had taken as a second husband.

She had early a love for society, and it was her lot to
be introduced to the best. In 1742, she was married to
Edward Montague, Esq. of Denton Hall, in Northumberland, and Sandleford Priory, in Berkshire, grandson of
the first Earl of Sandwich, and member in several successive Parliaments for the Borough of Huntingdon. By his
connections and her own, she obtained an extensive range
of acquaintance, but selected as her especial friends and
favourites, persons distinguished for taste and talents.
By Mr. Montague, who died without issue in 1775, she
was left in great opulence, and maintained her establishment in the learned and fashionable world for many years
with great eclat, living in a style of most splendid hospitality. She died in her eightieth year, at her house in Portman Square, Aug. 25, 1800.

She had early distinguished herself as an author; first,
by " Three Dialogues of the Dead," published along with
Lord Lyttelton's; afterwards by her classical and elegant
" Essay on the Genius and Writings of Shakspeare," in
which she amply vindicated our great poet from the gross,
illiberal, and ignorant abuse, thrown out against him by
Voltaire.

Few persons had seen more of life than Mrs. Montague,
and of that part of mankind, who were eminent either for
their genius or their rank; and for many years her splendid
house in Portman Square was open to the literary world.
She had lived at the table of the second Lord Oxford, the
resort of Pope and his contemporaries; she was the intimate friend of Pulteney and Lyttelton; and she survived
to entertain Johnson, Goldsmith, Burke and Reynolds,
till their respective deaths.* Dr. Beattie was frequently

* She formed a literary Society, which for some years, was the
topic of much conversation, under the name of the *Blue Stocking
Club*. Various accounts have been given of the origin of the title,

her inmate, and for many years her correspondent; and
Mrs. Carter was, from their youth, her intimate friend,
correspondent, and visitor.   Since her death four volumes
of her epistolary correspondence have been published by
her nephew and executor, Matthew Montague, Esq. but
in consequence of some violent criticism, he declined to
publish the remainder, which has been severely regretted
by the literary world; had the whole series been completed, a just idea might have been formed of Mrs. Montague's character, and the result, we may venture to pre-
dict, would have been highly favourable.

The Rev. Dr. Alexander Geddes. This learned writer
was a native of Arradowl, in the parish of Ruthven, and
County of Banff, in Scotland; he was bred a Roman
Catholic, and educated at the Scotch College in Paris.
Here school divinity and biblical criticism occupied the
principal part of his time; and he endeavoured also to
make himself master of the Greek and Latin languages,
and of the French, Spanish, German, and Low Dutch.
    After finishing his education, he was successively priest
of several Roman Catholic Congregations in Scotland. In
1780, he quitted his native country in consequence of
having been deposed from his office by Bishop Hay for
having occasionally attended the ministry of Mr. Buchanan,
The same year the University of Aberdeen granted him a
diploma for the degree of Doctor of Laws, being the only
instance it is said, in which that honour had been conferred
on a Roman Catholic; he officiated for twelve years at
the Imperial Ambassador's Chapel in London; and after
that was shut up, at the Chapel in Duke Street, Lincoln's
Inn Fields. At an early age, he distinguished himself
as an Hebraist, and turned his attention to biblical criticism, and having examined many rare MSS. both at Paris,
and after his return from the continent, he began, in 1782,

but it is generally said to have arisen from the circumstance of a
person excusing himself from going to one of its very early meetings,
on account of his being in a deshabille, to which it was replied :
" No particular regard to dress is necessary in an assembly devoted
to the cultivation of the mind ; so little attention, indeed, is paid
to the dress of the parties, that a gentleman would not be thought
very outré who should appear in *blue stockings*."   This lady
was, for many years noticed for the benevolent peculiarity of giving
an annual dinner on May-day to all the little climbing boys,
apprentices to the chimney-sweepers of the metropolis.   Perhaps
her attention to these too frequently distressed children, led to
those humane regulations, which, through the exertions of Mr.
Jonas Hanway, were determined on by Parliament.

a new translation of the Bible, of which he published a prospectus in 1786; in 1792, he brought out the first volume, containing the Pentateuch and the Book of Joshua, under the patronage of Lord Petre, from whom, during several years, and till the death of that nobleman, he experienced the most generous and active friendship. Previously to the publication of this work, great expectations having been raised by the known learning of the author, a most respectable subscription was obtained for it, graced by the names of the most eminent literary characters, both at home and abroad, from among the different denominations of Christians. On its appearance, however, it was found to abound in passages which were not only deemed exceptionable and disgusting by members of the Church of England, but were so much disapproved by those of his own community, that public censures were passed upon him by the Vicar Apostolic of the London district. Regardless of these censures, Dr. Geddes, in 1797, published a second volume, containing the books of Judges, Samuel, Kings, and Chronicles: and in the preface openly avowed opinions hostile to the belief of the inspiration of the Scriptures, as assented to both by his church and our own. His reputation for learning, was very considerable in Scotland, and he was one of the literati who took a very active part in the Institution of the Society of Antiquaries at Edinburgh. In their volume for 1792, he wrote " A Dissertation on the Scoto-Saxon Dialect," and " The first Eklog of Virgil," and " The first Idyllion of Theocritus, translatitt into Scottis vers," in the former of which the Edinburgh dialect is chiefly imitated, and in the latter the Buchan. Besides these Dr. Geddes wrote many fugitive pieces, essays, poems in the Newspapers and Magazines, and was a considerable contributor to the Analytical Review. In the year 1793, Dr. Geddes took a house in Allsop's Buildings, New Road, where he continued to reside till his death, which happened on the 26th of February, 1802. Dr. Geddes's funeral was attended by many eminent divines of very different religious persuasions; he was buried in the church-yard at Paddington, where is a plain upright stone to his memory, put up in 1804, at the expence of Lord Petre, with the following inscription:

" Rev. Alexander Geddes, LL.D. Translator of the Historical Books of the Old Testament, died, Feb. 26, 1802, aged 65."

" *Christian* is my name, and *Catholic* my surname, I grant that you are a Christian as well as I, and embrace you as my fellow disciple of Jesus; and if you were not a disciple

of Jesus, still I would embrace you as my fellow man."—
Extracted from his Works.
"*Requiescat in Pace.*"
There is a life of Dr. Geddes, in 8vo. with his portrait
prefixed, written by John Mason Good, .M. D. who was
his particular friend, and published in 1803.

The Rev. Basil Woodd. This gentleman was born at
Richmond, in Surrey, on the 5th of August, 1760. On
leaving his paternal roof, he became the pupil of the Rev.
Thomas Clarke, Rector of Chesham Bois, and at the age
of seventeen, was entered student of Trinity College,
Oxford, where he took the degree of Master of Arts. On
the 10th of March, 1783, he was ordained deacon, at the
Temple Church, London, by Dr. Thurlow, Bishop of
Lincoln, and Sept. 19, 1784, was ordained priest, at
Westminster Abbey, by Dr. Thomas, Bishop of Rochester;
at this time he frequently officiated at St. Paul's, Deptford;
but was shortly afterwards chosen Lecturer of St. Peter's
Cornhill, which situation he filled for twenty-four years.
In February, 1785, Mr. Woodd received the appointment
of Morning Preacher at Bentinck Chapel, of which he
purchased the lease in 1793, and where he continued his
labours with diligence and success up to the time of his
death. In the year 1808, he was presented by Lady
Robert Manners, to the Rectory of Drayton Beauchamp.
In addition to Mr. Wood's ministerial duties, he rendered himself exceedingly active in establishing schools;
under his superintendence more than 3000 children have
received their education in the schools connected with
Bentinck Chapel: he was also the founder of several excellent benevolent institutions, and was particularly instrumental in establishing a fund for the relief of the sick
and afflicted within the range of his observations. As an
author Mr. Woodd never appeared in any voluminons
work, but several Tracts and Discourses from his pen
have obtained a considerable circulation.
In 1785, Mr. Woodd introduced public worship on
Sunday Evenings, at Bentinck Chapel; this was deemed
a novel proceeding and met with great opposition; he
however persevered, and such is the effect of laudable
example, that opposition was succeeded by imitation;
Evening Lectures having been successively established
at the Parish Church and the other Chapels.
Mr. Woodd resided at Paddington. where he died
sincerely lamented by all who knew him, on the 12th of
April, 1831, and was interred in Paddington Churchyard,

where a splendid monument by *Rossi*, has been erected to his memory.

James Brooke, Esq. This gentleman was well known to the chief wits of his time ; and was particularly intimate with Johnson, Garrick, Churchill, Wilkes, Lloyd, Murphy, &c. as well as with most of the *Bon Vivants* of his early days, though his own habits were very temperate. He possessed considerable literary talents, which were chiefly exercised in numberless political pamphlets, prologues, epilogues, songs, &c. He conducted " *The North Briton,*" after it was relinquished by Wilkes, till the final termination of that once popular work. He was thoroughly acquainted with mankind, and abounded in anecdotes, which he related in a very easy, lively and entertaining manner. A daughter of this gentleman, a most amiable and accomplished lady, who died in the prime of life, was married to the late Philip Champion Crespigny, Esq. King's Proctor, and formerly M. P. for Sudbury and Aldborough. Mr. Brooke retained his faculties, as well as his vivacity and humour, almost to the close of his life ; and died after a short illness, at his house in Rathbone Place, Oct. 23, 1807.

Count Simon Woronzow. This distinguished Nobleman was born at Moscow in the year 1744, of a noble family, which in point of rank and antiquity was inferior to none in the Russian Empire. After active service in the army during the war between Russia and the Ottoman Porte in 1770-1-2-3, he retired to Italy, where he remained till 1781. He was appointed Russian Minister at Venice in 1782, and was sent on a special mission to the Court of London in 1789, where he soon after became resident Minister and Ambassador. He, however, retired from the service of the Emperor Paul, when that monarch formed an alliance with the First Consul Buonaparte. The Count was re-appointed Ambassador to the Court of St. James's, on the accession of Alexander. He visited Russia in 1802, but soon returned to England, and, after the marriage of his daughter to the Earl of Pembroke in 1808, he never quitted this country, except for short excursions to France in 1815, and 1819, which he undertook to visit his son Count Michael, who was Commander-in-Chief of the Russian corps, forming part of the European Army of Observation.

His Excellency was highly esteemed in the elevated circle in which he moved. He died at his house in Mansfield Street, on the 21st of June 1832, in the 88th year of

his age, and his remains were deposited in a vault underneath the Parish Church of St. Mary-le-bone, which also
contains the remains of one of his grandsons. By his
death, numerous charitable Institutions of this country,
have lost a constant and liberal benefactor. He distributed in charity more than £.4700 a year.

Sir George Leonard Staunton, Bart. F. R. S. This
gentleman was Secretary to Lord Macartney in his Embassy to China, and was a Member of the Royal Institution. He was son of a gentleman of small fortune in the
County of Galway, in Ireland ; and sent early to study
physic at Montpelier, whence he proceeded M. D. On
his return to London, he translated Dr. Storck's " Treatise on Hemlock," and drew up a " Comparison between
the literature of England and France." for the *Journal
Etranger*, in France. He married a daughter of Benjamin
Collins, Esq. Banker, at Salisbury ; and, before he embarked for the West-Indies, wrote a farewell letter to Dr.
Johnson, inserted in his Life by Boswell. He resided
there some years ; and his fortune increasing by his practice, he purchased an estate in Grenada, where he obtained
the friendship of Lord Macartney, the Governor, acting
as his Secretary, and as Attorney-General of the Island ;
having exchanged the medical profession for that of the
law, soon after his arrival out ; on the capture of that
Island by the French he returned to England, and on his
Lordship's appointment to the Government of Madras, he
accompanied him as his Secretary, and was appointed one
of the Commissioners to treat of peace with Tippoo Sul-
taun. On his return to England, the India Company
settled on him a pension of 500*l.* per annum; the King
created him a Baronet, and the University of Oxford conferred on him the degree of LL.D. In the Embassy to
China, he was not only appointed Secretary of the Legation, but had the title of Envoy Extraordinary and Minister
Plenipotentiary, to be ready in case of accident, to supply
the Ambassador's place. He afterwards published an
Account of the Embassy, and died at his house in Devonshire Street, Portland Place, Jan. 31, 1801, after long
suffering under a paralytic affection.

Richard Brothers. During the years 1792-3-4, the
minds of the credulous had been much disturbed by the
prophecies of this man, who had been a Lieutenant in the
Navy ; among other extravagancies promulgated by Mr.
Brothers, he styled himself the ' Nephew of God ;' and
predicted the destruction of all Sovereigns, the downfall

of the Naval power of Great Britain, and the restoration of the Jews, who under him as their Prince and Deliverer, were to be re-seated at Jerusalem: all these events were to be accomplished by the year 1798. His writings, founded on erroneous explanations of the Scriptures, at length made so much noise, that Government found it expedient to interfere; and on the 14th of March 1795, he was apprehended at his lodgings, No. 58, in Paddington Street, under a warrant from the Secretary of State. After a long examination before the Privy Council, in which Mr. Brothers persisted in the divinity of his legation, he was committed into the custody of a State Messenger. On the 27th he was declared a lunatic, by a Jury appointed under a Commission of Lunacy, assembled at the King's Arms in Palace Yard; and was subsequently removed to a private Madhouse at Islington, where he remained till the year 1806, when he was discharged by the authority of Lord Chancellor Erskine. After his liberation, he resided some time in the neighbourhood of the Edgware Road, and afterwards in Upper Baker Street, where he died on the 25th of January, 1824. Mr. Brothers was seen in the streets a few days before his death, walking with great difficulty, and apparently in the last stage of a consumption. It is a singular fact, that the minister died of a broken heart, and that the doctor under whose care he was confined, committed suicide.

Eccentric Characters.

John Elwes, Esq. The family name of Mr. Elwes was Meggot, and his father was a brewer of great eminence. His dwelling house and offices were situated in Southwark, which borough was formerly represented in Parliament by his grandfather Sir George Meggot. He purchased, during his life, the estate now in possession of the family, at Marcham, in Berkshire, of the Calverts, who were in the same line. His father died while the late Mr. Elwes was only four years old.

At an early period of his life he was sent to Westminster School, where he remained for ten or twelve years. He there exhibited great application, and became an excellent classical scholar.

From Westminster School, Mr. Elwes, removed to Geneva, where he soon entered upon pursuits more agreeable to his taste; he became passionately fond of horses, and from his constant attendance in the Riding Academy there, became one of the first riders in Europe.

On his return to England after an absence of two or three years, he was introduced to his Uncle, Sir Harvey Elwes, who then lived at Stoke, in Suffolk, perhaps the most perfect *picture of human penury* that ever existed. On the death of Sir Harvey, his fortune which amounted to at least 250,000*l.* fell to his nephew, Mr. Meggot, who by will, was ordered to assume the name and arms of Elwes.

To this property Mr. Elwes succeeded when he had advanced beyond the fortieth year of his age, and when his own private property was supposed to be very little inferior. For fifteen years previous to this period, it was, that he was known in the more fashionable circles of London. He had always a turn for play, and it was only late in life, and from paying always, and not always *being paid,* that he conceived disgust at the inclination. The theory which he professed, " *that it was impossible to ask a gentleman for money,*" he perfectly confirmed by practice ; and he never violated this feeling to the latest hour of his life.

The manners of Mr. Elwes were so gentle, so attractive, so gentlemanly and so engaging that rudeness could not ruffle them, nor strong ingratitude break their obervance. He retained this peculiar feature of the *old Court* to the last.

It is curious to remark, how in his early life, he then contrived to mingle small attempts at saving, with objects of the most unbounded dissipation. After sitting up a whole night at play for thousands with the most fashionable and profligate men of the time, amidst scenes of unrivalled splendour, he would walk out about four in the morning, *not* towards home, but into Smithfield, to meet his own cattle, which were coming to market from Thaydon Hall, a farm of his in Essex, There would this same man, forgetful of the scenes he had just left, stand, in the cold or rain, bartering with a carcase butcher *for a shilling!* Sometimes, when the cattle did not arrive at the hour he expected, he would walk on in the mire to meet them ; and, more than once has gone on foot the whole way to his farm without stopping, which was seventeen miles from London, after sitting up the whole night.

To see him setting out on a journey was truly curious; his first care was to put two or three eggs, boiled hard into his great coat pocket, then, mounting one of his hunters, his next attention was to get out of London, into that road where turnpikes were the fewest. Then, stopping under a hedge where grass presented itself for his horse, and a little water for himself he would sit down and refresh himself and his horse together. Here presenting a new species of brahmin, worth 500,000*l*.

The chief residence of Mr. Elwes, previous to the death of his uncle, was in Berkshire, at his own seat at Marcham. Here it was he had two sons born, who inherit the greater part of his property under his will made in 1786.

The keeping fox hounds was the only instance, in the whole life of Mr. Elwes, of his ever sacrificing money to pleasure, and may be selected, as the only period when he forgot the cares, the perplexities, and the regret, which his wealth occasioned. But they were kept with such a strict regard to rigid economy, that the whole fox hunting establishment, huntsman, dogs, and horses, did not cost him 300*l*. a year.

As instances of his inordinate passion for saving: he would walk home in the rain in London, sooner than pay a shilling for a coach: he would sit in wet cloaths sooner than have a fire to dry them: he would eat his provisions in the last stage of putrefaction sooner than have a fresh joint from the butcher's; and he wore a wig for above a fortnight, which he picked up out of a rut in a lane through which he was riding.

Mr. Elwes from his father, Mr. Meggot, had inherited some property in houses in London; particularly about the Haymarket, not far from which Mr. Elwes drew his first breath—for, by his register, it appears, he was born in St. James's Parish. To this property, he began now to add, by engagements with one of the Adams's about building, which he increased from year to year to a very large extent. Great part of Mary-le-bone soon called him her founder. Portland Place and part of Portman

Square, the barracks and stables of the 2d Regiment of Life Guards, and buildings too numerous to name, all rose out of his *pocket ;* and had not Lord North and his American war kindly put a stop to this rage for building, much of his property would have been laid out in bricks and mortar.

Mr. Elwes had resided thirteen years in Suffolk, when the contest for Berkshire presented itself on the dissolution of parliament; and when, to preserve the peace of that county, *he* was nominated by Lord Craven. Mr. Elwes, at once agreed to the proposal made to him, it coming farther enhanced by the agreement, that he was to be returned by the freeholders free of expense. It is said, that all he did, was dining once at the ordinary at Reading, and that he got into Parliament for 1*s.* 6*d.*

He was first chosen for the County of Berks, in the year 1774, and sat as Member during three successive Parliaments, a period of about twelve years, and it is to his honour, that in every part of his conduct, and in every vote he gave, he proved himself to be what he truly was an *independent* country gentleman. In all his parliamentary life he never asked a single favour. He, however, supported the celebrated *coalition* which became so unpopular, and with that coalition, ended the parliamentary life of Mr. Elwes.

The spring of 1786, Mr. Elwes passed at Stoke, he then removed to his farm-house, at Thaydon Hall, where, having been taken ill, he lay nearly a fortnight without assistance, but recovering, he made his will, in which he bequeathed the whole of his property, to be equally divided between his two sons, George Elwes, Esq. of Marcham in the County of Bucks, and John Elwes, Esq. of Stoke in the County of Suffolk, formerly Lieut. of the 2d Regiment of Life Guards. The entailed estates fell to Mr. Timms son of Richard Timms, Esq. Lieut.-Col. of the 2d Regiment of Life Guards. The will is dated the 6th of August, 1786.

The summer of 1788, Mr. Elwes passed at his house in Welbeck Street. His chief employment used to be that of getting up early in a morning to visit some of his houses in Mary-le-bone, which during the summer were repairing. During the year 1789, his memory

visibly weakened every day; and from the unceasing
wish to save money, he now began to apprehend he
should die in want of it. He was, however, persuaded
to allow himself to be taken *gratuitously* into Berkshire,
where at his seat at Marcham, he was taken ill on the
18th of Nov. and after lingering eight days, he expired
on the 26th, in presence of his two sons, with the ease
with which an infant sleeps on the breast of its mother,
worn out with the rattles and toys of a long day.

Mr. Custance. A very eccentric, yet worthy character. He was originally a carpenter, but for many
years past followed an employment more congenial to his
wishes, leaving him more time to prosecute his studies.
His indefatigable application to observations, both with
the telescope and microscope, rendered him an acute
observer of the works of creation, from its minutest
object to the more sublime appearance of the heavenly
bodies, in both of which departments of science the
many important discoveries he made are sufficient to
rescue his name from oblivion. He excelled, in a high
degree, in the art of preparing vegetable and other bodies,
for the purposes of microscopical inspection, of which
he has given the world many curious and unequalled
specimens; and left a valuable and excellent philoso-
phical apparatus behind him, which his economical and
abstemious way of living for many years had enabled
him to purchase. His apartment formed a complete
museum; and what with books, instruments, pictures,
natural curiosities, together with a large finger-organ,
he had scarcely room left for his bed and a few chairs.
Among many other eccentricities, he never suffered any
person to do any thing for him; he kept no servant, nor
was ever married; he cooked and did every thing for
himself, and was never in any house of public entertainment for thirty-five years. He was temperate, pious,
and of the strictest integrity; while his communicative
disposition and attentive assiduities endeared him as
much to those who had the pleasure of knowing him, as
his many peculiarities of living and dress attracted the
notice of those who were but superficially acquainted with
his character. He died at his apartments in Upper
Mary-le-bone Street, on the 11th of Jan, 1799.

REMARKABLE EVENTS.

Cato Street Conspiracy.

This Conspiracy was one of the most atrocious, though extravagant plots recorded in history. Its ultimate end was to effect a revolution; its immediate object, the assassination of the Ministers. The framer of this plot was Arthur Thistlewood. Born about the year 1770, he started in life originally with some fortune, and with a fair proportion of the advantages of education. He was a subaltern officer, first, in the militia, and afterwards in a regiment of the line, stationed in the West Indies. After having resigned his commission, and spent some time in America, he passed into France, where he arrived shortly after the fall of Robespierre. There he imbibed all the opinions of which that unhappy country was the propagator and the victim, and adopted the belief, that the destruction of the Institutions of his country was the only object worthy of the labours of a man. He had been deeply engaged in the absurd scheme of Dr. Watson. Having, like the Doctor been acquitted, he thought proper soon afterwards, to send a challenge to Lord Sidmouth, for which Thistlewood was tried, found guilty, and punished by fine and imprisonment.

After his liberation in Aug. 1819, actuated by a spirit of revenge, he employed himself in forming connections with the most degraded of the lowest and poorest class. Ings, a Butcher, Tidd and Brunt, Shoemakers, and a man of colour named Davison, were his principal confidants. These men held meetings in a hired room in the neighbourhood of Gray's Inn Lane, where the necessity of murdering the Ministers and subverting the Government was frequently discussed. At length, at a Meeting held on Saturday the 19th of Feb. 1820, it was resolved that poverty did not allow them to delay their purposes any longer, and that, therefore, the Ministers should be murdered separately, each in his own house, on the following Wednesday. Meetings were held on the Sunday, Monday, and Tuesday, and the whole plan was arranged. On the latter day, however, Thistlewood was informed by a conspirator named Edwards, who was a spy in the pay of Government, that a Cabinet dinner wa^s to take place at Lord Harrowby's house in Grosvenor Square on the morrow. Thistlewood immediately procured a Newspaper, and, on reading the announcement, exclaimed, " It will be a rare haul to murder them all together !" Fresh arrangements were determined on, and it was agreed that one of their number was to go to the door with a note, and when it was opened, the others were to rush in; and while a part secured the servants, the remainder were to force themselves into the apartment where the Ministers were assembled, and murder them without mercy; it was particularly specified that the heads of Lords Sidmouth and Castlereagh were to be brought away in a bag. The other parts of the plan were so absurd and extravagant, that it is not necessary here to specify them.

The Wednesday was spent in preparing weapons and ammunition, and in writing proclamations; and towards six in the evening, the conspirators assembled in a stable situated in Cato Street, Edgware Road. The building contained two rooms over the stable, accessible only by a ladder; in the larger of which, a sentinel having been stationed below, the conspirators mustered, to the number of twenty-four, or twenty-five, all busy in preparing for the bloody catastrophe.

The Ministers, however, had been made acquainted by Edwards, with every step that had hitherto been taken; and a man named Hidon, who had been solicited to join in the plot, had warned Lord Harrowby of it, on Tuesday. The preparations for the dinner were continued, lest the conspirators should take alarm, though no dinner was in fact to be given.

In the mean time, a strong party of Bow Street Officers, headed by Mr. Birnie, proceeded to Cato Street, where they were to be met and supported by a detachment of the Coldstream Guards, under the command of Captain Fitzclarence. The officers arrived about 8 o'clock, and entering the stable, mounted the ladder, and found the conspirators in the loft, on the point of proceeding to the execution of their scheme. Smithers, one of the officers, attempting to seize Thistlewood, was pierced by him through the body and immediately fell. The lights

P

were then extinguished, and some of the conspirators escaped through a window at the back of the premises. The military detachment now arrived, and by the joint exertions of the soldiers and officers, nine were taken that evening, and conveyed to Bow Street. Thistlewood was among those who had escaped, but he was arrested next morning, in bed, in a house near Finsbury Square. Some others were seized in the course of the next two days.

On the 27th of March, true bills of indictment for High Treason were found against eleven of the prisoners, and on the 17th of April, Thistlewood was put on his trial. The principal witness was a conspirator of the name of Adams, who had escaped from Cato Street, but had been taken on the following Friday, and had remained in custody up to the time he was produced in Court to give evidence. After a trial which lasted three days, the accused was found guilty of High Treason, by having conspired to levy war against the King. Ings, Brunt, Field and Davison were afterwards severally tried and convicted. The remaining six, permission being given to withdraw their former plea, pleaded guilty. One of them, who appeared to have joined the meeting in Cato Street, without being aware of its true purpose, received a pardon; and the other five had their sentence commuted to transportation for life. Thistlewood with the four above-named prisoners, was executed on the 1st of May; all of them, excepting Davison, who was very repentant, glorying in what they had attempted, and regretting its failure, rather than repenting of their atrocious guilt.

The discovery of this plot created a great sensation throughout the kingdom, and some were found to complain of the use which government had made of spies on this occasion. But as the guilt of the prisoners was established by evidence altogether independent of Edwards, the case was free from the circumstance, which renders the use of spies most objectionable, viz. the hazard of confiding in the testimony or information of men, who are professedly pursuing a system of deceit and treachery. The plot was clearly proved to be the result of most infuriated depravity; and it is also fully established, by the declaration of Thistlewood, made immediately before his execution, that Edwards was neither its instigator or framer; it was therefore absurd to talk of the seduction of men, who, in a court of justice, defended assassination as a virtue, and even on the scaffold, exulted in the remembrance of their scheme of murder, as a picture, with the contemplation of which their fancy could never be satiated.

Sir Charles Warwick Bampfylde, Bart. was shot in the street, in the open day, shortly after he had come out of his house in Montagu Square, on the 7th of April, 1823. J. Morland, the assassin, had formerly been in his service, and his wife was in Sir Charles's service at the time. Upon seeing that his aim had taken effect, Morland discharged a second pistol into his own mouth, which killed him on the spot. This horrible deed was committed while under the influence of jealousy, which has since been proved to have been entirely groundless. Sir Charles lingered till the 19th, when he expired in great agony. The jury which sat on the body of the murderer, having returned a verdict of *felo de se,* his body was buried in the cross road, opposite St. John's Wood Chapel. Sir Charles was descended from one of the most distinguished families in Devonshire, and was in his 71st year.

On the 21st of June, 1825, the square of houses formed by Great Titchfield Street, Wells Street, Mortimer Street, and Margaret Street, was nearly all destroyed by a dreadful fire, which commenced in the workshops of Mr. Crozet, carver and gilder, in Great Titchfield Street; caused by a kettle containing a compound called French polish, boiling over, which set fire to some shavings of wood. The flames spread rapidly to the premises of Mr. Woolley, a stable-keeper; Mr. Stoddart, a pianoforte-maker; Mr. Stout, who had a mahogany and timber-yard; Mr. Messer, a coachmaker; Messrs. Bolton and Sparrow, Upholsterers; the Chapel of Ease in Margaret Street; Mr. Pears, perfumer; Mr.

Arnold, grocer; Miss Storer and Mrs. Vennes. In Mortimer Street, the houses of Mr. Wales, cabinet-maker; Mr. Hunt, card-maker; Mr. Reid, sofa and chair-maker; Mr. Kensett, cabinet-maker; and Messrs. Holt and Scheffer, were in a short time reduced to ruins. A party of the guards soon arrived at the spot, and assisted the police officers in aiding the firemen, and preventing plunder. But all the exertions of the firemen, with a plentiful supply of water, appeared to have no effect in extinguishing the flames. In the whole, not less than 30 houses and shops were destroyed; more than 100 families were thus deprived of a home; and many who were lodgers, lost all they possessed, excepting the property they carried about their persons. Among the property burnt were some of the valuable carvings belonging to the Duke of Rutland, which were deposited in one of the warehouses, and on which an insurance to a large amount had been effected in the Westminster Fire Office. His late Royal Highness the Duke of York, and several of the Nobility, visited the ruins and set on foot a liberal subscription for the sufferers.

Joanna Southcott. This notorious impostor was a native of Exeter, and, in conjunction with others, had long practised on the ignorance and credulity of the lower classes, by a series of the most gross and impious absurdities. It is also lamentable to record that very many persons of respectable condition in life, from whom better things might have been expected, suffered themselves to be deluded by her irrational and abominable pretensions. She died at her house in Manchester Street, Manchester Square, Dec. 27, 1814. The silencing of her preacher Tozer, and shutting up of the chapel, which he had opened, had by no means diminished the number of her believers, nor had the non-completion of her pro-phecies decreased, apparently, their faith. Her corpse, after having been examined by the surgeons, was re-moved, on the 31st to an undertaker's in Oxford Street, where it remained till the interment. On the 3d of January, it was carried in a hearse, so remarkably plain as to give it the appearance of one returning from, rather than proceeding to church, accompanied by one coach, equally plain, in which were three mourners. In this manner they proceeded to the new cemetery adjoining St. John's Wood Chapel. So well, indeed, had their measures been concerted, to avoid notice, that there was scarcely a person in the ground unconnected with it. A fourth person arrived as the body was being borne to the grave. This was supposed to be Tozer. The grave was taken, and notice given of the funeral, under the name of *Goddard*. Neither the Minister of St. John's, who read the service, nor any of the subordinate persons belonging to the Chapel, were apprised of the real name of the person about to be buried, till the Funeral reached the Chapel. For the inscription to her memory, see p. 142, ante.

DISTRICT SOCIETIES.

In addition to the numerous Charities already mentioned in this volume, there are four District Societies, established for the purpose of visiting and relieving the Sick and Poor at their own habitations. The funds distributed in this way, are raised by voluntary contributions, and principally by Ladies, who take an active part in the management.

It appears from the abstract of the accounts of the four District Societies, submitted to the General Meeting on the 25th of April, 1832 ; that the gross amount of the Receipts for the year ending the 25th of March 1832, was 2422*l*. 16*s*. 8*d*. of which sum was expended 2326*l*. 11*s*. 6*d*. in relieving 5017 Cases of various descriptions, with Money, Provisions, and Fuel; and in providing Linen, Blankets, Shoes, Medicine, &c. Of this number 910 were Lying-in cases relieved by the Ladies.

St. Mary-le-bone Bank for Savings.

This Institution, constituted and enrolled according to Act of Parliament, 9th George IV. cap. 92. was established under the patronage of His Grace the Duke of Portland, at the Old Court House, in July 1830; but has been recently removed to No. 14, Henrietta Street, Cavendish Square.

The Objects of this Bank, are, under the sanction and protection of the Legislature, to receive such small sums as may be saved by *Tradesmen, Mechanics, Servants, Labourers,* and persons of a similar description, as well as their *Children,* not only residing in this Parish, but in *other adjacent Parts;* also from *Friendly and Charitable Societies,* to invest the Deposits in Government Securities, and to manage the same for the benefit of the Depositors: and thus enable the industrious and frugal, by commencing early in life with saving only a few shillings weekly, to make a provision for times of need, or to purchase an annuity, or in some other way to provide for independence in old age.

Sums are received at this Bank (as it suits the Depositor's convenience) as low as *One Shilling* at a time; and as soon as they amount to *Five Shillings,* and have been deposited one month, they will become entitled to a Monthly Interest.

Auditors.

Stephen Cleasby, Esq.   George Robert Paul, Esq.
Sampson Hodgkinson, Esq.

Secretary and Actuary.   Mr. Finney.

Assistant Secretary.
Mr. Douglass Finney.

319

The Queen's Bazaar.

Is situated in Oxford Street, nearly opposite the Pantheon, and comprises a Ladies Bazaar for the Sale of Miscellaneous Articles; and galleries for the reception and display of works of art: this Bazaar is much frequented by the Nobility and Gentry. The pictures now exhibiting at this Establishment, are Mr. D. Roberts's Grand Picture of the "Departure of the Israelites out of Egypt, painted with Dioramic effect, by H. Sebron, pupil of Mr. Daguerre," and the Physiorama, containing Twelve Views, arranged in a gallery two hundred feet long. The Public are admitted to both Exhibitions, for 1s. each person.

THE END.

ERRATA.

P. 14, *line* 29, for Rector, *read* Minister.
P. 148, *line* 8, *read* "The pipes underneath Stratford Place, are very numerous, and cross each other in so many different directions, as to present the appearance of reticulated lace-work."

LONDON:
PRINTED BY JOHN SMITH, 49, LONG-ACRE.

For EU product safety concerns, contact us at Calle de José Abascal, 56–1°,
28003 Madrid, Spain or eugpsr@cambridge.org.

www.ingramcontent.com/pod-product-compliance
Ingram Content Group UK Ltd.
Pitfield, Milton Keynes, MK11 3LW, UK
UKHW010351140625
459647UK00010B/984